TOTAL TENNIS TRAINING

CHUCK KRIESE

mp
MASTERS PRESS

Published by Masters Press (a subsidiary of Howard W. Sams),
2647 Waterfront Parkway E. Dr., Indianapolis, IN 46214

© Copyright Masters Press, 1988
Fourth printing, July, 1992

All rights reserved. No part of this publication may be reproduced, stored in a retrieval system, or transmitted in any form or by any means, electronic, mechanical, photocopying, recording, or otherwise, without the prior permission of Masters Press.

Printed in the United States of America

Library of Congress Cataloging-in-Publication Data

Kriese, Chuck, 1950-
    Total tennis training: realizing your physical, mental, and emotional potential / Chuck Kriese.
      p.   cm.
    Bibliography: p.
    ISBN 0-940279-24-X
    1. Tennis–Training.   2. Tennis–Psyshological aspects.
    3. Tennis–Coaching.   I. Title.
GV1002.9T7K74 1988
796.342'07—dc19   88-22100   CIP

All photographs are by Scott Harke except for the following, which are by Rob Biggerstaff from the Clemson University Athletic Department: pp. 34, 38, 84, 100 (all), 103, 104, 109, 128, 133, 135, 142, 147(all), 157, 159, 174, 179.

Front Cover photograph by Rob Biggerstaff

Back Cover photograph by Scott Harke

Models: Kris Huff, Bill Randolf, Richard Matuszewski, Joe Defoor

An adapted portion of Chapter 14, contributed by Coach Chuck Kriese, appeared in *The ITCA Guide to Coaching Winning Tennis* by David A. Benjamin, 1988, Reprinted by permission of the publisher, Prentice-Hall, Inc., Englewood Cliffs, New Jersey.

The list of clinical names for excuses in Chapter 17 first appeared in *Life and Health*, 3rd ed., by Ralph Grawunder and Marion Steinmann, 1980, published by Random House, Inc. New York, New York. Used with permission.

Table 2-1 and variations of Figures 2-1 and 2-2 first appeared in *Interval Training* by Edward L. Fox and Donald K. Matthews, 1974, published by W.B. Saunders Co., Philadelphia, Pennsylvania. Used with permission.

TABLE OF CONTENTS

FOREWORD v

PREFACE vii

ACKNOWLEDGMENTS ix

KEY TO DIAGRAMS x

INTRODUCTION xi

PART ONE: THE PHYSICAL ONE-THIRD
Chapter 1: Be Specific in Your Physical Training 3
Chapter 2: Train for Anaerobic Endurance 7
Chapter 3: Train for Strength and Flexibility 15
Chapter 4: Train Other Important Motor Skills 33
Chapter 5: Support Your Training with Good Nutrition 37
Chapter 6: Develop Your Technical Skills and Stroke Production 41
Chapter 7: Prevent and Treat Athletic Injuries 77

PART TWO: THE MENTAL ONE-THIRD
Chapter 8: Build Your Best Game 83
Chapter 9: Concentrate on Your Pre-Match Preparation 89
Chapter 10: Observe Important Checkpoints for Match Play 101
Chapter 11: Use the Power of Momentum to Control Match Flow 105
Chapter 12: Take Time to Evaluate Your Match 117

PART THREE: THE EMOTIONAL ONE-THIRD
Chapter 13: Use Your Ability, Desire, and Opportunity 125
Chapter 14: Develop Your Motivational Program 129
Chapter 15: Set High Expectations and Understand Pecking Order 139
Chapter 16: Develop Your Optimal Level of Emotional Arousal for Competition ... 145
Chapter 17: Eliminate Excuses and Defense Mechanisms 149

PART FOUR: INDIVIDUAL AND TEAM COACHING CONSIDERATIONS
Chapter 18: Build a Team in an Individual Sport 153
Chapter 19: Use Timely Positive and Negative Feedback 165
Chapter 20: Train Your Team's Doubles Skills 173
Chapter 21: Use Effective Drills to Sharpen Your Team's Skills 183

NOTES 208

BIBLIOGRAPHY 209

FOREWORD

My work as a sports psychologist and tennis coach has convinced me of the necessity for a total developmental approach to performance enhancement. As you move upward in tennis from one level to the next, you will be challenged emotionally, physically, and strategically. Getting to the next level of performance is never just "all in your head." It involves fundamental training in all aspects of your game.

In the past few years, there have been many volumes published suggesting quick fixes to get you to the top. *Total Tennis Training* is not one of those books. Chuck Kriese has combined years of experience into a simple and practical three-pronged approach to tennis development. There are no easy answers in this text—only time-tested advice that has worked for players and coaches at all levels. Chuck Kriese's no-nonsense approach to development is evident in *Total Tennis Training*. This book is a must for any player or coach committed to excellence through hard work.

Dr. William B. Moore
East Carolina University

PREFACE

I was not looking for profound wisdom as I sat in a restaurant with my mother on a cold rainy evening in Charlotte, North Carolina.

We were both solemn and concerned over my brother-in-law, John, and the diagnosis of colon cancer that had just been given to him. At 35, John had moved up the corporate ladder until it looked like only a matter of time before most of his goals in business would be realized. He also was, and had been, my best friend in life.

John would suffer through a terrible 18 months before dying. During that time, he would show me what courage really is and much about true friendship. In those last months, he helped me with coaching and personal problems, and he seemed to gain strength and enthusiasm from doing so.

That evening in Charlotte, when we first received the bad news about John, I had been moaning about some of my problems. I had shared my deep concerns, as I often still do, with my mother. Mostly, I complained of my inability to properly motivate the players on my team. "It seems that it means so much more to me than it does to them," I complained. "I do everything I can for them—early morning workouts, individual one-on-one training, the best equipment. We have great facilities and the opportunities to compete with the best, but I still feel that I'm not able to motivate them completely. They won't make a total commitment. They go 80 percent of the way and then back off. What am I doing wrong?"

My mother reached across the table and rested her hand on mine. She looked at me and began to speak softly of the Great Depression. She said that during hard times people had to develop an "inner need," or determination to survive. Then she spoke of the war and the prosperity of the 1950s and how the memory of not having much made all parents eager to provide generously for their children to give them all the things they themselves had never had. Ironically, she said, this, along with the emphasis our country has placed on external performance at the expense of internal values, has had a crippling effect. My mother often speaks in phrases, and one of my favorites is, "Our strengths are often our weaknesses and our weaknesses are often our strengths." I felt I was beginning to understand her message.

She continued. "Let me explain it this way. When I was a young girl, I would go to my grandmother's farm in Indiana. I would often stay for hours and watch the baby chicks in the incubator fight their way into the world by pecking and struggling to break their shells. It took what seemed to be forever, watching it through the eyes of an eight-year-old. If you've ever watched it, son, the baby chick will peck and peck and work and work and it always seems that they wouldn't or couldn't make it."

"One day as I watched, one of the chicks got its head stuck popping out. And it just stayed there for the longest time. I was sure he couldn't get out, and as anyone who is kind and thoughtful would do when someone is in a jam, I wanted to help. I asked Grandma if I could help him by breaking him out of his shell. It seemed so easy for me to see and so hard for him to do. She quickly replied with a stern, 'No! You mustn't, and you won't. If you open his shell, his lungs will be too weak and he will die. As he opens his own shell, he gains strength enough to survive in his new environment.' So I learned about baby chicks and about life."

As parents and teachers, we have often opened our children's shells for them, and this is the greatest mistake we can make. This story provided a very valuable lesson for me early in my career as a coach, and it came to be my guide as I watched John, my brother-in-law and friend, build inner strength from his struggle with cancer.

This book is dedicated to my mother, who shared her wisdom, and to John who proved its truth.

Chuck Kriese
Clemson University
July, 1988

Postscript

In the autumn of 1988, two weeks after this book was published, my mother passed away after battling with cancer. She was able to see the book, and I was able to feel her deep pride for the work I had completed before she passed. As in her living, her death was one filled with strength and without fear. She stated her faith and belief in God, and that made a potentially unbearable situation very joyful and comforting for our family. The lessons that she taught were many and will always be remembered.

Chuck Kriese
Clemson University
May, 1989

ACKNOWLEDGEMENTS

In writing this book, there are many people who have provided valuable assistance. I would like to express my appreciation to the Clemson University Athletic Department as well as Bobby Robinson, Clemson's athletic director, and Dwight Rainey, the associate athletic director, for giving me a break from my normal duties to devote more time to this book. My coaches, Larry Ware at Tennessee Tech, and also Bill Green, John McLeod, Alan Cornelious, Paul Ditzenberger, and Br. Roland Driscoll taught me the value of hard work and helped me develop as an athlete and a person.

I am indebted to George Dostal and Reno Wilson for their counsel and to Pat Jensen for her direction at many stages of this project. My thanks to Jerry Baskin for his help on the technical skills and stroke production section, and to Bob Johnston and Lebron Bell for giving me training in exercise physiology. I am grateful to Pam Watkins who spent many hours typing the manuscript, to Bill Koon who read the manuscript and made valuable suggestions about the format, and to Laura Chlopecki and Kristy Rudeen for doing the necessary legwork.

A special thanks must be extended to the entire Kriese family, especially my parents, for their patience and support throughout this project. Finally, I would like to thank **Debra Kriese**, Andy Johnston, Cheryl Martin, and Marshall Green, four of my best friends in life, who never wavered in providing encouragement and guidance.

Chuck Kriese
Clemson University
July, 1988

Note: While not wishing to minimize the full participation of women in tennis or their contribution to the sport, to facilitate smooth reading and to avoid awkward phrasing, the editors of this book have chosen to use masculine pronouns when referring to both genders.

KEY TO DIAGRAMS

Player	P (P_1, P_2, etc.)
Coach	C
Player Movement	⟶
Ball Movement	‑ ‑ ‑ ⟶
Volley	V (V_1, V_2, etc.)
Ball	
Boundary Line	. . . .

INTRODUCTION

Quality is never an accident. It's always the result of high intention, sincere effort, intelligent direction, and skillful execution.
— The American School,
Chicago, Illinois

HOW DO I REALIZE MY POTENTIAL?

How does a player improve his skills in the very difficult and complex game called tennis? Does he just play sets against better players and hope that some of the skills will rub off? Or does he do drill work, over and over again, simulating the shots and situations that he faces in competition?

What about physical conditioning? What about the relatively new area called mental training? What about strategy and learning what to do and when to do it? Do the skills that are needed so much in this game just evolve if the game is played long enough? Does a player have time to wait for it all to evolve?

Skill Growth

The following graph illustrates growth for most motor skills. At first improvement comes quickly, with little more than time and effort. As the player improves, his expectations rise, sometimes unrealistically, and it appears that success will be only a matter of working a little harder and longer than the next person. This is true until the player reaches the 50th or 60th percentile of his abilities, when the plateau in growth starts to occur. A player should anticipate later growth to come in small increments. This irregular progress can be frustrating to both players and coaches.

In the early stages, a good system for training must be developed. It is the coach's job to help the player learn the fundamentals and to guide him in the development of the right areas at the right pace.

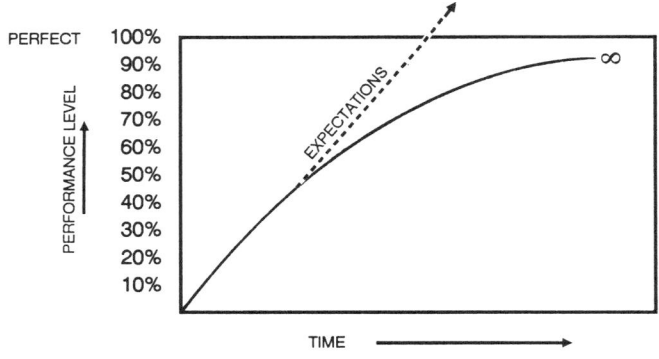

The skill growth curve

Hard work is important, but working harder does not always mean working better. When the plateau in the learning curve occurs, hard work alone will not always bring improvement, so the goal of the coach and the player should be to work hard and to work smart. The athlete must find the ingredient, whether it is physical, mental, or emotional, that will bring growth. Frustration on the part of the athlete and coach occurs when this solution cannot be found, especially when the athlete's hard and obsessive work produces little result.

Once it's understood that plateaus and barriers do exist, the athlete and coach can plan the next few percentages of improvement. It's exciting to discover that a one percent improvement for the athlete who is at the 70th percentile is a huge jump and may separate him from many other players.

There are many examples of this in tennis. The rapid growth and great improvements that John McEnroe made in 1978 and that Boris Becker made in 1985 are good examples. Ironically, both players made the jump as a result of excellent performances at Wimbledon, the most prestigious of all tennis tournaments. It's ridiculous to think that such improvement took place entirely in the space of a few days and a few wins at a big tournament. More accurate is the observation that both players were physically capable of the feat before that tournament, and as they gained momentum from each win, they became confident in their physical capabilities. The next phase of growth, the most critical one, was being comfortable with their new roles and the host of responsibilities that accompanied them. Often players collapse and retreat after advancing to a new level because of a reluctance to accept all that it takes to stay there; often they cannot deal with the new expectations that success brings them.

What is Total Player Development?

Philosophers, psychologists, and teachers all testify to the three areas of human development that are critical to growth: the physical, the mental, and the emotional. A tennis player must also develop his whole person in order for his game to benefit. He must be physically capable of the skill, he must mentally recognize and have confidence in that capability, and lastly and most importantly, he must be emotionally comfortable with each new level of play and its new responsibilities.

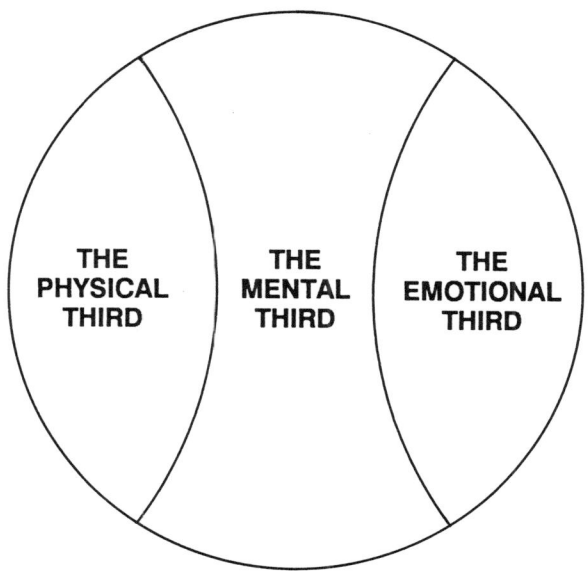

Total player development

In the early stages of development, the physical skills must be emphasized. They are the foundation without which the other areas cannot be developed. Later, the mental aspect is developed, enabling the physical to become functional. The last area to be developed is the emotional, which either allows the mental and the physical to work together, or if it is lacking, becomes the monkey wrench that eventually breaks down the machinery.

The coach must be discerning in picking out the area of growth that the athlete needs. He must be able to recognize that, in the learning stages, development must progress from the physical, to the mental, and then to the emotional (outside-in), but that in the functional stage, it must operate in the exact opposite sequence, from the emotional, to the mental, and then to the physical (inside-out). Inside-out performances can be possible only with an understanding that the emotional areas allow the mental areas to function, which in turn, allow the physical areas to engage fully.

Each area has unique components and, for the total development of the athlete, each must be trained. Athletes have a tendency to go through physical motions robotically without engaging the mental and emotional aspects. Too often, the athlete relies on the coach to supply these areas. The coach must be sure to put the responsibility back on the athlete and make sure that he engages fully in the workouts as well as in matches. In this way only can total player development take place.

PART ONE

THE PHYSICAL THIRD

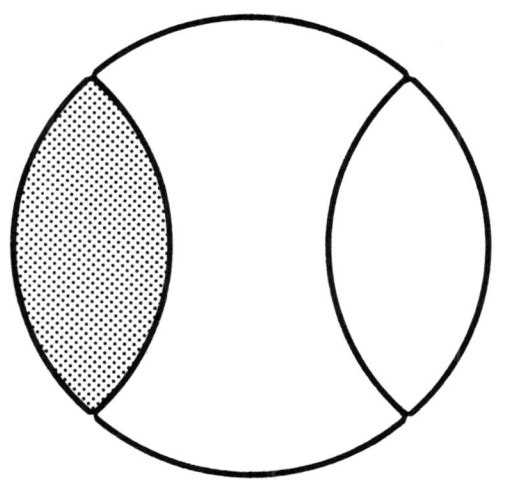

CHAPTER 1

BE SPECIFIC IN YOUR PHYSICAL TRAINING

"Pain is but for a moment, respect is for a lifetime."
—Anonymous

There are seven reasons why a comprehensive and thorough program of physical training will enhance a player's performance on the tennis court.

1. A rigorous and consistent program of physical training increases confidence in match situations.

If a person is prepared physically for a match, he will be prepared mentally. Being prepared mentally allows for emotional comfort. An athlete's physical training for a match makes him aware that his body is ready, and he will think to himself, "I have done all I can do and am now ready to play." This will enable him to play the match without pressing, rushing, or being tentative in his play.

2. A rigorous and consistent program of physical training improves technique production and power.

Tennis is becoming more and more a strength-related sport. Most of the top players are great athletes, and unless a player develops his athletic ability to its maximum potential, he cannot compete at the higher levels of the game.

3. A rigorous and consistent program of physical training reduces the number and severity of injuries.

If for no other reason than reduction of injuries, a tough physical training program should be followed. The tennis circuit is so strenuous now, even on the collegiate and junior levels, that the tennis player's body must undergo more strain from competition than ever before. A thorough program of physical training will not only reduce injuries but, in most cases, eliminate them. The training program must follow strict guidelines of flexibility and strength training, and it must also include a good running program.

4. A rigorous and consistent program of physical training delays fatigue in competition.

The development of muscular endurance through physical training allows an athlete to participate at a higher intensity for longer periods of time, thereby enhancing his performances later in the competition and helping him become a strong finisher in all events.

5. A rigorous and consistent program of physical training promotes a fast recovery after competition.

Muscular endurance developed through a good physical training program enables the body to recover much faster after a strenuous match, allowing an athlete to compete day after day with the same level of excellence in all of his performances. Most athletes can compete very well early in a tournament, but by the fourth or fifth day their bodies tend to break down under stress. A well-conditioned athlete can go many days in a row and recover quickly after each performance.

6. A rigorous and consistent program of physical training reduces the number of "tired hours" after training.

High school and college athletes have to study after practice. An athlete in top condition can recover quickly from his workout sessions, no matter how strenuous, and be ready to study. He will also be ready for the next day's activities with a minimal amount of rest.

7. A rigorous and consistent program of physical training helps the tennis player to become a better athlete.

Athletic ability is becoming very important in tennis. A strict training program will enable a tennis player to significantly improve his strength, flexibility, speed, agility, power, and other motor skills. Through the improvement of these areas, the athlete's overall performance will improve dramatically.

Figure 1-2. Physical training will improve your game.

Maximum benefit can be obtained from a specific physical training program, and Figure 1-1 shows a breakdown of the physical training that a tennis player should undergo in a week. It is essential for a player to follow a good flexibility program every day to relax the body before competition, to guard against the possibility of injury during the match, and to alleviate any soreness from previous performances. Static (nonmoving) stretching exercises should be done, but ballistic stretch exercises or any type of bouncing stretch exercises are not recommended. An anaerobic program of training should be followed from three to a maximum of four days a week, and it is a good idea for a tennis player to include some aerobic training at least one day a week.

BE SPECIFIC IN YOUR PHYSICAL TRAINING

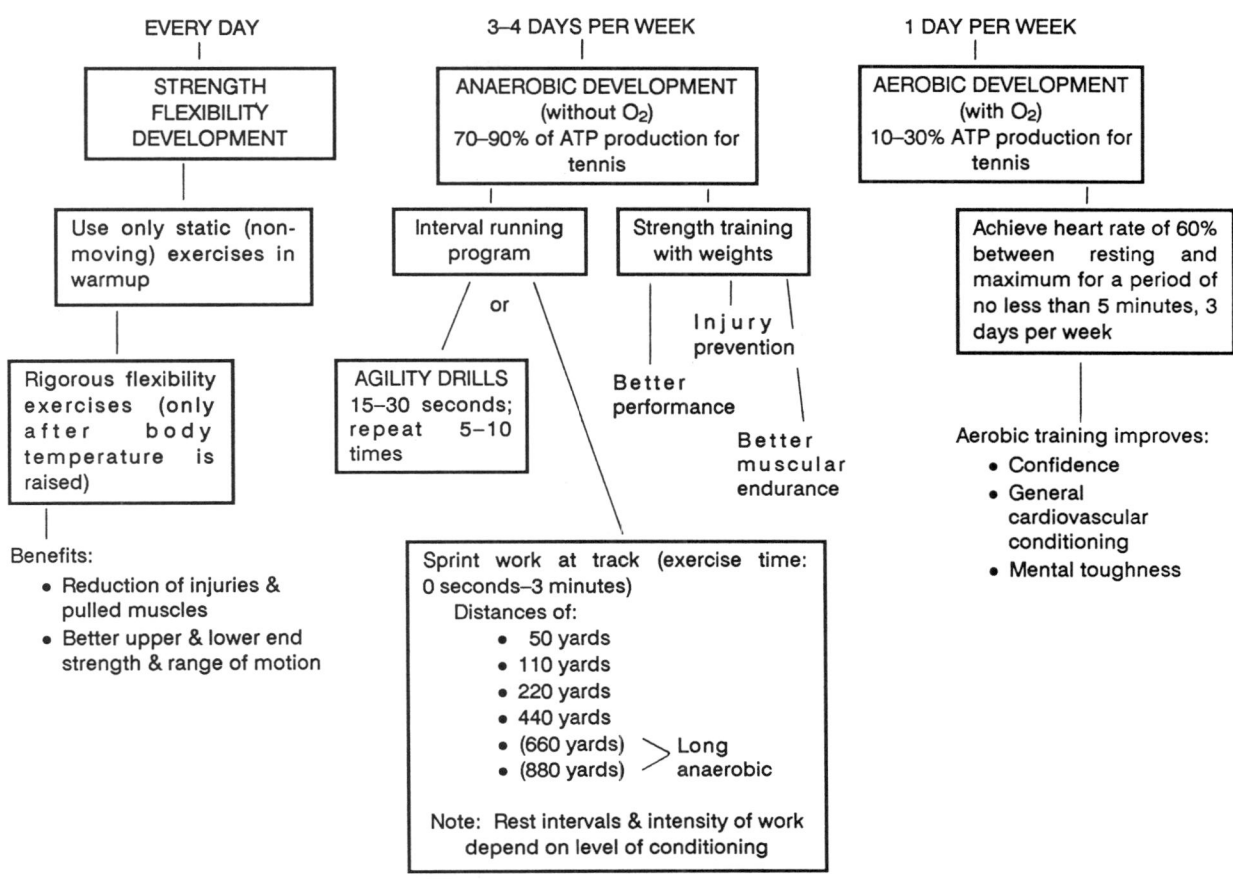

Figure 1-1. A weekly diagram outline of physical training for tennis.

SUMMARY

A specific, comprehensive physical training program will help a tennis player: 1) increase his confidence, 2) improve his technique and power, 3) reduce the number and severity of injuries, 4) delay fatigue, 5) promote fast recovery after competition, 6) reduce the number of "tired hours" after training, and 7) enable him to become a better athlete.

CHAPTER 2

TRAIN FOR ANAEROBIC ENDURANCE

"Fatigue makes cowards of us all."
—John Wooden, men's basketball coach, UCLA

Most athletes who compete in tennis realize that in order to be fit on the tennis court, they should follow some type of running program off the court. The players who improve their fitness through extra training are usually more likely to prevail in long, grueling matches.

Many athletes think that distance running develops the endurance needed to play a long match, and running long distances has been an acceptable training method for quite some time. Many junior, college, and professional players run great distances in an attempt to reach the fitness level they hope will give them the strength and endurance needed for long three-set matches. They run long distances religiously without ever asking themselves if distance running is the best way to train. It may be a surprise to many that it is not.

In distance running, the aerobic (oxygen) system is used, which is a different energy system than the system primarily used in tennis. A top-level tennis player must have the capability to replenish his anaerobic (without oxygen) system time after time following several high-intensity work periods. This is not the same as having the capacity to withstand a continuous, low-intensity work load for a long period of time, which is what you get when you run a long distance. A tennis player could run five or six miles a day and still be out of shape to play a match—this is comparable to a dash man preparing for his season by running distances instead of running at maximum intensity for shorter amounts of time with rest intervals between each effort. It has been shown, in Fox and Matthews's *Interval Training*,[1] that 70 to 90 percent of the energy expended by a tennis player must be derived from his anaerobic (without oxygen) system. This means that the body, in order to produce the energy needed to play tennis, uses the energy stored in the muscles. The chemical names of these energy sources are adenosine triphosphate (ATP) and phosphocreatine (PC), as well as glucose, which is broken down to lactic acid.

Each point in tennis is an all-out explosive type of exercise. Therefore, in order to gain maximal results, a training situation should simulate the playing of a point as closely as possible. The best physical training program for tennis includes exercises with short, explosive movements. Distance running, though, may be used for losing weight, for breaking the

SPORT	% ACCORDING TO ENERGY SYSTEMS		
	ANAEROBIC		AEROBIC
	ATP–PC & LA	LA–O_2	O_2
BASEBALL	80	20	—
BASKETBALL	85	15	—
FENCING	90	10	—
FIELD HOCKEY	60	20	20
FOOTBALL	90	10	—
GOLF	95	5	—
GYMNASTICS	90	10	—
ICE HOCKEY			
a. forwards, defense	80	20	—
b. goalie	95	5	—
LACROSSE			
a. goalie, defense, attack men	80	20	—
b. midfielders, man-down	60	20	20
ROWING	20	30	50
SKIING			
a. slalom, jumping, downhill	80	20	—
b. cross-country	—	5	95
c. pleasure skiing	34	33	33
SOCCER			
a. goalie, wings, strikers	80	20	—
b. halfbacks, or link men	60	20	20
SWIMMING AND DIVING			
a. 50 yds., diving	98	2	—
b. 100 yds.	80	15	5
c. 200 yds.	30	65	5
d. 400, 500 yds.	20	40	40
e. 1500, 1650 yds.	10	20	70
TENNIS	70	20	10
TRACK AND FIELD			
a. 100, 220 yds.	98	2	—
b. field events	90	10	—
c. 440 yds.	80	15	5
d. 880 yds.	30	65	5
e. 1 mile	20	55	25
f. 2 miles	20	40	40
g. 3 miles	10	20	70
h. 6 miles (cross-country)	5	15	80
i. marathon	—	5	95
VOLLEYBALL	90	10	—
WRESTLING	90	10	—

ANAEROBIC
  ATP–PC = Adenosine Triphosphate
  LA = Lactic Acid System

AEROBIC
  O_2 = Oxygen

Table 2-1. Energy system used for various sports activities.

monotony of a training routine, or for general cardiovascular exercise. A good way to choose a training method is to ask the question, "Should the physical training be more like a sprinter's or a distance runner's?" and then pattern the training method accordingly.

Table 2-1, from *Interval Training*,[2] lists the extent to which anaerobic and aerobic energy systems are used in a number of different sports.

INTERVAL TRAINING

The concept of interval training is to train at the most efficient intensity of the sport for short periods and follow that with a rest period during which the lactic acid level subsides and repetitions of the same duration can be done. Figures 2-1 and 2-2 illustrate why the interval method of training is more efficient than conventional training without rest periods.

The amount of work that can be done by muscle tissue depends greatly on lactic acid levels within that tissue. If the level is kept down with intermittent periods of rest, more work at greater intensity can be done by the muscle (see Figure 2-2). Without adequate rest periods between exercises, the lactic acid levels soar, thus paralyzing the muscle and preventing efficiency of performance (see Figure 2-1).[3]

After a period of intense interval training, a player can exercise for longer and longer periods, with reduced rest periods between until the intensity is great and the rest period is minimal.

Exercise periods must also be of at least equal intensity as the competition the athlete is training for or training effect will not be adequate for maximal performance. Anaerobic interval training, therefore, is recommended over aerobic training for the tennis player. High intensity sessions with adequate rest intervals are the key!

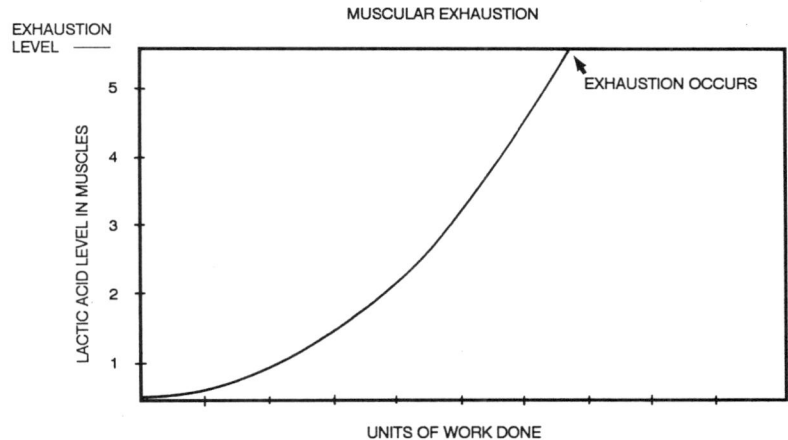

Figure 2-1. Conventional non-interval training.

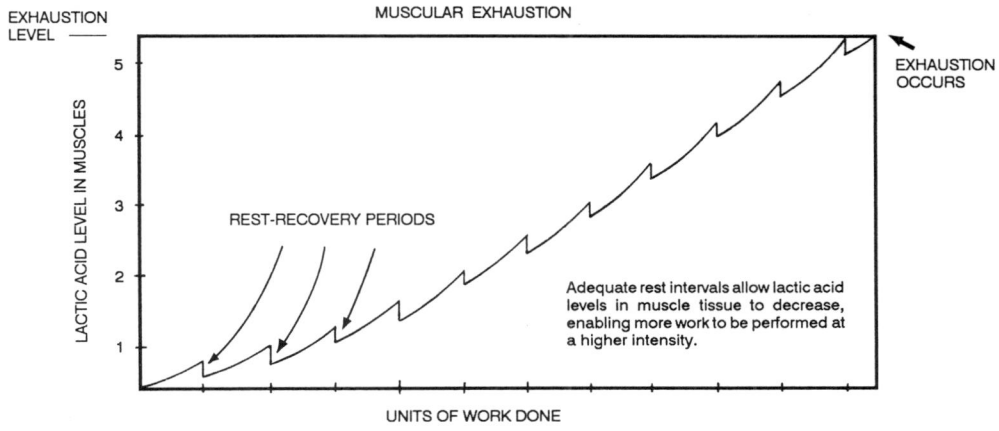

Figure 2-2. Interval training.

INTERVAL TRAINING EXERCISES TO TRAIN THE ANAEROBIC SYSTEM:

Running Drills

1. Sprint 50 yards 8-10 times with 1 1/2-2 minutes rest between each sprint.

2. Sprint 100 yards 6-8 times with 2-2 1/2 minutes rest between each sprint.

3. Sprint 220 yards 4-5 times with 3-4 minutes rest between each sprint.

4. Sprint 440 yards 2-3 times with 5-7 minutes rest between each sprint.

Note: The longer sprints should be done early in the training period and the shorter, more intense sprints after the athlete has a good base.

Agility Drills

1. Service box drill: Start in the center of the service box, facing the net. Shuffle as quickly as possible from one side to the other side, touching the center service line and the singles sideline using a cross over step and bending the back knee low to the ground simulating the proper volley footwork. You can also run forward and backward or at an angle to get a variety of movement. (Do this drill for 20 seconds at maximum rate and then repeat up to five times.) Rest for approximately one minute between each execution.

Figure 2-3. Service box drill.

2. Alley touch drill: For quicker feet, do the same drill as above, but using the 4 1/2 foot alley instead. Again, good footwork to simulate the volley should be used.

Figure 2-4. Alley touch drill.

3. Suicide line touch drill: Start at the doubles sideline and sprint first to the singles sideline and back, then to the center service line and back, then to the opposite singles sideline and back, and finally to the opposite doubles sideline and back again to the starting position. (Do this drill up to five times with approximately 30 seconds between each execution.)

Figure 2-5. Suicide line touch drill.

TRAIN FOR ANAEROBIC ENDURANCE

4. Ball drill: Two people are needed for this drill. Your partner kneels down with two balls and rolls them, one at a time, to your right side and then to your left side. You must retrieve the balls one at a time and toss them back to your partner, always remembering to face him and use good tennis footwork. Use the same hand in which you hold your racquet to pick up every ball so that you will be forced to put your body weight forward on the correct foot as if you were playing a shot.

Figure 2-6. Ball drill.

Jumping Exercises

1. Bench blasts: Place one foot on a bench (or chair) and keep the other on the ground. Push off as hard as possible using the leg on the bench, come back down, and then immediately push off again. Repeat 20 to 25 times on each leg for one set. Do three sets of exercises on each leg and rest up to one minute between each set. A bench low enough to give good resistance but not so high as to put undue strain on the knee joint should be used. If knee strain or lower back strain results from this exercise, it should be discontinued. This is a strenuous exercise and should be performed only by the most well-trained athletes.

Figure 2-7. Bench blasts.

2. Australian double-knee jump: Jump high enough into the air to touch the knees to the chest and then return to the ground. This should be done at maximum intensity 20 to 30 times for a set. Complete up to three sets with a 30 to 45 second rest between each.

Figure 2-8. Australian double-knee jump.

3. Power jumping: A weighted jump rope (preferably the Ultra-Rope®) is an excellent way to build anaerobic endurance, muscular endurance, and strength. A good work load would be five sets of 50 seconds of jumping of at least 75 revolutions per set, with 50 seconds rest between each set.

Figure 2-9. Power jumping with a weighted jump rope.

4. Speed rope jumping: A speed rope and a weighted jump rope complement each other very well. In the training routine the speed rope should be used for just that—speed. High intensity single or double jumps for periods of 30 to 45 seconds are excellent, and up to five sets should be done with equal rest intervals between sets.

Figure 2-10. Jumping with a speed rope.

SEVEN-WEEK INTERVAL TRAINING PROGRAM

Table 2-2 is a sample seven-week interval training program for the tennis player. The workouts start out with long sprints and middle distance type work. This gives a good base and prepares the player for higher intensity workouts later in the program. In the fifth, sixth, and seventh weeks, there are still some long anaerobic workouts, but most of the workouts are short, very high intensity anaerobic workouts to help the athlete peak in his conditioning for a tournament or competition.

SUN.	MON.	TUES.	WED.	THURS.	FRI.	SAT.
Rest	Flexibilities 4x440 @ 75 sec. 2x220 @ 30 sec. 2 min. rest intervals	6 agility drills	Flexibilities 2x440 @ 75 sec. 4x220 @ 30 sec. 2 min. rest intervals	6 agility drills	Flexibilities 6x220 @ 35 sec. 2x440 @ 75 sec. 2 min. rest int.	Distance run 1-3 miles
Rest	Flexibilities 2x220 @ 32 sec. 3x330 @ 48 sec. 2x440 @ 75 sec. 2 min. rest int.	6 agility drills	Flexibilities 1x880 @ 2 min. 50 sec. 2x440 @ 75 sec. 2x220 @ 35 sec. 2-3 min. rest int.	6 agility drills	Flexibilities 8x110 @ 15 sec. 1 min. rest int.	Distance run 1-3 miles
Rest	Flexibilities 1x mile for time	6 agility drills	Flexibilities 2x440 @ 70 sec. 2x330 @ 48 sec. 2x220 @ 31 sec. 2 min. rest int.	6 agility drills	Flexibilities 3x220 @ 31 sec. 3x440 @ 75 sec. 2 min. rest int.	Distance run 2-5 miles
Rest	Flexibilities 880 for time 10 min. rest int. 440 for time	6 agility drills	Flexibilities 4x330 @ 50 sec. 2 min. rest int.	6 agility drills	Flexibilities 2x220 @ 30 sec. 6x110 @ 14 sec. 2 min. rest int.	Distance run 2-5 miles
Rest	Flexibilities 1x440 for time 5 min. rest int. 1x440 for time	6 agility drills	Flexibilities 6x220 @ 30 sec. 2 min. rest int.	6 agility drills	Flexibilities 10x110 @ 15 sec. 1 min. 30 sec. rest int.	Distance run 3 miles
Rest	Flexibilities 1x mile for time	6 agility drills	Flexibilities 4x220 @ 30 sec. 4x110 @ 14 sec. 1 min. 30 sec. rest int.	6 agility drills	Flexibilities 5x110 @ 15 sec. 5x50 @ full speed 1 min. rest int.	Distance run 3 miles
Rest	Flexibilities 880 for time 5 min. rest int. 440 for time	6 agility drills	Flexibilities 4x110 @ full speed 4x50 @ full speed 1 min. rest int.	6 agility drills	Flexibilities 12x50 @ full speed 45 sec. rest int.	Distance run 3 miles

Table 2-2. Seven-week interval training program.

SUMMARY

Most of the energy used in playing tennis is anaerobic energy, and therefore it is important for an athlete to follow a good anaerobic endurance training schedule. Interval training, or training with high intensity for short periods followed with rest periods, can be used to train the anaerobic system.

CHAPTER 3

TRAIN FOR STRENGTH AND FLEXIBILITY

"I see no virtues where I smell no sweat."
—Francis Quarles

STRENGTH TRAINING

For years the prevalent school of thought was that strength training, especially when done with weights, was not good for a tennis player's development. Many people believe that weight training tends to make a tennis player clumsy and restrict his movement, hampering the broad range of motion of all limbs that he needs to play the game. But, in fact, most of what is taught about strength work in tennis has little or no scientific backing and it has been shown that good muscular strength is important for the following reasons:

1. It reduces the number and severity of injuries and delays muscular fatigue.

2. It decreases recovery time from training stress, thereby reducing the number of "tired hours" after training. Therefore, it is possible to have more consecutive days of good physical performance.

3. It increases confidence in athletic ability, because it enhances better technique, stroke production, power, and speed of movement.

FLEXIBILITY STRENGTH

Flexibility is defined as the range of motion of any joint in the body. The greater the range of motion, the greater the flexibility. Players today are discovering that the one most important and distinguishing quality top players have is flexibility strength. Contrary to some beliefs, strength and flexibility can work together. Strong muscles will not hamper flexibility if they are developed through exercises employing a wide range of motion. The perfect example of flexibity strength is a gymnast, who has the strength of a linebacker and the flexibility of a dancer.

The players winning the most tournaments today are those with much athletic ability and great flexibility strength. Therefore, the best fitness program for a tennis player's physical development is one that combines both strength training and flexibility exercises. Most benefit is obtained if strength work is done three days per week, alternating workouts with a good anaerobic running or agility program. Work on balance, agility, and stretching should be done daily. Figure 3-1 is a sample of a weekly flexibility strength training program.

MON.	TUES.	WED.	THURS.	FRI.	SAT.	SUN.
– Anaerobic exercises – Endurance work – Speed work	– Strength-flexibility training – Optional agility drills	– Anaerobic exercises – Endurance work – Speed work	– Strength-flexibility training – Optional agility drills	– Anaerobic exercises – Endurance work – Speed work	– Strength-flexibility training	– One-day rest or light aerobic workout

Figure 3-1. Flexibility strength training program.

The most intense periods of physical conditioning should be in the off-season and the pre-season. After the season starts, the program should be tapered depending on the physical demands of the player, but the program must never be abandoned. After a base of fitness is established in the pre-season, it can be maintained with timely workouts that are well planned and geared to the schedule and rest periods that are needed by the athlete. Optimally, a program of 60 to 70 percent physical work should be done in the early season, tapering back to 30 to 40 percent in the late season.

FLEXIBILITY STRENGTH TRAINING EQUIPMENT

Nautilus equipment increases the range of motion of each joint and stretches the muscle properly when exercised. When free weights or a universal gym are used, special attention should be paid to the range of motion and the specificity of each exercise to maintain and perhaps increase flexibility.

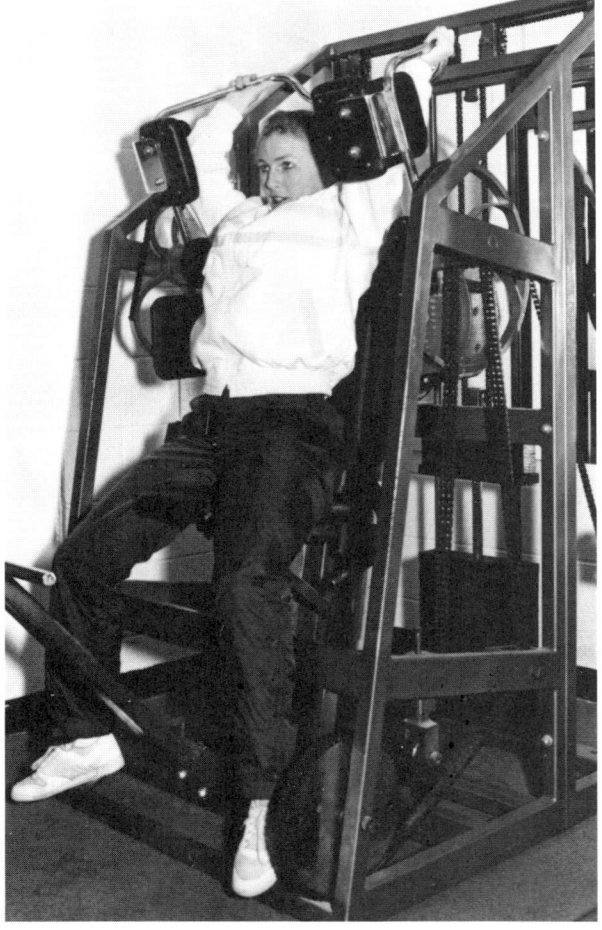

Figure 3-2. Nautilus euipment.

TRAIN FOR STRENGTH AND FLEXIBILITY

I. Pectoral (Chest) Strength Exercises

1. Men's deep chair aided push-up.

Strokes aided: High forehand and forehand volley.

Description: Unlike conventional push-ups on the ground that only allow half of the full range of motion, three chairs can be used to get a greater overload and at the same time get a pre-stretch factor and a complete range of motion for the pectoral muscles and triceps.

Place your feet on one chair and a hand on each of the other two chairs. Do regular push-ups, making sure to lower your chest as close as possible to the ground between the two chairs.

Figure 3-3. Universal gym equipment.

Figure 3-4. Men's deep chair aided push-up.

The use of a proper weight load is critical for strength development. Too little weight does not give the quality results that heavier weights give. However, when too heavy a weight is used, proper exercise technique cannot be executed. Therefore, a weight heavy enough to gain training effect, and not too heavy to inhibit proper technique, must be used. (The same principle relates to racquet weight. If your racquet is too heavy or too light, the proper technique of strokes cannot always be executed.) Usually, eight to 12 lift repetitions work well. Try to follow the interval training guidelines as they relate to muscular work and energy expenditure.

2. Women's deep chair aided push-up.

Strokes aided: Forehand volley and high forehand.

Description: Use the same method described in the men's version, except keep the feet on the ground instead of using a third chair.

FLEXIBILITY STRENGTH EXERCISES

If a player does not have access to a weight training facility, the following exercises can be used to increase flexibility strength. Notice how many of them have been adapted to increase the range of motion. Note: In the following exercises, quality is much better than quantity for maximum efficiency and to gain strength. For example, it is better to do six to 10 repetitions at maximal intensity or with a heavier weight than to do 30 consecutive repetitions at a lower intensity or with a lighter weight. The suggested exercise load is two or three sets of 10 repetitions with one-half to one minute rest between sets, and three to four workouts per week.

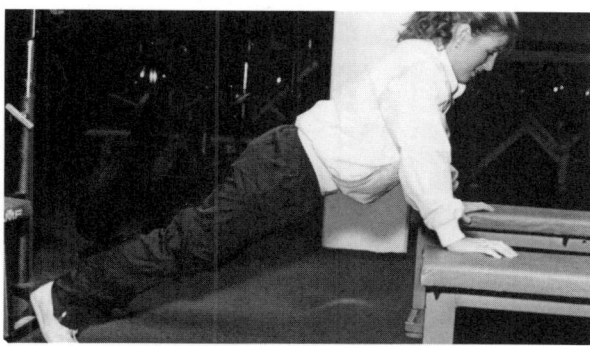

Figure 3-5. Women's deep chair aided push-up.

II. Posterior Deltoid and Shoulder Strength Exercise

1. Supine lateral raise.

Strokes aided: Backhand and backhand volley.

Description: Lie on a bench or couch on your side so that your right arm comes across your chest and hangs freely to the floor. Hold a small dummbell or weight in your right hand and elevate it in a backhand motion, using only the shoulder. Repeat on the left side.

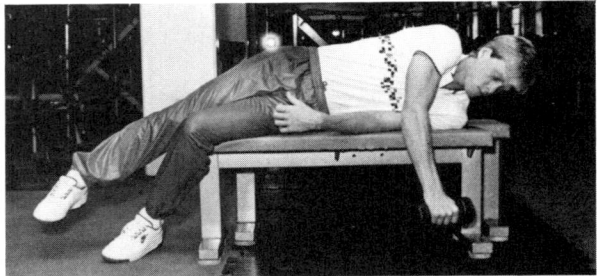

Figure 3-6. Supine lateral raise.

III. Tricep Strength Exercises

1. Tricep press or French curl.

Strokes aided: Service and overhead smash. This exercise will improve your power in the serve dramatically in one to two months. The tricep is the primary muscle used for the service motion. Its contraction straightens the arm out. The three joints used in serving are the shoulder, the elbow, and the wrist.

Description: Stand and hold a dumbbell or hand weight in your right hand and point your elbow up toward the ceiling (it may be supported by the opposite arm). Using only your tricep, straighten your arm out and up. Repeat using the opposite arm.

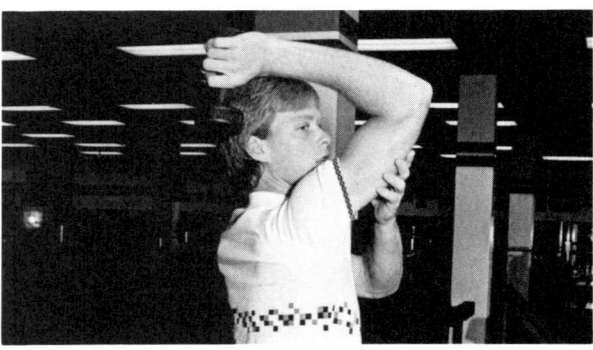

Figure 3-7. Tricep press.

2. Chair dip.

Strokes aided: This exercise aids in the development of the tricep for serving and promotes good shoulder strength for all strokes, especially high ground strokes, volleys, and out-of-position shots. It is often used by pole vaulters to develop tricep strength.

Description: Place both hands behind your back and on one chair and place your feet on another chair. Using only the elbow joint, lower your body and then raise it back to the starting position.

Figure 3-8. Chair dip.

IV. Wrist Strength Exercises

Good wrist strength is needed for playing the net. The easiest way to exercise the wrists is to use a tennis racquet that is weighted in the head of the racquet. Enough weight should be used to create an overload situation. The suggested exercise load for wrist exercises is one to two sets of 10 to 12 repetitions with adequate rest periods in between.

Figure 3-9. This low volley shows the need for good forearm and wrist strength when playing the net.

TRAIN FOR STRENGTH AND FLEXIBILITY

1. Wrist curl or flexion spin (flexors).

Description: With the palm of the hand facing up, use the wrist only to elevate the racquet and weight to a fully flexed position and then lower it. Strength gain will occur in the forearm.

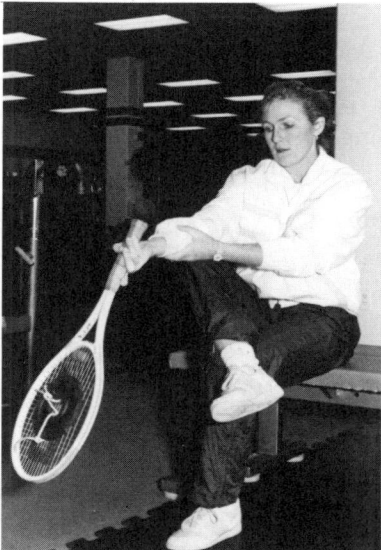

Figure 3-10. Wrist curl.

2. Wrist extension (extensors).

Description: With the palm of the hand facing down, use the wrist only to elevate the racquet and then lower it. The back of the forearm receives the strain.

Figure 3-11. Wrist extension.

3. Neutral position curl.

Description: With the racquet held in an eastern forehand grip (racquet head perpendicular to the ground), elevate the weight using only the wrist. This helps to keep the racquet up on volleys.

Figure 3-12. Neutral position curl.

4. Wrist pronation and supination.

Description: With the racquet head pointed straight up, use the wrist to twist the racquet to the left and then to the right. This will strengthen your pronator and supinator muscles for added help in hitting top spin on both sides.

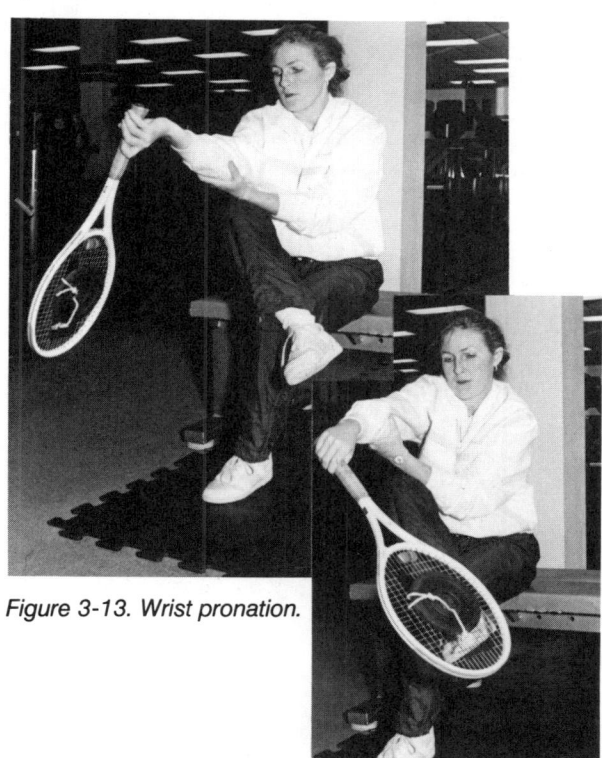

Figure 3-13. Wrist pronation.

Figure 3-14. Wrist supination.

V. Abdominal Exercises

Special attention should be paid to the development of abdominal strength, because power for stroke production and athletic performance originates in the stomach. The hyperextension exercises of the abdominal area not only significantly increase the strength of that area, but also increase flexibility of the abdominal muscles for prevention of injuries. The suggested exercise load for abdominal exercises is eight to 15 repetitions in two to three sets.

Note: If a Roman bench is not available, the following exercises can be done on a regular bench or table, or with the use of a partner to hold the legs in position.

1. Roman bench sit-up.

Strokes aided: Overhead smash, serve.

Description: Sit at the edge of a Roman bench and lean down as far as possible to extend the abdominal muscles to the point of slight discomfort. Then proceed to do sit-ups.

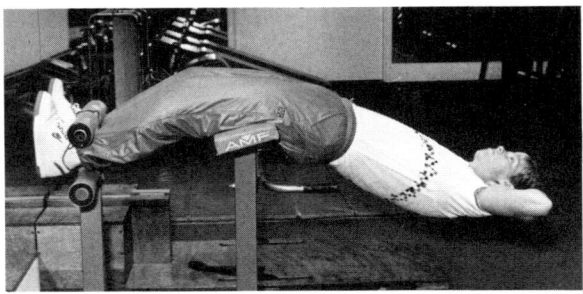

Figure 3-15. Roman bench sit-up.

2. Roman bench back raise.

Description: Using either a Roman bench or having a partner restrain your legs, lie face down with your lower abdominal area touching the edge of the bench. Go from a flexed position to a fully extended position, arching your back upward.

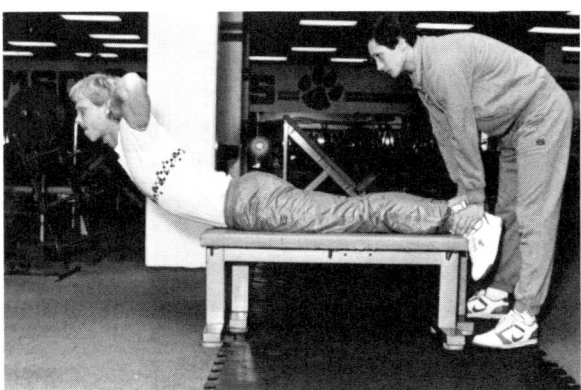

Figure 3-16. Roman bench back raise.

3. Roman bench external oblique exercise. This exercise strengthens the side abdominal muscles.

Stroke aided: Serve.

Description: Lie on your side on a Roman bench with your upper body off the bench and cross your legs so that firm support can be given by a partner who holds your feet. Lower your upper body to the ground as far as possible until slight discomfort is felt in your side abdominal muscles and then return to the starting position.

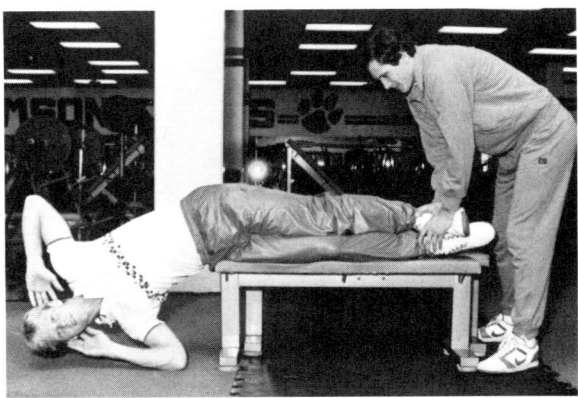

Figure 3-17. Roman bench external oblique exercise.

Figure 3-18. The athlete must use his abdominal strength in this coiling action of the serve.

FLEXIBILITY TRAINING

Flexibility training should be done daily in a tennis player's preparation for practice or for matches. Two flexibility programs are detailed: a one-man static stretching program that is familiar to most athletes, and a two-man program devised by George Dostal. A stretching program is also recommended after performances to aid in the partial removal of lactic acid from the tired muscles which, in turn, helps decrease recovery time.

STATIC STRETCHING PROGRAM (ONE-MAN STRETCHING ROUTINE)

To perform static stretching exercises, a joint is held for about 30 seconds in a position that stretches the tissue to its maximum controllable length without undue stress. Static (nonmoving) stretching is safer than ballistic (balancing or oscillating) methods because it does not impose sudden stress upon the involved tissue, yet does the work intended. Proper stretching will aid in relieving tension from daily stress.

Static Stretching Guidelines:

1. Never force a stretching muscle during the exercise to a level of discomfort or pain. Do not overstretch.
2. Be patient; work within your limits.
3. Stay relaxed in all areas of the body.
4. Maintain good posture and body alignment at all times.
5. Do not hold your breath—breathe normally.
6. Always do some sort of aerobic warm-up exercises before stretching.
7. Use equal time intervals between exercises to let the muscles relax (10 to 30 seconds).

1. Standing hamstring stretch.

Muscles stretched: Hamstring, lower back muscles, upper calf muscle.

Description: Stand upright with the knees locked. Bend forward slowly, moving the hands toward the ankles until tightness is felt in the hamstrings. Hold this position for 30 seconds, and then slowly return to the original position.

Figure 3-19. Standing hamstring stretch.

2. Hurdler's hamstring stretch.

Description: Sit on the floor with one leg turned backward, but not as to put excess strain on the knee joint, and the other extended forward (hurdler's position). Bend the torso down toward the knee until tightness is felt. Hold this position for 30 seconds, and then slowly return to the original position.

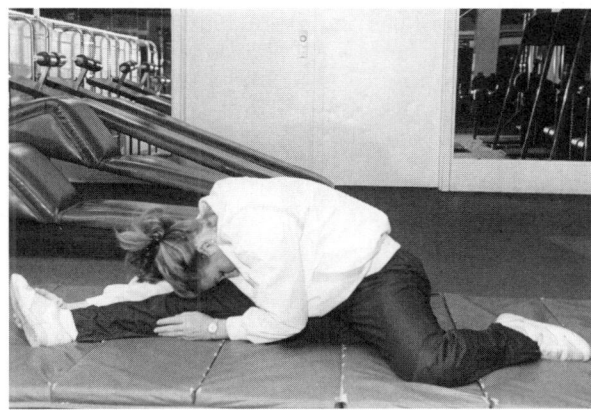

Figure 3-20. Hurdler's hamstring stretch.

3. Sprinter's stretch.

Muscles stretched: Groin area muscles, gastrocnemius (calf), hamstring, quadriceps, upper back muscles.

Description: Stand in an upright position with the knees locked. Slowly spread the legs apart forward and backward as far as you can. Slowly move the hands toward the right ankle until tightness is felt in the hamstring and gastrocnemius, and hold this position for 30 seconds. Return to the original position and repeat for the left leg.

Figure 3-22. Pretzel stretch.

Figure 3-21. Sprinter's stretch.

4. Pretzel stretch.

Muscles stretched: Lower back, buttocks, upper shoulder.

Description: Sit with the right leg bent at the knee with the upper leg flat on the floor. Raise the left knee and place the left foot flat on the floor next to the right knee. Slowly twist the torso to the left. The right arm should be placed outside the raised knee to facilitate twist. Hold for 30 seconds and return to the original position. Repeat the procedure on the opposite side.

5. Cobra stretch.

Muscles stretched: Abdominal muscles, upper quadriceps.

Description: Lie flat on your stomach. Push your upper body off the floor with hands extending up to full stretch. Hold for 30 seconds. Slowly return to the original position.

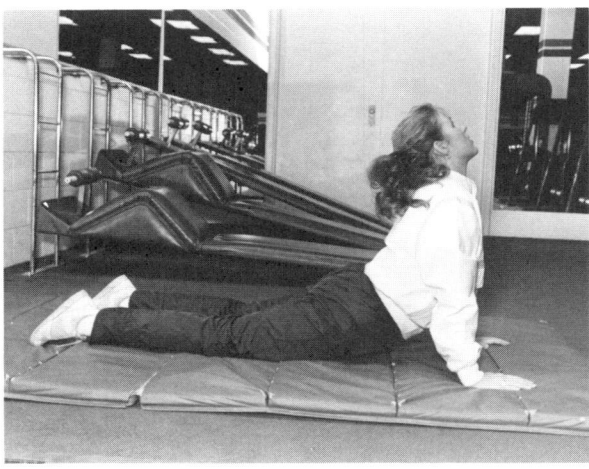

Figure 3-23. Cobra stretch.

TRAIN FOR STRENGTH AND FLEXIBILITY

6. Static groin stretch.

Muscles stretched: Groin muscles.

Description: Sit down, and pull your heels together toward the groin. Slowly push down on your knees with your elbows until tightness is felt in the groin area. Hold for 30 seconds and return to the original position.

Figure 3-24. Static groin stretch.

7. Hurdler's quadricep stretch.

Muscles stretched: Quadriceps, shin muscles.

Description: Lie on your back with your legs together. Grasp your left ankle with your left hand, slowly pull the ankle toward your waist, and lower your head toward the floor until tightness is felt in the quadriceps. Hold this position for 30 seconds. Slowly return to the original position and repeat with the right leg.

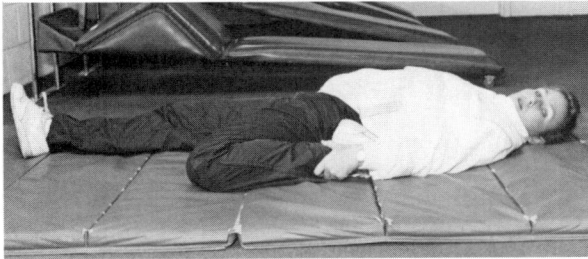

Figure 3-25. Hurdler's quadricep stretch.

8. Sitting shoulder stretch.

Muscles stretched: Shoulder and neck muscles.

Description: Sit down with the legs together pointing forward. Your arms are behind your body, with your palms on the floor and your fingers pointing toward your body. Slowly lean back and increase the angle between your arms and your trunk until maximum stretch is achieved. Hold this position for 30 seconds and return to the original position.

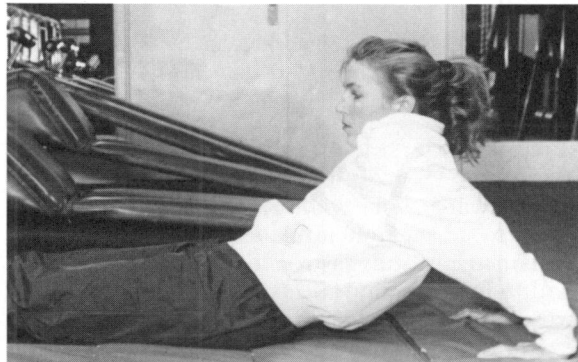

Figure 3-26. Sitting shoulder stretch.

9. Standing shoulder stretch.

Muscles stretched: Front and back shoulder and neck muscles.

Description: Stand with your arms straight out to your sides and hold a stationary object. Turn slowly to the left and slowly stretch the shoulder until tightness is felt. Hold this position for 30 seconds. Return to the starting position and repeat, turning to the right.

Figure 3-27. Standing shoulder stretch.

10. Scissor back stretch.

Muscles stretched: Lower back muscles, buttocks, upper hamstrings.

Description: Lie on your back with your legs together and your arms extended out at the sides. Slowly rotate the left hip and raise the right leg to reach the left arm. Hold this position for 30 seconds. Return to the original position and repeat, this time raising the left leg to reach the right arm.

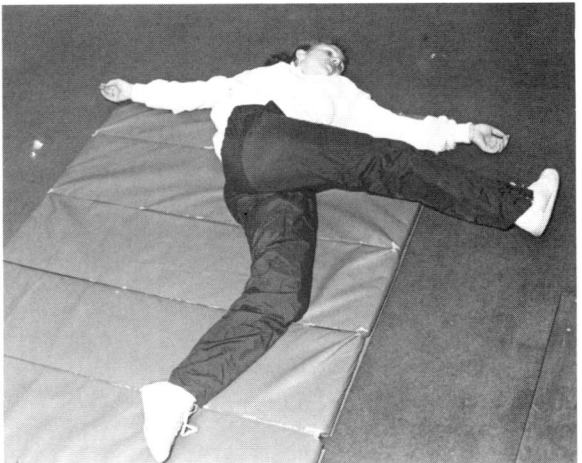

Figure 3-28. Scissor back stretch.

11. Calf stretch.

Muscles stretched: Calf, lower hamstrings.

Description: Stand erect with your feet together and both heels on the ground. Lean forward against a wall or immovable object. Then lean farther until tightness is felt in the calves and achilles tendons. Hold this position for 30 seconds and then return to the original position.

Figure 3-29. Calf stretch.

12. Standing shin stretch.

Muscles stretched: Tibialis anterior, shin and ankle muscles.

Description: Stand erect with your back to a wall and your feet flat on the ground. Lean backward until tightness is felt in the shin muscles. Turn the toes outward, and then inward for different angles. (This may be done with one leg or both legs at a time.) Hold each position for 30 seconds and then return to the starting position.

Figure 3-30. Standing shin stretch.

Exercises for Wrist Flexors and Extensors

Pre-stretch position and initial exercise: The following wrist exercises should be done in a contract-relaxation manner and are easily done by one person. The opposite hand should be used as the resisting force to allow the isometric contraction. Extension should be done to the point of muscle tightness and slight resistance. The wrist should then be extended slightly farther and the exercise should be repeated. Three extensions and contractions should be sufficient for each exercise.

1. Wrist flexor stretch.

Description: The palm of the racquet hand should be facing up. With the opposite hand, pull the racquet hand and fingers downward so that the muscles and connective tissues of the wrist are extended.

TRAIN FOR STRENGTH AND FLEXIBILITY

Figure 3-31. Wrist flexor stretch.

2. Wrist extensor stretch.

Description: The palm of the racquet hand should be facing down. With the opposite hand, press the hand and fingers downward, extending the muscles and connective tissues of the wrist.

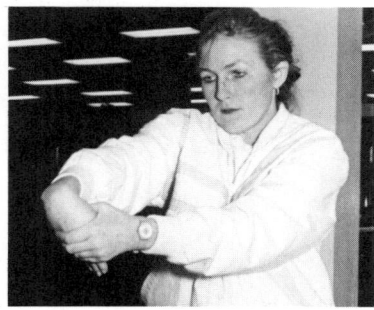

Figure 3-32. Wrist extensor stretch.

3. Pronation muscle stretch.

Description: Hold a racquet with the racquet head pointing straight up (12 o'clock position) and then rotate it clockwise to a 3 o'clock or 4 o'clock position. At this extended position, the opposite hand is used as the resister and the contract-relaxation exercise is done. The racquet is then rotated farther to a 4:30 or 5 o'clock position, and the exercise is repeated.

Figure 3-33. Pronation muscle stretch.

4. Supination muscle stretch.

Description: Hold a racquet with the racquet head pointing straight up (12 o'clock) and then rotate it counterclockwise to an 8 o'clock or 9 o'clock position. Provide resistance with the opposite hand and do contract-relaxation exercises. The racquet is then rotated farther to a 7 o'clock or 7:30 position and the exercise is repeated.

Figure 3-34. Supination muscle stretch.

5. Neutral position stretch.

Description: Hold the racquet in an eastern forehand grip, with the racquet head perpendicular to the ground. Let the racquet head face forward toward the ground, extending the muscles on the top part of the wrist. Keeping the racquet head in this neutral position, add slight pressure for a very gradual stretch.

Figure 3-35. Neutral position stretch.

6. Tricep and service stretch.

Description: Hold the racquet behind your back. The racquet should be dropped straight down the middle of your back as a slow gradual stretch is done.

Figure 3-36. Tricep and service stretch.

THE DOSTAL FLEXIBILITY TRAINING PROGRAM (TWO-MAN SYSTEM)

This contract-relaxation flexibility program combines strength with flexibility. Because strength gain is relative to the joint angle for the muscles being exercised, it is important to follow correct procedure at the proper intensity to develop greater flexibility. Before starting this program, the athlete should jog or jump rope to elevate the body temperature to the breaking of a sweat. This will allow efficiency in the exercise while preventing any injury.

Athletes perform stretching exercises in order to accomplish one or more of the following objectives:

1. To reduce injuries due to tearing of muscle tissue.
2. To increase the amplitude of movements inherent in the activity.
3. To promote muscle relaxation.
4. To increase metabolism in muscles, joints, and associated connective tissues.

General Procedure for the Dostal Flexibility Training Program

All exercises in the Dostal method should be done using the general procedure described for the hamstring stretch. Mastery of this method is quick, and improvement will be experienced at the initial workout. The exercises should be performed daily for maximum benefit, preferably before specific sport training begins. For added flexibility, the Dostal exercises should be repeated after training.

Hip Extensors Stretch Example

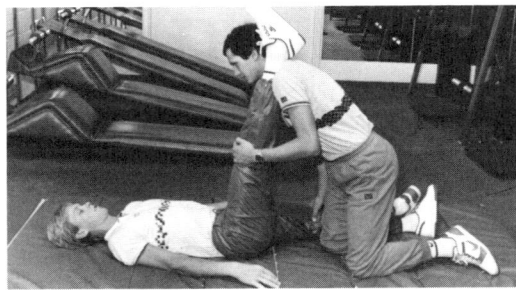

Figure 3-37. Pre-stretched, contracted position—hip extensors stretch.

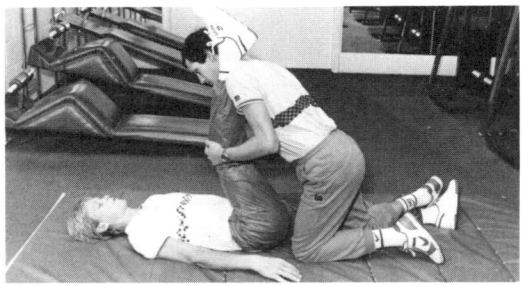

Figure 3-38. Stretched, extended position—hip extensors stretch.

In Figure 3-37, the athlete (P1) lies on his back with the leg to be stretched lifted as far as possible from the floor with the knee extended. The opposite leg remains on the floor throughout the exercise with the knee extended. The partner (P2) is positioned so that he serves as an immovable object when the athlete begins to exercise. With the hamstrings in a lengthened position, the player begins the exercise by attempting to push his leg back toward the floor. This effort is resisted by P2, who does not permit the leg to move, thus causing an isometric contraction. In the first two seconds of the contraction, P1 gradually builds to a maximum or near maximum effort, and he should sustain the contraction for an additional four seconds. The entire six-second exercise should be counted aloud by P2.

After the initial six-second effort, P1 lifts his leg toward his head by contracting the opposite muscle group. This concentric contraction pulls the leg to a new position as the result of increased flexibility of the hamstrings and surrounding connective tissue. This maneuver should be aided by slight pressure from P2. Slight discomfort may be felt, but if P1 experiences pain, the exercise should be stopped immediately. The isometric contraction should never be explosive, but should always be a gradual increase in effort.

In Figure 3-38, P1 has moved to a new position as a result of the initial exercise. The entire procedure is then repeated three or four times. This is followed by the same sequence applied to the opposite leg.

1. Hip extensors stretch (hamstrings).

Description: P1 lies on his back, with one leg on the floor, and the other raised as high as possible. Both legs remain straight throughout the exercise. P2 is on one knee, with the opposite foot on the floor and the shoulder against the back of P1's leg. P2 holds the non-exercising leg to the floor. P1 attempts to push his raised leg to the floor. P2 resists this effort causing an isometric contraction. After the six-second contraction, P1 pulls the leg toward his head. P2 assists with light pressure. P1 then repeats this procedure from the new stretched (extended) position two or three more times.

2. Hip abductors stretch I (groin muscles).

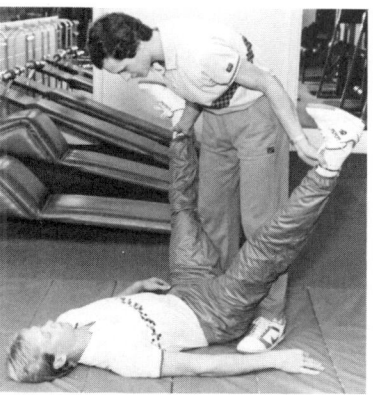

Figure 3-41. Pre-stretch position—hip abductors stretch II.

Description: P1 sits with his back and legs straight, with his legs as far apart as possible. P2 is positioned in front of P1, holding both P1's legs above the ankles. P1 attempts to bring his legs together, making sure to keep them straight, and P2 resists. After the six-second isometric contraction, P1 spreads his legs (abducts the hip joint), and P2 assists with light pressure. P1 then repeats this procedure three times from the new stretched (extended) position.

Figure 3-42. Stretched position—hip abductors stretch II.

3. Hip abductors stretch II.

Description: P1 lies on his back, with his legs spread apart as far as possible and raised to form a ninety degree angle with the floor. P2 stands in front of P1, and holds both P1's legs below the knee. P1 attempts to squeeze his legs together, and P2 resists. After the six-second isometric contraction, P1 pulls his legs apart (abducts his hips) as far as possible. P2 assists with light pressure. P1 then repeats this procedure three times from the new stretched (extended) position.

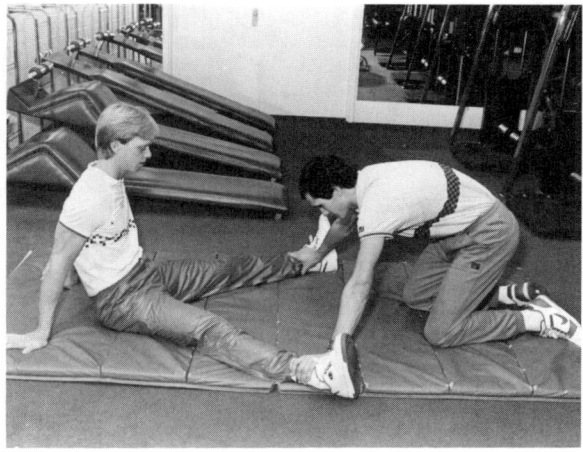

Figure 3-39. Pre-stretch position—hip abductors stretch I.

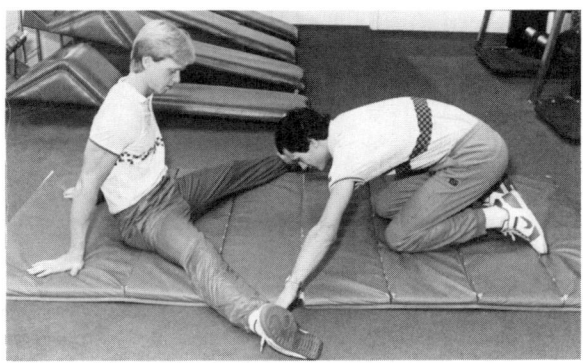

Figure 3-40. Stretched position—hip abductors stretch I.

4. Hip flexors stretch I.

Description: P1 lies prone with his right leg flexed at the knee and raised as high as possible. P2 is behind P1, resting on his right knee, with his left foot on the floor. P2's right hand is placed under P1's raised knee, and his left hand is placed slightly above P1's right buttock. P1 attempts to pull his knee downward to the floor. P2 resists. After the six-second contraction, P1 lifts his leg higher, and P2 assists with light pressure. P1 then repeats this procedure three times from the new stretched (extended) position.

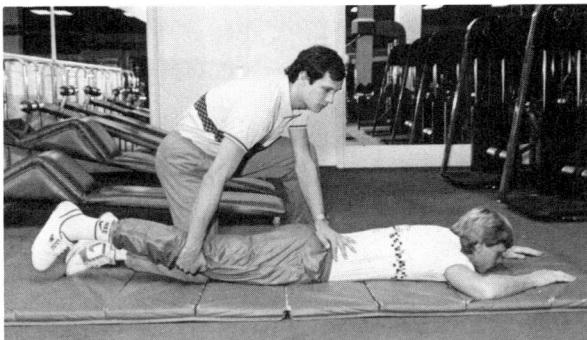

Figure 3-43. Pre-stretch position—hip flexors stretch I.

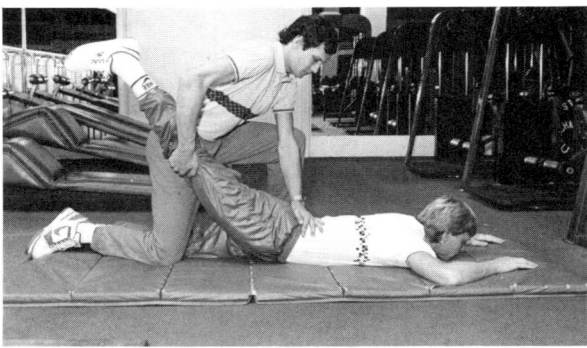

Figure 3-44. Stretched position—hip flexors stretch I.

5. Trunk extensors stretch (lower back muscles).

Description: P1 sits down, with his legs straight out in front of him and his trunk flexed forward as far as possible. P2 stands behind and slightly to the side of P1 and places his hands on P1's neck and the central portion of his upper back. P2's rear foot should be braced against an immovable object. P1 attempts to straighten up and extend his trunk. P2 resists. After the six-second isometric contraction, P1 pulls his trunk down toward his legs, and P2 assists with light pressure. P1 then repeats this procedure three times from the new stretched (extended) position. Note: This exercise should be performed with less than maximum effort until the athlete is accustomed to it and is confident that no injury will result.

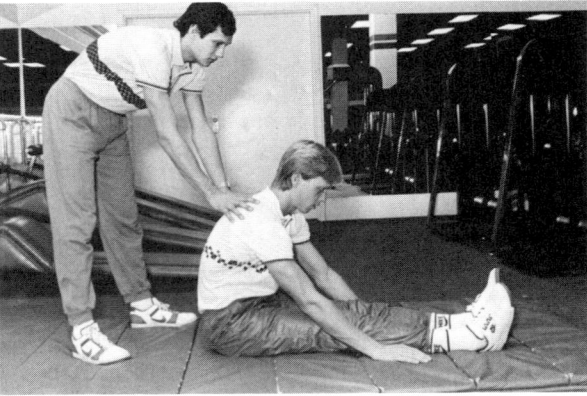

Figure 3-45. Pre-stretch position—trunk extensors stretch.

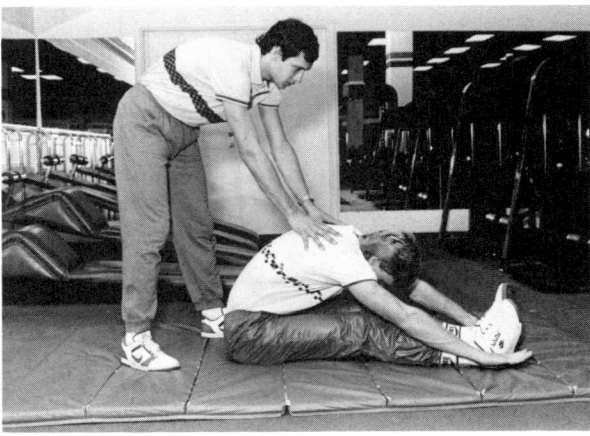

Figure 3-46. Stretched position—trunk extensors stretch.

6. Combination: Trunk extensors, groin, and hamstrings.

Description: P1 sits with his legs spread and his trunk flexed as far as possible toward his right leg, with his hands stretched toward his foot. P2 stands behind and slightly to the side of P1, with his hands on P1's upper back. P1 tries to straighten up (extend trunk). P2 resists. After six-second isometric contractions, P1 pulls his trunk down toward his leg, and P2 assists with light pressure. Repeat this procedure from the new stretched (extended) position. P1 then repeats the sequence, this time reaching down his left leg, and then repeats, reaching straight ahead to stretch his middle groin area (Figures 3-49 and 3-50). Note: This exercises should be performed with less than maximum effort until the athlete is accustomed to it and is confident that no injury to the groin area or lower back will result.

TRAIN FOR STRENGTH AND FLEXIBILITY

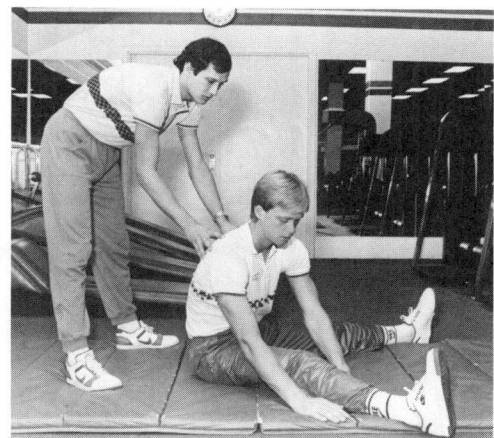

Figure 3-47. Pre-stretch right leg — combination.

Figure 3-48. Stretched position right leg — combination.

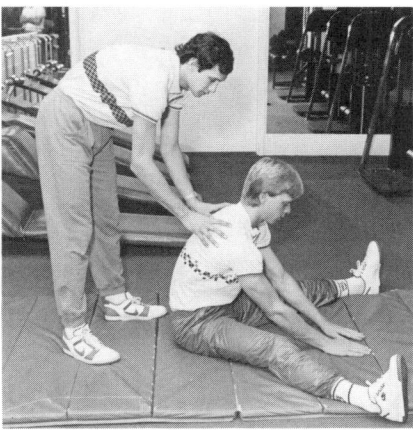

Figure 3-49. Pre-stretch middle groin — combination.

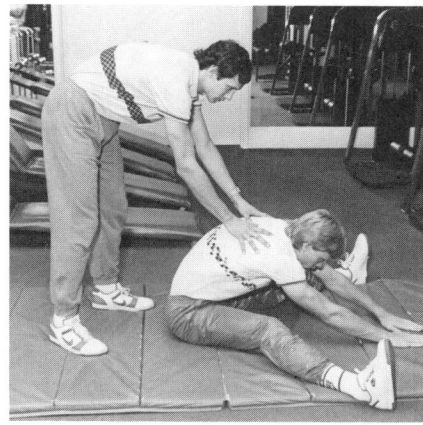

Figure 3-50. Stretched position middle groin — combination.

7. Trunk lateral flexors (external obliques).

Description: P1 stands with his feet shoulder width apart, with his left hand resting on the left side of his head. He bends his trunk to his right side. P2 stands on P1's left side, with his left hand on P1's waist, and his right hand holding P1's raised elbow. P1 attempts to pull his body to the upright position. P2 resists this effort to cause an isometric contraction. After the six-second isometric contraction, P1 pulls his trunk downward. P2 assists with light pressure. P1 repeats this procedure three times from the new stretched (extended) position.

Figure 3-51. Pre-stretch position—trunk lateral flexors.

TOTAL TENNIS TRAINING

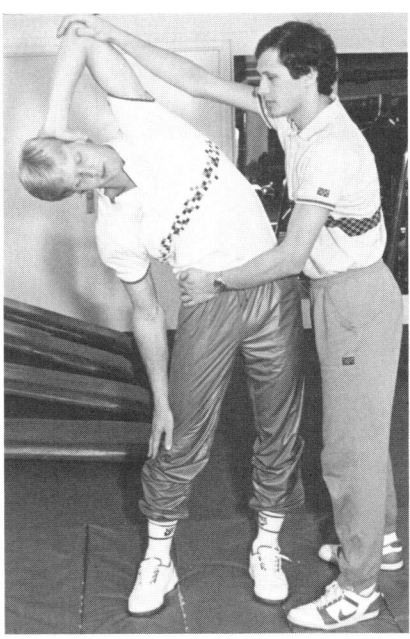

Figure 3-52. Stretched position—trunk lateral flexors.

8. Shoulder extensors.

Description: P1 sits down with his back straight, his legs extended straight out in front of him, his arms straight up, and his shoulders stretched as far as possible. P2 stands behind P1, standing backward with the back of his legs resting against P1's spine (or P2 can stand facing forward with one foot near P1's body with his knee resting against P1's spine). P2 holds both P1's forearms. P1 attempts to pull his arms toward his legs, keeping his elbows straight. P2 resists. After a six-second isometric contraction, P1 pushes his arms backward. P2 assists with light pressure. P1 then repeats this procedure from the new stretched (extended) position.

Figure 3-53. Pre-stretch position—shoulder extensors.

Figure 3-54. Stretched position—shoulder extensors.

9. Shoulder horizontal abductors.

Description: P1 sits down with his legs straight out in front of him, his back straight, and his arms raised straight out to his sides to shoulder level. P2 stands behind P1, with one foot near P1's body and his knee resting against P1's spine. P2 holds both P1's forearms (use of a pad or towel may prove helpful). P1 attempts to pull his arms forward, keeping his elbows straight. P2 resists. After a six-second isometric contraction, P1 pushes his arms backward, and P2 assists with light pressure. P1 repeats this procedure from the new stretched (extended) position.

Figure 3-55. Pre-stretch position—shoulder horizontal abductors.

TRAIN FOR STRENGTH AND FLEXIBILITY

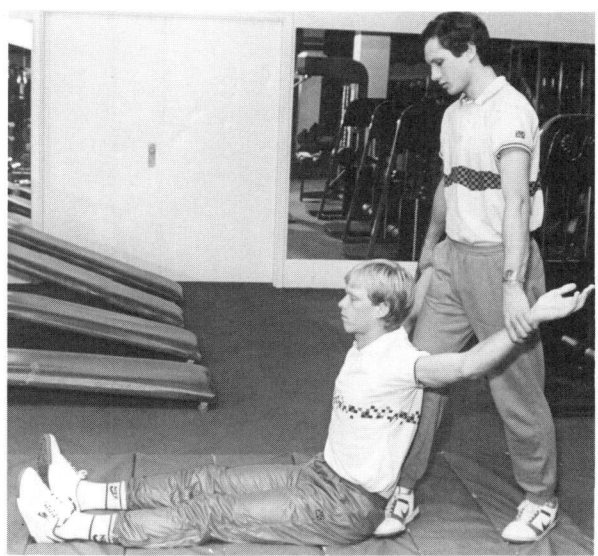

Figure 3-56. Stretched position—shoulder horizontal abductors.

10. Shoulder internal rotators.

Description: P1 stands erect, with his arm raised to shoulder level, and his elbow flexed to 90 degrees, with his shoulder rotated out as far as possible. P2 stands in front and to the side of P1, with one hand on P1's wrist, and the other on P1's arm slightly above the elbow. P1 attempts to rotate his shoulder inwardly (throwing motion), and P2 resists. After a six-second isometric contraction, P1 rotates his shoulder outwardly. P2 assists with light pressure. P1 then repeats this procedure from the stretched (extended) position.

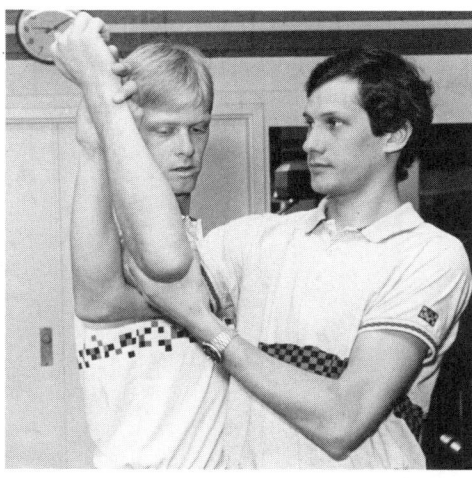

Figure 3-57. Pre-stretch position—shoulder internal rotators.

Figure 3-58. Stretched position—shoulder internal rotators.

SUMMARY

A thorough, systematic flexibility program can only aid the athlete. Good sense and judgment should be used, and a consistent program should be followed. The idea behind stretching is to get the muscles to a state of readiness so that they can endure the heavy ballistic action that occurs during competition. It is important to recognize that stretching behond the normal movement capacity for a joint may be detrimental in many ways to the athlete. Both overstretching and understretching, therefore, should be avoided. With experience, the athlete will learn his own limitations in flexibility training.

CHAPTER 4

TRAIN OTHER IMPORTANT MOTOR SKILLS

"Do not wish for quick results, nor look for small advantages. If you seek quick results, you will not attain the ultimate goal. If you are led astray by small advantages, you will never accomplish great things."

—Confucius

MOTOR SKILLS: SPEED, AGILITY, AND BALANCE

Tennis is an extremely complex sport, in part because of the many different motor skills that are involved. Speed, agility, balance, reaction time, quickness, power, and hand-eye coordination are all important. There is not enough time in practice to work on each of these areas alone, so most coaches try to incorporate a training program that encompasses many of them. Those of primary importance to tennis are speed, agility, and balance.

Speed in athletics is defined as "the rate at which a person can propel his body, or parts of his body, through space."[1] When we talk about speed in tennis we are usually referring to a player's foot movement. Can he move from point A to point B on the court quickly? Can he run down balls that are out of reach for the average player?

Many more motor skills are involved, though, than just running speed. Every time a tennis player hits a ball, his reaction time, quickness, and power are important factors. Reaction time, or "the time between the stimulus and the initial response," becomes a key ingredient in any quick exchange of shots. Quickness is a term that refers to an athlete's short spurts of speed. Power is defined as speed plus strength. Power has often been categorized as the greatest individual determinant of athletic ability. But in tennis, the saying, "Power thrills, but speed kills," is very true. Train them both for good results on the court.

Agility is defined as "the physical ability which enables an individual to rapidly change positions and direction in a precise manner." In tennis, the need for this motor skill is quite obvious, because all stroke production is based on the ability to get from one part of the court to another, to set up, to keep on balance, and to change direction.

Speed agility refers to a player's ability to move as quickly as possible while remaining in perfect balance so that a quick stop and change of direction can be made. Without the ability to get to the ball and then set up for a good stroke, good technical skills are useless. Lack of this combination of speed and agility can prevent a player from progressing to a new level in his game.

When a player starts losing a match, he often makes comments like, "I can't feel the ball," or "I don't know why I'm missing the ball." What he means is that he is not able to set up for his shots, and his shots are not effective. He does not have enough speed.

Professional players' careers falter when they lose their speed and balance and cannot make effective shots. In fact, speed is always the first thing to go as a player ages or if he does not train. Again, though, it should be emphasized that speed alone is not lost, but speed, agility, and balance, the three key ingredients to effective stroke production. Without them, it does not matter what the body is doing from the waist up.

Balance, or the ability for a person to hold a stationary position, is also a very important ingredient needed for a tennis player's athletic achievement. Solid and well-placed shots cannot be made without this important motor skill. The researcher Bass states there is evidence to indicate that the ability to balance easily depends upon the functions of the mechanisms in the semicircular canals; the kinesthetic sensations in the muscles, tendons, and joints; the visual perception while the body is in motion; and the ability to coordinate these three sources of stimuli. Balance is very much an inherited skill but it should be worked on as any other important motor skill in the tennis player's training routine.[2]

All running and agility drills done in practice should emphasize good balance. Speed is of great help to a player with good balance as well. In all stroking work done in practice, the reminder, "Head down, and feet on the ground," is critical to good development of the balance of good stroke produc-

Figure 4-1. Pender Murphy's training for speed, agility, and balance pays off in a match.

tion. Good balance allows a player's technical skills to remain effective long into his career. Good balance allows maximum leverage for stroke production for power and accuracy even if the athlete is not strong.

The following sample 45-minute training routine incorporates many of the components needed for the development of important motor skills in tennis. All drills should closely simulate the speed, agility, and balance that is used in tennis. The footwork, when possible, should be the good fundamental footwork used when executing a stroke.

1. **Five minutes:** Light jog and flexibilities (warm-up period should allow the body temperature to rise approximately one degree, or when sweat breaks).

2. **Five minutes:** 30 seconds jump rope, 30 seconds rest (five times), alternate the weighted rope with the speed rope.

3. **Ten minutes:**
   a. Box drills: two sets (30 seconds rest).
   b. Bench blasts: two sets each leg (30 seconds rest).
   c. Alley quick step drills: two sets (30 seconds rest).
   d. 30-yard sprints: six sets (10 seconds rest).

4. **Five minutes:** Foot control ball drills (dribble a tennis ball alternating feet in order to improve balance and control).

5. **Two minutes:** Jump rope, cool down.

6. **Five minutes:** Rest break.

7. **Two minutes:** Loosen up using a jump rope.

8. **Five minutes:** Lateral court movement drills, ball pickup drills, lateral movement.

9. **Three minutes:** Power jump rope, alternate 45 seconds exercise, 15 seconds rest.

10. **Two minutes:** Bench blasts.

11. **Two minutes:** Jump rope, cool down.

Of additional importance when we talk about speed is an understanding that strength is a very important component for its development. A misconception was held for years that strength development was detrimental to speed. Research by Zorbas, Karpovich, Wilkin, Masley, Endres, and Chui proved exactly the opposite.[3] These educators discovered that strength development, primarily through weight training, significantly improved the athlete's speed of movement.

Figure 4-2. Training for motor skills.

It is also important to understand the relationship between fast twitch and slow twitch muscle tissues. The body's striated (skeletal) muscles contain two types of fibers: dark fibers and light fibers, also referred to as slow twitch and fast twitch fibers. Dark muscle fibers have slow contractions but great endurance, whereas light muscle fibers have quick contractions but little endurance.

This relationship is easily understood by looking at a chicken or a quail. Both these birds have light muscle fibers in the breast and dark muscle fibers in the legs. Neither can fly far, but each has strong legs to walk on. A duck's breast has only dark muscle fibers that aid his long, slow flight to Canada and back. We see this relationship in fish as well. The dark muscle tissue of salmon and trout gives them the endurance they need to travel great distances upstream to spawn. Bass and bream have light muscle tissue that allows their quick bursts of speed, but both these fish fatigue easily.

In a human being, dark and light muscle fibers are interspersed throughout all the muscles. It may be true that sprinters have a higher proportion of light muscle fibers, whereas distance runners have a higher proportion of dark fibers. Regardless, training of the tennis player should be geared for both types of muscle tissue. Tennis is predominantly an anaerobic sport that requires high intensity and ballistic speed, so a program of training should be done for the fast muscle. Exercises like bench blasts, double-knee jumps, sprints, suicide line drills, and speed jump rope work are all excellent for this. On the other hand, training of the slow twitch muscles is also important for injury reduction, for joint and connective tissue strength, and for muscular endurance. Excellent slow twitch work can be done with Nautilus equipment, other weight programs, or exercises designed to improve strength and speed.

SUMMARY

A tennis training program should incorporate work on speed, agility, balance, reaction time, quickness, power, and hand-eye coordination. Drills can be used to develop these skills, and it should be remembered that all drills should simulate actual match play. Exercises should be done to develop both the slow twitch and the fast twitch muscles.

Figure 4-3. Strength development increases a tennis player's speed.

CHAPTER 5

SUPPORT YOUR TRAINING WITH GOOD NUTRITION

"If you are what you eat, then the average young athlete is a hamburger and an order of fries."
—Cheryl Martin, State Farm Insurance

TWO MONTHS OF TRAINING OUT THE WINDOW

We had been training for six weeks in preparation for our first major tournament at the University of Miami. All the details had been taken care of and the players were in top shape. I was particularly concerned about the heat and humidity in southern Florida and the fact that the players would sweat more there. During the week before the tournament, each player took a steam bath for 10 to 15 minutes every day and, in addition, the players wore nylon rainsuits during their workouts to make them perspire more than they normally did in the cool winter temperatures.

I thought I had taken care of all details, but I had forgotten one thing—I had not monitored the eating habits of my team. We were playing the University of California at Irvine in a morning match. Halfway through the second set, one of my returning All-Americans was playing very poorly and looking sluggish. I walked to his court and asked him what was the matter. He said he really did not know, except that he could not focus properly on what he was doing. At first I was upset with him and told him to concentrate and get going. I said to him, "You've got to get tough. Get your rear end in gear. What the heck is going on here?" As he played another game, I saw a determined but exhausted expression on his face, and I knew he was trying hard to concentrate, but something was wrong. I went over to him at the next crossover. He had his head between his legs and looked totally exhausted. I wondered if I had the guys properly trained. I also wondered if this player had been out on the town the night before, breaking training. Then a thought struck me. I walked over to him and asked him what he had eaten for breakfast. He replied, "pancakes with syrup, a danish, and a glass of orange juice." Then I realized what was happening: he was experiencing a sugar crash from all the sugar he had eaten that morning. It made me wonder if our six weeks of training and preparation for the trip were to no avail because of an order of pancakes and danish. The match was lost over a very simple detail that I should have monitored.

Figure 5-1. The results of good nutrition.

BASIC NUTRITIONAL GUIDELINES FOR THE TENNIS PLAYER

A proper diet is essential to good athletic performances, but many athletes give little or no thought to their eating habits and dietary needs. The following nutritional guidelines are important for all athletes to know and follow.

Food Groups

Food is composed of seven basic substances: carbohydrates, fats, proteins, vitamins, minerals, water, or indigestible materials. Each one of these has specific functions in providing nourishment for the body. For the athlete, it is of critical importance to recognize what each does to his body under the physical, mental, and emotional strain of competition.

Carbohydrates: All forms of refined sugars, including honey, are carbohydrates. Carbohydrates are metabolized very easily into glucose (blood sugar) to be used for quick energy or the athlete's primary energy source. Carbohydrates enable the athlete to feel alert, strong, and energetic, and they help to maintain proper blood sugar levels. Too much sugar intake can cause lightheadedness, fatigue, and concentration lapse.

Carbohydrates provide four calories of energy per gram. The best sources of carbohydrates are fruit, vegetables, pastas, breads, and cereal products. Carbohydrates are used up very quickly in the athlete's body and should be replaced often.

Fats: At nine calories per gram, fats provide more a long-term energy source. The body uses fat for energy metabolism after carbohydrate supplies are depleted. It is also used for insulation and for padding for the body's organs. Fat is much harder to digest than carbohydrates, and too much fat in the diet can cause health problems. Fats are found in many foods.

Athletes who avoid eating refined sugar products have little trouble converting from carbohydrates to fat for energy metabolism. Sources of fats are butter, oils, peanuts, and meats.

Proteins: Tissue repair and growth are the primary job of protein, and protein should be an important part of an athlete's diet. In addition, proteins are used by the body as an energy source after carbohydrates and fats are used. Actually, protein is very difficult to convert to energy, and for this reason, it should be consumed on days the athlete is not competing, or a few hours after competition.

Protein provides four calories per gram. Meat, fish, poultry, dairy products, eggs, nuts, legumes, wheat germ, and bean sprouts are good sources of protein.

Vitamins: Vitamins assist body functions and metabolism. They are necessary for cell activity, and are therefore critical to the proper function of the athlete's body.

Vitamins A, D, E, and K are fat soluble. They are stored in the fat, and it is not necessary to eat them every day. In fact, excessive quantities of fat soluble vitamins can cause sluggishness or indigestion.

Vitamins B and C are water soluble. They are not stored in the body and must be replaced, and any excess will be removed in the urine. A low level of B-complex vitamins in the body may cause muscular fatigue, cramps, and loss of concentration.

A well balanced diet containing all the food groups is recommended because a limited diet cannot supply all of the vitamins needed for the athlete.

Minerals: Like vitamins, minerals are essential to the proper functioning of the body. They participate in hormone and enzyme production and give structure to the bones and other parts of the body.

Calcium, magnesium, phosphorus, sulphur, sodium chloride, and potassium are needed in large amounts. Others needed in trace amounts are iron, selenium, manganese, fluoride, copper, molybdenum, zinc, chromium, cobalt, and iodine.

Water: Water is important for every bodily function, and, in fact, about 60 percent of the athlete's body is water. Water allows the cells to work, is a component of blood, and is an important part of the body's cooling system, lymphatic system, and nervous system.

Almost all foods contain water but, of course, the best way to obtain it is by drinking fluids. Water contains no calories, but it is primarily responsible for all energy metabolism.

A recent study showed an athlete training on a treadmill to the point of exhaustion, with no water intake. His endurance was just over one hour. Then the same athlete exercised again with two water breaks when he was given as much water as he wanted, and he doubled his time on the treadmill. The third time the same athlete was given frequent small amounts of water, and he was able to exercise up to four times as long as his original time. The lesson for the tennis player is to drink early in the day of competition and frequently from the start to the finish of the match, before thirst occurs.

Indigestible materials—fiber and roughage: Cancer of the colon is now the second most common type of cancer in America. Many doctors and nutritionists blame high meat and fat diets, preservatives added in so many foods, and diets lacking in foods rich in fiber.

Harmful Foods

Sugar: The harmful effects of all types of refined sugars are far-reaching. Two hundred years ago the average American ate about four pounds of sugar per year. Today, Americans eat an average of 129 pounds of the substance, or about two two and one-half pounds per week.[1] Sugar is added to many processed foods, and consumers should be sure to read the ingredient panel on packages of food.

Sugar can cause a condition called reactive hypoglycemia, in which the blood sugar level rises quickly, giving a high feeling of energy. Very quickly the body's balancing system reacts by sending insulin into the bloodstream, which produces a crashing effect with depression and reduced concentration. Appetite is controlled by the blood sugar level, and this crash causes great hunger pangs, and if these pangs are satisfied by more sugar, an even greater crash is created. Appetite is best controlled by eating complex carbonydrates such as fruits, vegetables, and eliminating refined sugars.

Sugar's harmful effects:

—Over many years, sugar consumption results in decreased ability of the cells to use their ordinary materials such as glucose.

—Sugar has been implicated in acne and other skin disorders.

—Cancer, leukemia, and gout may be correlated with high sugar intake.

—The digestion of sugar uses up B vitamins, thus causing a possible B vitamin deficiency.

White flour: White flour is missing many of the important nutrients found in wheat. Whole wheat or other whole grain breads, therefore, are more nutritious than white bread.

Salt tablets: Sodium, magnesium, and potassium are the minerals that are lost through exercise. They are replaced well by fruits and vegetables and fruit juices. The average American gets far too much salt in his diet already, and the ingestion of salt tablets can lead to serious dehydration, possible heat exhaustion, and stroke.

Alcohol and beer: Alcohol has a long-lasting effect on athletic performance. One can of beer can lower some athletes' heat tolerance for 24 to 48 hours, and three or more drinks can reduce heat tolerance for days. Uncoordination may persist until 24 hours after alcohol consumption.

Juice supplements: There has been much discussion about what is the best drink before and during competition. Juice supplements contain varying amounts of potassium, but they contain much less potassium than do whole milk or orange juice. Milk should not be drunk either immediately before or after competition. Perhaps the best drink is a mixture of three parts water and one part fruit juice.

THE PRE-GAME MEAL

The old idea of a steak and potato before the ball game is no longer considered a good one. Protein takes a long time to digest, and meat can sometimes sit in the stomach for hours before entering the digestive tract. Carbohydrates, including pasta, breads, fruits, vegetables, and plenty of liquids are the best pre-game meal. Fats are also hard to digest, but are important for an endurance event. Dairy products should not be ingested before competition, because the calcium in them may interfere with the magnesium uptake that is important in energy expenditure.

THE POST-GAME MEAL

Athletes are often so hungry after a competition that they run out and grab whatever food they can find, and, more often than not, they choose sugar-filled foods. There is great harm in this practice because sugar interferes with the body's metabolism and regulating system, and the following day the athlete's muscles feel heavy, he is disoriented, and he may be emotionally sensitive.

To prevent this practice, a great college basketball coach used to closely monitor the diets of his players after a tough ball game. He would always make sure to have juices, fruit, bread, and peanut butter sandwiches in the locker room immediately after the game to help to take the edge off the players' appetites so they would not go out and load up on sugary foods. He discovered, too, that a well-balanced meal made his athletes feel better the day after a match.

SUMMARY

Good nutrition is essential for an athlete's good performance; his diet should be high in carbohydrates, moderate in proteins, and low in fat. Athletes should avoid sugar, salt tablets, white flour, and alcohol. Fluid replacement on the day of competition is crucial, and athletes should drink frequently in small amounts when competing. The best pre-game or post-game meal is one that is high in carbohydrates.

Figure 5-2. A proper diet will help an athlete reach his physical, mental, and emotional potential.

CHAPTER 6

DEVELOP YOUR TECHNICAL SKILLS AND STROKE PRODUCTION

"The greatest thing a person can do in this world is to make the most possible out of the stuff that has been given to him. This is success and there is no other.

—Orison Slepp Marden

LEARN YOUR STROKES FROM THE INSIDE OUT

I was fortunate enough after college to work for Harry Hopman, who was the Australian Davis Cup Coach for over 20 years. Hopman has been recognized as one of the greatest coaches of all time, and his results with players such as Rod Laver, Ken Rosewall, and Roy Emerson may never be equaled in the sport of tennis. Having had little formal tennis training at that point, I approached my new job expecting to learn all the new techniques and the mechanics of hitting the ball.

In my first month of working for Hopman, I was shocked, surprised, and somewhat disappointed to find out that I was not learning all the fancy schoolbook techniques of the great players that I had heard so much about. Hopman was working with current junior players John McEnroe, Peter Fleming, and Vitas Gerulaitis. He would put them on workout courts and make them hit thousands of balls as he ran them from side to side and up and back, while encouraging them to push themselves physically beyond their limits. Very seldom did I hear Hopman talk about certain shot techniques, and when he did, it was always in a way that gave leniency to the player's individual form and style and allowed the player to immediately adapt.

At first I did not understand Hopman's approach. After three months of working with him, however, I started to realize the genius of this man who knew how much more important it was to train the inner part of an athlete than it was to just train an athlete's technical skills. I think what Hopman gave top-notch athletes with a bit of rebellion in them (like McEnroe, Fleming, and Gerulaitis) was discipline and a tremendous pride that came from their hard work. Seeing how this pride grew was a great help to me as I developed my own coaching methods.

But I realized that there was much more to his style that just that. I started asking myself questions about teaching and playing styles. Why were the strokes of the top 10 players in the world so completely different? Why were some players baseline players, and why were others net rushers? Why did almost all the players use different grips to hit the ball? I thought of all the coaches who were teaching structured styles and forcing their pupils to play in certain ways. Then I would watch Hopman. I saw how he could coax the inner part of a player to get the results that he wanted, but always in a unique way, suiting each player's personality.

During that year, a young Swedish player named Bjorn Borg was quickly coming to international attention. Borg had a revolutionary style that included extremes for stroking on both the forehand and backhand sides. Very few players had ever used a two-handed backhand before, and very few players had ever strayed far enough to use the severe western forehand grip that Borg used. At that point, no one knew the impact that Borg would have on the tennis world. As I watched him play, I wondered if someone had actually taught him those strokes. Did someone tell him to hold the racquet as he did and to hit two-handed, and to loop the ball with such heavy top spin? Or, did he develop the strokes on his own?

I realized that although certain fundamental skills are important to deliver a ball with the right force, spin, and direction, a player's strokes are developed pretty much according to his temperament and his own style. This was a revelation for me as a coach, and it gave me new insight in training players. I realized Hopman's genius more than ever.

Forcing a certain structure on an athlete may be confusing to him, and often keeps his outer and inner selves from "meeting," thus preventing him from reaching his full potential. As coaches, we may train an athlete in a certain way and drill the fundamentals into his head, but unless he develops the inner determination necessary to become the best, he will not reach his full potential.

I have often wondered what would happen if a coach provided no instruction, but instead delivered thousands of balls to a very coordinated athlete to hit with different strokes. Would the athlete develop into a fine player? My guess is that he would.

But good basics *are* very important, and just hitting balls is not enough. In the early stages of development, strict attention should be paid to fundamentals—helping a player execute the forehand, backhand, serve, volley, approach shot, return serves, passing shots, and overhead shots. Only when a player is able to execute these, will he be able to develop an individual style of play and shot delivery.

Providing instruction to a tennis player is like providing instruction to a painter or musician. Painters and musicians learn the fundamentals of fingering and brushwork, but artists only become artists when they are able to give physical expression to the world inside themselves. It is the same with tennis players. Athletics is one of the purest forms of art. What a tragedy it is when an individual's inner self is prevented from surfacing by either a coach's inability to let the athlete play according to his personality as he reaches advanced stages, or at the other extreme, a lack of knowledge of the fundamentals that should have been learned earlier in the athlete's career!

A coach must understand that each player will play according to his personality. If the player is conservative, he will probably have a conservative style of play. If the player is reckless, he will probably have a reckless style of play. It is interesting that in critical match play situations, a player will do exactly what his personality dictates. A coach's most important job is to get the outside of the athlete to work comfortably and confidently with the inside of the athlete and vice versa. This union is the key to reaching maximum potential as a player. The coach should spend about 90 percent of his time in the early stages of a player's development working on technical skills and fundamentals. As a player progresses to a solid base of skills, the coach should work 50 percent on fundamentals and 50 percent on the mental and emotional parts of the athlete. As the player's fundamentals are firmly ingrained, nearly a complete range of freedom should be given to the athlete to play from the inside out as his temperament dictates, with the coach keeping a watchful eye on technical flaws that may prevent the athlete from developing to the next level.

THE TOOL BOX OF SKILLS: CONSISTENCY, PLACEMENT, DEPTH, SPIN, POWER

In tennis, the development of skills should follow a logical progression beginning with consistency and progressing to placement, depth, spin, and then power (see Figure 6-1). To be consistent with limited shots is the first step, and placing balls consistently from corner to corner follows. Next is the ability to use both under spin and top spin as deep balls are hit consistently to each corner, and lastly is the ability to add power to those shots. Most players work on bits and pieces of each of these skills throughout their development, but it is important to understand that each skill builds on the previous skills. The most obvious mistake most players make is to try to learn power before they learn the other skills that are necessary to control power.

Consistency

Consistency is the ability to get the ball back and into the opponent's court time and time again. This should be a player's first goal as a new stroke is learned.

Placement

Placement is the ability to direct the ball from side to side. Being able to do this gives the player the control needed to run his opponent.

Depth

Depth is the ability to keep an opponent deep in the court. This prevents the opponent from being offensive and at the same time gives a player many options. Controlling depth may also mean the player's ability to hit short balls and to bring his opponent purposely to the net from time to time.

Spin

Spin is the ability to control the ball and give it spin. It also means being able to deliver a ball that the opponent does not like to hit. Being able to hit a ball with top spin, under spin, or side spin opens multiple dimensions of the game.

Power

Power is the ability to win points outright and to force an opponent into errors. It is exciting and enjoyable to have power, but it should be the last skill to be developed, although many make it their first. The elements that dictate power are speed of the racquet head and good timing.

TOOL ONE: GRIPS

There are nearly as many ways of holding a tennis racquet as there are people playing the game. Although each player should learn the fundamentals of grip and stroke technique, each person's style and and grip will eventually be as unique as his signature.

Tennis instructors and coaches are often too rigid in their teaching of grip. Like golf, in which different clubs, and sometimes different grips and swings, are required for each shot, tennis requires some flexibility as well. Different court surfaces and conditions can demand different grips. Clay courts provide a slow, high bounce; hard concrete or asphalt courts provide a medium height and medium paced bounce; and gym floors or grass courts provide a very low, very fast bounce. For each surface, a different grip and wrist position is needed to hit the ball for the best impact and leverage.

Figure 6-1. Stroke development: Learn your strokes from the inside-out.

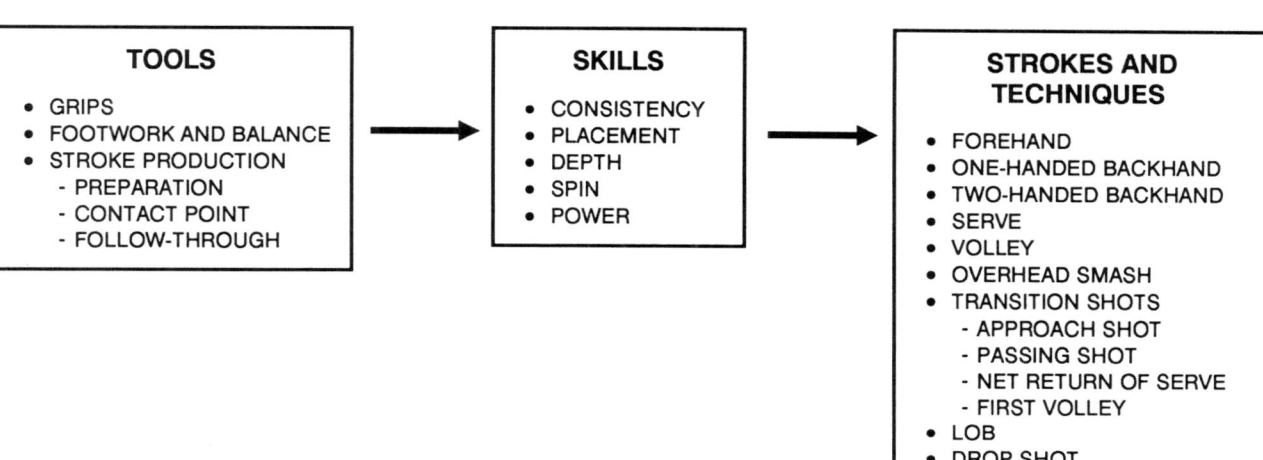

It is also necessary to use different grips for the different balls hit at a player on the same surface by the same opponent. Sometimes balls are high, sometimes low, sometimes wide and away from the player, and sometimes close to the player. Some are fast, some are slow, and almost all are delivered with a different spin. In order to use the same grip to hit all balls, a player would have to move fast enough to set up for the same bounce every time. This is often possible on ground strokes because they give a player more time to judge the bounce. A novice player becomes comfortable with a particular grip, usually based on the court surface that he is used to playing on. As his skills develop and he must hit balls of different heights and speeds, it becomes necessary to vary his grip.

A player should choose a grip to enable him to make contact with the ball in the optimal strike zone. Four basic grips are used by probably ninety percent of the world's tennis players, including the world's top players. They are the continental, the eastern, the semi-western, and the western grips. Figure 6-2 shows the approximate contact zone for each grip for the forehand. The experienced player will learn that for shots other than the forehand, a slightly different grip and hand position may be used for maximum effectiveness. It is not true that only one grip is acceptable at all times for each stroke.

Figures 6-3 through 6-10 illustrate each of the grips and show a player using each grip to hit a forehand in a different contact zone.

Figure 6-2. Approximate contact zones for different forehand grips.

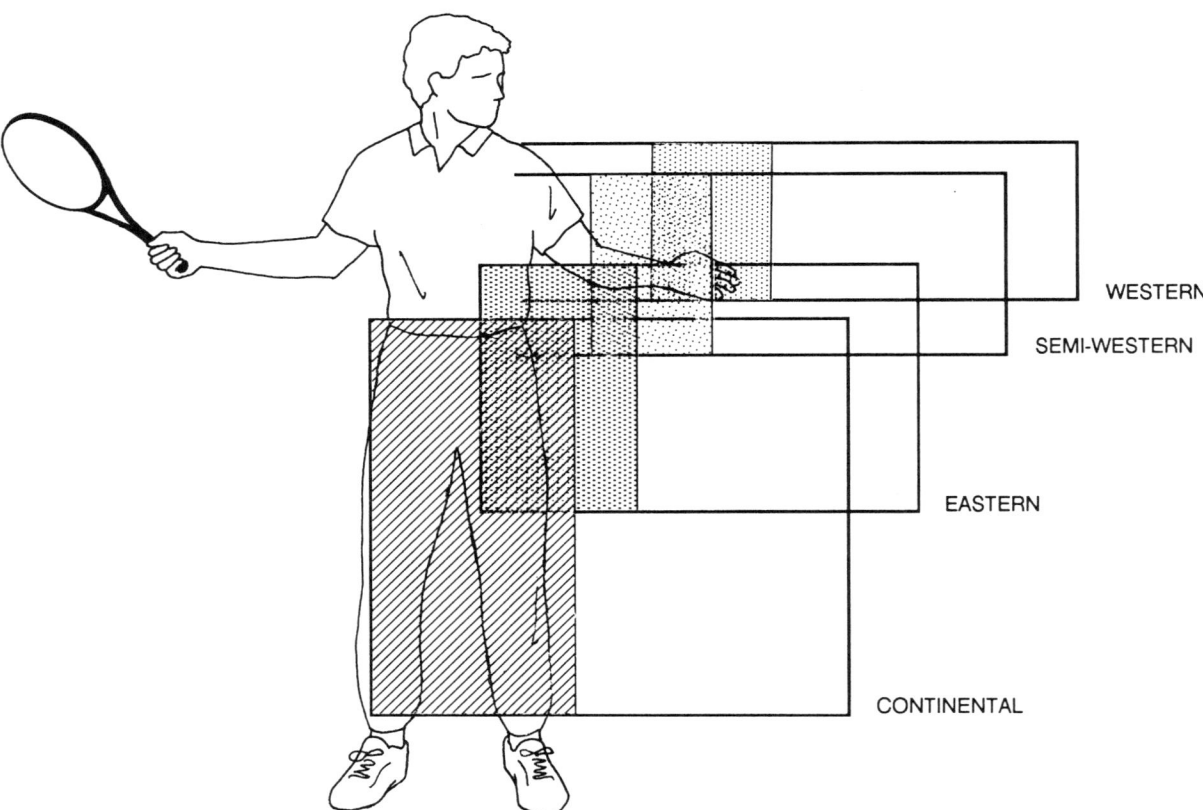

DEVELOP YOUR TECHNICAL SKILLS AND STROKE PRODUCTION

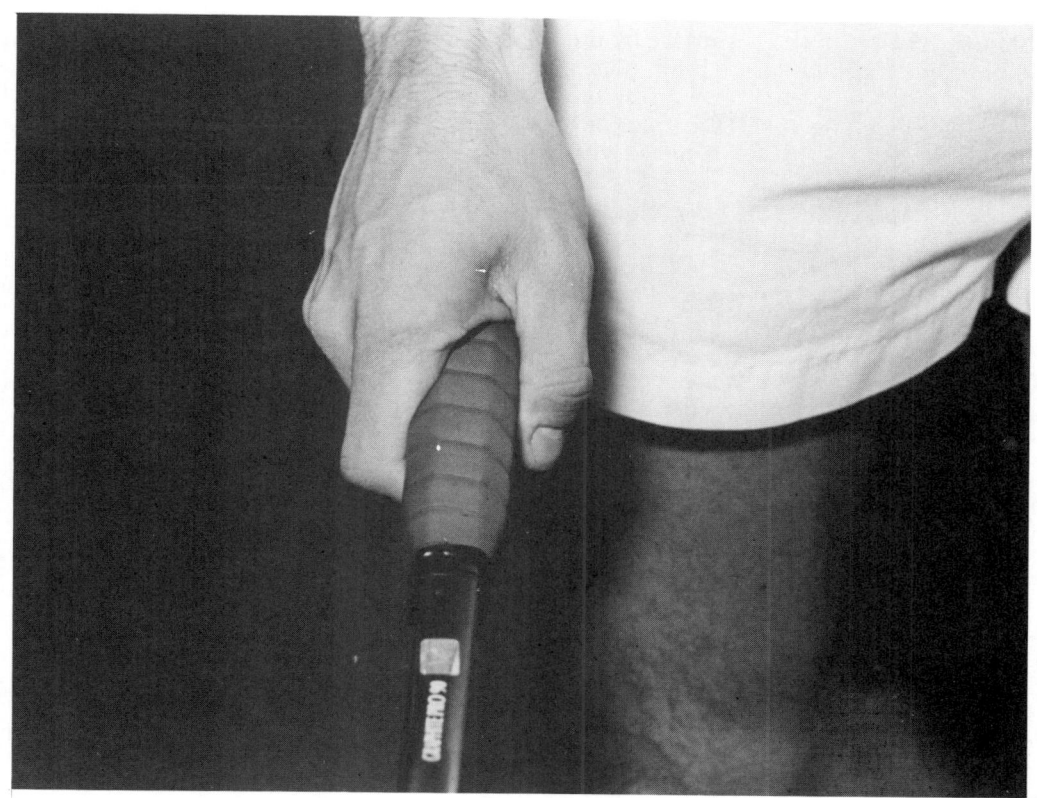

Figure 6-3. Continental grip.

Figure 6-4. Continental grip contact point.

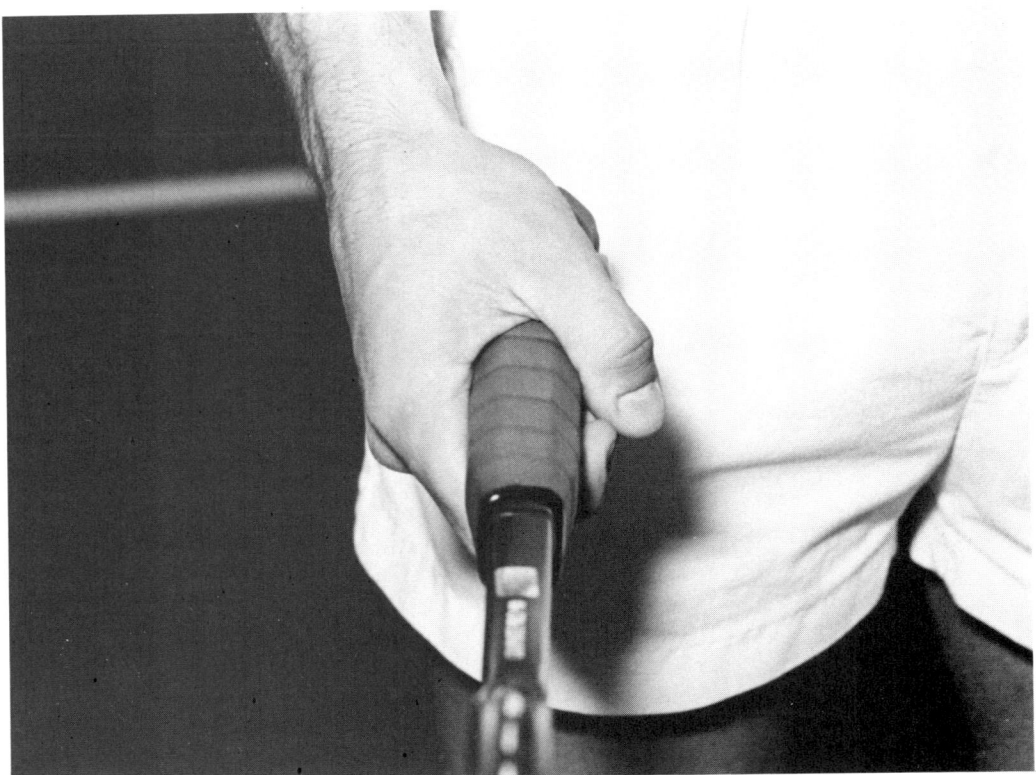

Figure 6-5. Eastern grip.

Figure 6-6. Eastern grip contact point.

DEVELOP YOUR TECHNICAL SKILLS AND STROKE PRODUCTION

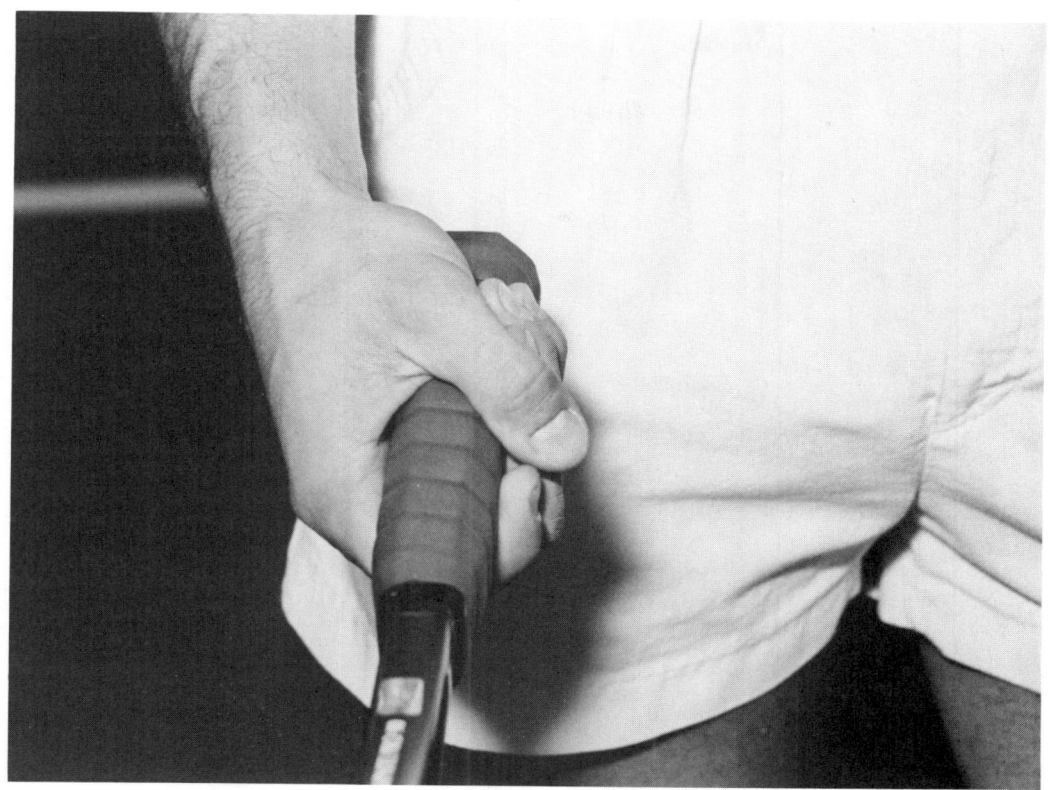

Figure 6-7. Semi-western grip.

Figure 6-8. Semi-western grip contact point.

TOTAL TENNIS TRAINING

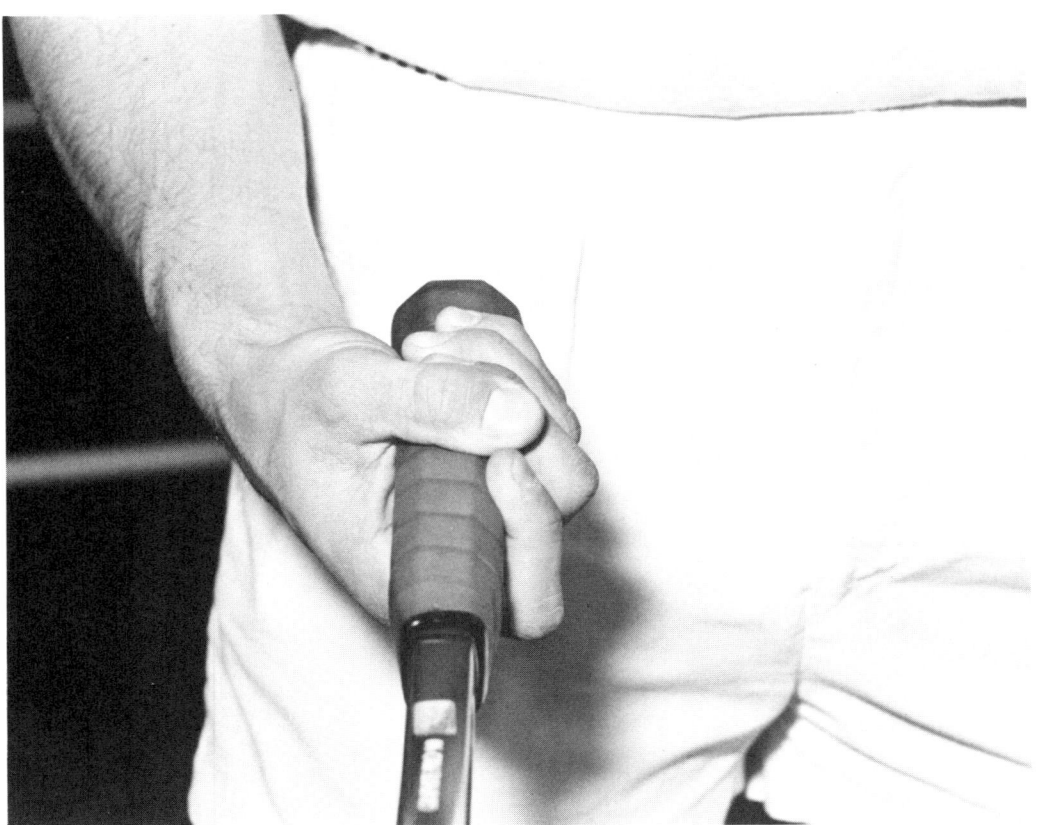

Figure 6-9. Western grip.

Figure 6-10. Western grip contact point.

TOOL TWO: FOOTWORK AND BALANCE

Stroking technique and proper grip can work effectively only if the player can get into position to use them. In his development, it is important for a player to learn proper footwork and to acquire the ability to be on balance to hit each shot.

Proper Footwork

Two things are important to maintain good balance and leverage when hitting any stroke: the head should be kept down and both feet should be on the ground. Keeping the head down allows good control of the entire body—if the head comes up, so will the arms, legs, and the rest of the body, thereby preventing optimal balance, leverage, and weight transfer through the ball.

Footwork Variations

The two variations of footwork that are used for all strokes are the closed stance and the open stance. In both variations, the upper body is the same position, with the shoulders and side turn in a coiled position to face the net. However, in the closed stance both feet are somewhat perpendicular to the net, and in the open stance both feet are more parallel to the net.

TOOL THREE: STROKE PRODUCTION

Preparation

The key to preparation for any stroke in tennis is to turn the shoulders to face the net as soon as possible. The shoulders and racquet should move together like a coil or whip, so that the force can be transferred into the racquet head and through the ball. If a player turns and coils his shoulders, the racquet will automatically go back, but leverage on the stroke can easily be lost if the racquet goes back but the shoulders do not turn to coil. On ground strokes, where leverage for racquet head speed is needed, a player should concentrate on turning his shoulders and coiling his hips to allow the uncoiling action to generate this racquet head speed. For stroke leverage generated from the backswing, the player should move the racquet and shoulders, and then the hips. For the uncoiling or swing movement, the player should move his hips first, and then his shoulders and racquet.

Figure 6-11. Closed stance—forehand.

Figure 6-12. Open stance—forehand.

Figure 6-13. Coiling action of shoulders and hips for the two-handed backhand.

Figure 6-14. Contact point: the uncoiling.

The contact point varies somewhat for each stroke and each grip, but the general principle is the same: it must be the point where maximum leverage can be achieved. In general, though, the ball must be hit in front of or slightly off the front foot or the line of the body. Weight must be shifted from the back foot to the front foot in order to generate force through the ball.

Follow-through

The ball is far away from the strings of the racquet when the follow-through is taking place, but the follow-through should be observed to show how a ball is hit. The important thing to note is the movement of the racquet head, because where it finishes shows where it has been and how it started. A follow-through that is too high shows perhaps too much top spin and a short ball, whereas a follow-through that is too low shows too much slice on the ball. A long follow-through usually indicates a longer stroke that produces a deeper ball. A shorter upward or downward follow-through indicates a shallower shot with more spin on the ball.

Figure 6-15. Proper follow-through.

DEVELOP YOUR TECHNICAL SKILLS AND STROKE PRODUCTION

Figure 6-16. Short, cramped follow-through.

The follow-through also gives a good indication of a player's confidence level. A shortened, jerky, or rushed follow-through usually indicates that a player is pressing or is feeling a bit too much pressure. A smooth follow-through shows confidence, control, and trust in the stroke.

THE JOBS: FOREHAND, BACKHAND, SERVE, VOLLEY, OVERHEAD SMASH, TRANSITION SHOTS, LOB, DROP SHOT

The flight of a tennis ball after a racquet hits it is determined by the laws of physics. It is important for a player to have an understanding of these laws to understand the physical elements of stroke production.

JOB ONE: THE FOREHAND

The continental and western grips are the most difficult grips to adjust to hit balls of different heights. The continental grip is best suited for hitting low balls and is difficult to use to hit high balls. Conversely, the western grip, which is suited best for high balls, is difficult to use to hit low balls. Both the eastern and the semi-western grips are more responsive to low or high balls. A player using an eastern grip has very few problems in adjusting for a low ball and only moderate difficulty in adjusting for a high ball. The player using the semi-western grip has little problem adjusting to a high ball and only minor difficulties in adjusting to hit a low ball. The hardest thing to do is to make an adjustment from the continental range to the western range and vice versa. The execution of the forehand is shown in Figures 6-17 through 6-20.

Figure 6-17. Shoulders and hips turn and coil as the racquet comes back.

Figure 6-18. Racquet head extends and releases to a position from above to below the ball.

Figure 6-19. Forward racquet movement is from low to high, and contact point is in front of body.

DEVELOP YOUR TECHNICAL SKILLS AND STROKE PRODUCTION

Table 6-1. Physical relationships of the forehand.

SKILL DEVELOPMENT AREA		THE TOOLS		STROKE PRODUCTION		
		Grips	Footwork	Preparation	Contact	Follow-through
CONSISTENCY	high balls ↔ low balls	WESTERN: best for high bouncing balls; slow courts SEMI-WESTERN: good for high balls, fair for low balls EASTERN: good for low balls, fair for high balls CONTINENTAL: best for low & stretch balls	Open Stance: requires spin for control Closed Stance: requires a flatter ball	Shoulders & hips to the side →→→→→	In front on higher balls Even with body on lower balls →→→→→	Low to high for smooth follow-through Left arm in front for balance Catch racquet on follow-through for balance, to drive shoulder, & to turn through to the ball →→→→→
PLACEMENT	hit early ↔ hit later	WESTERN: hardest to change direction SEMI-WESTERN: fair for changing direction EASTERN: fair for changing direction CONTINENTAL: best for changing direction	Closed Stance: better for placement			
DEPTH	shallow balls ↔ deep balls	WESTERN: hardest to hit deep SEMI-WESTERN: fair for deep balls EASTERN: good for deep balls CONTINENTAL: best for deep balls	Closed Stance: better for depth			
SPIN	top spin ↔ under spin	WESTERN: best for top spin, hardest for slice SEMI-WESTERN: good for top spin, fair for slice EASTERN: fair for top spin, good for slice CONTINENTAL: best for slice, hardest for top spin	Open Stance: better for spin			
POWER	high ball power ↔ low ball power	WESTERN: power good on high balls only SEMI-WESTERN: best power EASTERN: best power CONTINENTAL: power good on low balls only	Open Stance: good for circular momentum (spin player) Closed Stance: good for linear momentum (flat player)			

TOTAL TENNIS TRAINING

Figure 6-20. The follow-through is long and extended.

Backhand Grips

The one-handed backhand grip: The one-handed backhand can be hit well with either the eastern backhand grip or the continental grip. The eastern grip allows a wrist angle that favors a ball hit with top spin or hit low to high. The continental grip makes it very easy to slice the ball or to hit a flatter shot. Although some players can generate top spin using the continental grip, proper leverage with this grip is difficult, which can make it quite difficult to control.

The two-handed backhand grip: The two-handed backhand is used to hit the same balls used in the western and semi-western forehand: high balls and for offensive shots when the ball is sitting up. With this grip, the left side of the body of a right-handed player does most of the work, so the grip used with the left hand is of prime importance. The left hand should be placed on top of the right hand, and an eastern or semi-western grip should be used. Although the power for the stroke does not come from the right hand or the right side of the body, the right hand should also grip the racquet with an eastern or a continental grip because this grip will help the player when he stretches to hit wide, low, and other out of position balls that force a one-handed to be hit. The stroke is very similar to the left-handed forehand in that it allows the shoulder to rotate through the ball. It is different from the one-handed backhand, where the left side of the body freezes to shift leverage to the right.

JOB TWO: THE BACKHAND

The one-handed and the two-handed backhands are both accepted and used by players of all levels and abilities. The one-handed backhand is used in the same situations as the continental or eastern forehand grips, and it was developed by grass court or fast court players because it works well with low hard balls or when the player is stretched out. The two-handed backhand is used to hit higher, bouncing balls that are closer to the body, and it works well for clay court or slow court players. Ideally, a player should be versatile enough to use a one-hander for low, skidding balls and for balls away from the body, and also for approach shots and drop shots. The two-hander could be used more as an offensive weapon when the ball is sitting up and easy to make contact with. Table 6-2 lists and describes these relationships in more detail. Figure 6-21 through 6-24 show the execution of the one-handed backhand.

DEVELOP YOUR TECHNICAL SKILLS AND STROKE PRODUCTION

Table 6-2. Physical relationships of the backhand.

SKILL DEVELOPMENT AREA		THE TOOLS		STROKE PRODUCTION		
		Grips	Footwork	Preparation	Contact	Follow-through
CONSISTENCY	high balls ↔ low balls	TWO-HANDED: best for high balls ONE-HANDED Eastern: fair for high balls Continental: best for low and wide balls	Closed stance: best for consistency	Shoulders & hips to the side →	High balls and two-handers to the front. Slice is met further back for more control →	Two-handed: shoulders rotate through the ball with high extension, follow-through as if hitting a left-handed forehand One-handed: left arm & left side of body freeze, shifting the leverage or force to the right side of the body →
PLACEMENT	hit early ↔ hit later	TWO-HANDED: difficult to change direction ONE-HANDED Eastern: fair for changing direction Continental: better for changing direction	Closed stance: best for placement			
DEPTH	shallow balls ↔ deep balls	TWO-HANDED: difficult to hit deep ONE-HANDED Eastern: fair or good for deep balls Continental: best for deep balls	Closed stance: best for depth			
SPIN	top spin ↔ slice	TWO-HANDED: best for top spin ONE-HANDED Eastern: good for top spin Continental: best for slice	Open stance: can be used for under spin Closed stance: for top spin			
POWER	high ball power ↔ low ball power	TWO-HANDED: circular power for high balls ONE-HANDED Eastern: linear power for high & low balls Continental: linear power for lower balls	Closed stance: best for one-handed and linear power			

TOTAL TENNIS TRAINING

Figure 6-21. Shoulders and hips turn and coil as racquet comes back.

Figure 6-22. Racquet head extends and releases to a position from above to below the ball.

Figure 6-23. Forward racquet movement is from low to high, and the contact point is in front of the body.

Figure 6-24. Follow-through is long and extended, and the shoulders face the net.

Figures 6-25 through 6-28 show the execution of the two-handed backhand.

Figure 6-25. Preparation—shoulders and hips uncoil.

Figure 6-26. Racquet head extends and releases.

Figure 6-27. Contact point.

JOB THREE: THE SERVE

The serve is the most important shot in tennis—it is used every point, and it is the only shot that is not dependent on how the ball is delivered off the opponent's racquet. Its proper execution can make a person progress to a new level of play.

Service Grips

It is very important for a player to learn the fundamentals of the stroke—consistent placement, depth, spin, and power. Proper execution takes many hours of repetitive practice. The eastern forehand grip may be used in the novice stages of development, and this grip will allow the player to learn consistency and placement. Once these skills are learned, however, the player should begin to use a continental grip and then an eastern backhand grip, because using these grips will make it possible to learn depth, spins, and power. The backhand grip is the best grip to use for the serve, as it allows the wrist action to produce the most varieties of spin and also the racquet head speed for the greatest power.

Figure 6-28. Follow-through.

However, the continental grip is suitable for most serves, and many advanced and novice players do not advance beyond the use of the continental grip.

Service Deliveries

Most advanced players learn at least three deliveries of the serve: a flat serve, a slice (or side spinning) serve, and a top spin serve. Some players also become adept at the reverse action or the American twist serve. The eastern backhand grip allows the wrist action to produce all four of these serves. Figures 6-29 through 6-33 illustrate these four deliveries.

DEVELOP YOUR TECHNICAL SKILLS AND STROKE PRODUCTION

Figure 6-29. Flat serve—basic, compact delivery, contact is made behind the ball.

Figure 6-30. Player hits a slice serve as if he is going to cut the ball with his wrist action. Contact is made at 2 o'clock.

Figure 6-31. Top spin serve—contact is made by hitting upward at 12:30.

TOTAL TENNIS TRAINING

Figure 6-32. American twist serve—where the toss should be delivered in order to put correct spin on the ball.

Figure 6-33. American twist serve—the pronation and the outward follow-through.

DEVELOP YOUR TECHNICAL SKILLS AND STROKE PRODUCTION

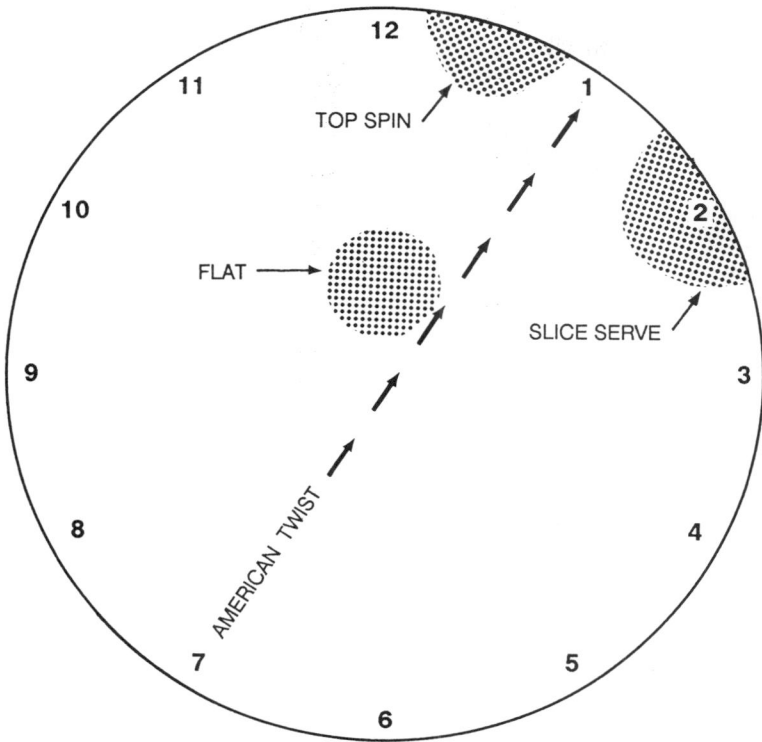

Figure 6-34. Approximate contact points with the ball for the four service deliveries.

Torque and power are delivered in the serve in much the same way they are delivered in the forehand and backhand ground strokes. The legs, shoulders, and hips coil and, as they release, the left side of the body freezes to transfer all the force to the racquet side of the body. Figures 6-35 through 6-38 show the service delivery.

Figure 6-35. Service preparation.

Figure 6-36. Coiling action and toss (notice arms working together).

Figure 6-37. Extension and contact.

Figure 6-38. Follow-through.

DEVELOP YOUR TECHNICAL SKILLS AND STROKE PRODUCTION

Service Footwork

The two most accepted service footwork methods are the crossover method and the thrust method.

The crossover method is much more easily learned, and it is very good for beginners or for players who do not have enough strength in their legs to get leverage from them. When serving with this method, the left foot is kept in place, and the right foot pivots with the service motion to shift the body weight through the ball. The crossover footwork method is shown in the serving sequence in Figures 6-35 through 6-38.

The thrust method is better for very good athletes who can thrust by using the coiling action of their legs as an additional power source. When serving with this method, the right foot is brought up behind the left as the ball is tossed and the legs coil. The legs then push upward as the body explodes to the ball. Unlike the crossover method, the left foot leads as the player makes contact with the ball, thus allowing the body to stay sideways as the left side freezes, which will allow the force to be transferred to the right side and into the shot. Staying sideways also forces the athlete to hit up on the ball and get maximum extension. Figures 6-39 and 6-40 show the thrust footwork method.

Figure 6-39. Thrust footwork.

Figure 6-40. Thrust footwork.

TOTAL TENNIS TRAINING

Table 6-3. Physical relationships of the serve.

SKILL DEVELOPMENT AREA		THE TOOLS		STROKE PRODUCTION		
		Grips	Footwork	Preparation	Contact	Follow-through
CONSISTENCY	easiest to learn ↔ best	EASTERN FOREHAND: easiest to learn CONTINENTAL: good for consistency EASTERN BACKHAND: hardest to learn initially	Crossover: easiest for consistency	Good balance Arms together in front and relaxed	Flat: contact to front & full extension Slice: make contact @ 1:30 on ball Top spin: make contact @ 12:30 on ball American twist: brush ball from 7:00 to 1:00, giving ball reverse spin	Flat: left arm is pulled in across chest Slice: Left arm is pulled in across chest Top spin: Left arm is pulled in across chest American twist: Follow-through is up and out away from body. Keep left arm up as long as possible to insure hitting up on the ball
PLACEMENT	easiest to learn ↔ best	EASTERN FOREHAND: easiest to learn CONTINENTAL: good EASTERN BACKHAND: best, but hardest to learn	Crossover: easiest for placement			
DEPTH	fair depth ↔ best depth	EASTERN FOREHAND: fair depth CONTINENTAL: good depth EASTERN BACKHAND: best depth	Thrust: gives best lift & depth			
SPIN	least spin ↔ most spin	EASTERN FOREHAND: flat and slice serve CONTINENTAL: flat, slice, top spin EASTERN BACKHAND: flat, slice, top spin and American twist	Crossover: best for slice, good for flat Thrust: best for top spin & American twist			
POWER	least power ↔ most power	EASTERN FOREHAND: least wrist action CONTINENTAL: good wrist action EASTERN BACKHAND: most wrist action	Crossover: flat serve is easier Thrust: best leg action for power			

DEVELOP YOUR TECHNICAL SKILLS AND STROKE PRODUCTION

Read the Receiver and Attack his Grips

It is a good idea for the server to look at the receiver's grip pattern, because he can then learn the restrictions and liabilities of the different grips used by the receiver. The idea is to deliver the serve away from the strike zone that the receiver's strokes allow. It is comparable to a pitcher throwing away from a batter's favorite hitting zone.

Serving against the western forehand grip: The western forehand grip is very vulnerable to flat or low balls that are moving away from the body. A slice or hard flat serve to pull this player wide in the deuce court will work very well. In this instance, the receiver will usually mishit or shank the return.

Serving against the continental forehand grip: The continental grip favors a flat, low ball outside, so a high kicking ball to this forehand is often hard for the receiver to handle. The receiver may be able to block back a shot, but he should not be able to hit an offensive return off of this serve.

Serving against the two-handed backhand: Reach is the chief liability of the two-handed backhand. If a good wide angle can be hit, the receiver will either have difficulty making a good return, or he will be pulled wide far enough to allow the server to control good court positioning. A poor wide kick, though, will allow the receiver to hit a ball perfect for his or her strike zone, therefore a low wide ball would be the best delivery to the two-hander. A serve aimed with some slice into the body also works quite well against the two-hander because it works to jam his stroke.

Serving against the one-handed backhand: If the receiver is not very strong, a high ball delivered to the one-handed backhand can work very well and will usually produce a weak or a floating return.

Figure 6-41. Forehand serving targets.

Figure 6-42. Backhand serving targets.

JOB FOUR: THE VOLLEY

The technique of the volley is much less complex than the technique of the forehand, backhand, and serve, because the movement is less complicated. When hitting ground strokes, there is enough time to make adjustments in grip, stance, technique, and court positioning, but often the volley happens very quickly, so adjustments are harder to make and movements must be more precise.

Volley Grip

The continental grip is the grip that is most adaptable for both the forehand and backhand volleys at nearly all heights and distances from the body.

Volley Technique

Contact with the ball should be made with a short blocking action in front of the body, and the racquet head should always be cocked above the wrist. Volleys should be made at eye level. This means that on low volleys, the knees should bend low to keep the racquet head up.

Unlike ground strokes, where the coiling action of the shoulders and hips comes first, the first movement a player must make in preparation for the volley is to lay his wrist back to prepare the racquet head for contact. He then turns his shoulders, but the racquet head and his hands should stay in front of his body. The weight is then transferred to the front foot via a crossover step, and contact is made in front of the body. Figures 6-43 through 6-48 show the correct volley techniques.

Figure 6-44. Forehand volley contact. Racquet head should stay above wrist. Weight comes forward to the left foot as contact is made.

Figure 6-43. Forehand and backhand volley ready position. Notice the weight is forward with racquet cocked up and out in front of body.

Figure 6-45. Forehand volley follow-through. Racquet head stays up as stroke finishes.

DEVELOP YOUR TECHNICAL SKILLS AND STROKE PRODUCTION

Figure 6-46. Backhand volley contact.

Figure 6-48. Low volley. Notice how the back knee is down to the ground, the back stays up, and the racquet head remains above the wrist.

Figure 6-47. Backhand volley follow-through.

JOB FIVE: THE OVERHEAD SMASH

A player's net game is only as good as his overhead smash. When a player is at the net, his opponent will usually try to hit over him. If a player has a good smash, it puts much more pressure on his opponent's passing shot. If a player's smash is weak, his opponent has a definite advantage.

Overhead Smash Technique

Although the fundamentals of the overhead smash are simple and straightforward, it takes a lot of time and practice to develop an effective and confident smash. The first movement a player must make from the ready position at the net is to simultaneously move the racquet head straight back into a cocked position and move his right foot one step backward. This will position him so his side faces the net, and once he is in this position, he can move anywhere on the court and be prepared to hit the smash. The ball should fall as if it were going to hit the player in the chest or the forehead. A very good drill to help a player learn to position himself under the falling ball is to have the player turn sideways with his racquet cocked and his free arm pointing up at the ball. As the ball falls, the player should reach up with his arm fully extended, and his hand pointed, and catch the ball.

The hitting action is the same as that in the flat serve. The body stays sideways and the ball is hit from a fully extended position at approximately 1 o'clock.

The Scissors Jump

If possible, both feet should be on the ground when the overhead smash is hit, because this position provides the best balance and gives a very solid stroke. When the ball is lobbed well and is too high for the player to stay on the ground, he may need to do a scissors jump. Although this action looks complicated, it is actually a very natural movement and is easy to do with some practice. The athlete must move backward quickly in a sideways position, push off the ground with his right foot, and land on his left foot, moving his legs like a scissors in the process. Figures 6-49 through 6-52 show the overhead smash with the scissors jump and the follow-through.

Figure 6-50. The right leg goes back, racquet is cocked, and the left arm is used to guide the ball.

Figure 6-49. Overhead smash ready position.

Figure 6-51. Scissors jump.

DEVELOP YOUR TECHNICAL SKILLS AND STROKE PRODUCTION

Figure 6-52. Contact is made.

JOB SIX: TRANSITION SHOTS

Transition shots are shots that allow a transition or change-up in the style of play in the point. Some transition shots are the approach shot, the passing shot, the return of serve, and the first volley. In each of these shots, except for the return of serve, a transition made from the baseline to the net by one player or his opponent.

Transition shots are the most missed shots in tennis. Many errors happen because the pattern of play changes and the rhythm of the point is broken up. One of the rules for my team is not to change the direction of the ball on a transition shot. The timing is tough enough as it is, and to change the direction of the ball into the open part of the court is to greatly increase the chance for a bad error or to deliver a ball that the opponent can easily take advantage of.

Returning the ball back to where it came from (not changing the direction of the ball), allows a player to make a shot that leaves the strings of his racquet at a right angle. This also keeps the court closed and forces the opponent to hit a ball that is behind him, tempting him to go to the open court (or change the direction himself).

Another rule for players is always to think of hitting two shots when they approach, two shots when they pass, two shots when they return serve, and two shots to volley. This makes him realize that the purpose of a transition shot is to set up the next shot—not to end the point. (If the purpose were to end the point, it would be called a putaway shot.)

Transition Shot One: The Approach Shot

In the summer of 1972, I sat as one of a group of summer camp counselors watching the televised Wimbledon final of Stan Smith versus Ilie Nastase. The camp director was Harry Hopman, and he too was present in the room. Mr. Hopman would often make a one-sentence comment about tennis or about life that would be so profound and wise that it would carve a permanent place in one's memory.

Nastase, the great shot maker, had just been forced into the corner of the court with a great Smith approach shot. On the dead run, Nastase hit a perfect down-the-line backhand passing shot that left Smith diving onto the grass. One of the instructors commented, "Wow, what a great shot." Hopman responded with, "No, it wasn't, that was the only shot he had," and that one sentence taught me more about the importance of proper placement on approach shots than did all the rest of my years of tennis.

Of course, what Hopman meant was that players are often physically able to make great shots, especially if they are forced into a position where they *have* to make them. In the Wimbledon match, Nastase's back was to the wall, and he threaded the needle down the line with the only chance he had. The fact that he made the shot this one time was not a great feat, any more than is a basketball player who throws a three-pointer, in desperation, as the shot clock runs down.

I learned from Hopman that day that an approach shot is just that—a shot that a player approachs the net with. The player's job is to handcuff his opponent but also to time the delivery of his shot properly so that he can get himself set up on the net. He may hit the ball short or deep, high or low, to the corner or to the middle, but his main objective is to find a vulnerable area in his opponent's passing shots. But I learned more than that—I learned that many times, if a player is forced into a corner, he can play "spinal chord tennis," that is, tennis played automatically without thought. Hopman loved the approach shot up the middle because it gave the opponent choices, and having choices is often the undoing of a talented shotmaker like Nastase. Hopman taught me that any opponent will sometimes make a great shot when a player comes to the net, but this should never deter the player from keeping his attacking game intact. When a player finds the right approach shot to use, his advantage of better court positioning on the net will pay off. Proper execution of the right approach shots may actually be the quickest way to rapid improvement in a player's game.

Technique of the approach shot: As in other strokes, first the shoulders turn to face the net. As the player moves into position, the anchor foot is placed down (left foot on backhand, right on forehand), and the weight is shifted from the anchor foot, with force exerted through the ball, onto the front foot. The stroke is similar to the volley but with more backswing and follow-through. Under spin is recommended to keep the delivery low and to give the approaching player time to get to a balanced and ready position at the net. Note: If top spin approach shots are used, they are best played up the middle or to the stroke that has difficulty with high balls.

Figure 6-53. This player has an excellent approach shot form.

Transition Shot Two: The Passing Shot

This section should be called "Passing Shots" because it usually takes two shots to pass. The first shot is to put the net man off balance, and the second is to pass him with only a small degree of difficulty. A player can go for a great passing shot on his first attempt, but the percentages will not favor him unless his shot is a lot better than the opponent covering the net. To go for the passing shot on the first whack at the ball is comparable to a basketball team that puts the ball up with a thirty-footer immediately after bringing it over the 10-second line. When a player takes the first shot to set up the second or third passing shot, it is more like a basketball team that passes the ball two or three times to get a much higher percentage shot. Of course, the best teams can hit the quick 30-footers as well as pass the ball three or four times to get an easier shot. Likewise, the best tennis player can make a great passing shot when he has to, but understands the importance of being able to hit through an opponent once or twice to get the high percentage final passing shot.

A player's key to passing effectively is to take the first ball early and return it to where it came from. This should catch the opponent off balance and force him to pop the volley up so that it can be returned with an easy passing shot.

Transition Shot Three: The Return of the Serve

The return of the serve is perhaps the second most important shot in tennis because, like the serve, it must be used in every point of the even or odd games. It is also probably the most boring stroke to practice. It is a shot in which a player is reacting to his opponent, and a good return has very few dimensions. Again, since it is a transition shot, a good general rule is not to change the direction of the ball, thus eliminating many errors that may be caused by trying to make a difficult shot instead of hitting through the opponent. Good returners use their opponent's pace and try to use a short backswing for good weight transfer, and to take the ball early and hit the ball right back where it came from.

Reading a server: Most servers have a serving pattern. For example, the first serve is flat and to the backhand, and the second serve is a top spin serve to the backhand, or the first serve is wide, and the second serve is up the middle. A good rule for a player to follow in returning serve effectively is to watch for the server's pattern in the first few returning games and to gauge his returns accordingly. For example, if the server hits his first serve flat to the backhand most of the time, the player should wait with a backhand grip and in a position for a backhand. If the serve is to the backhand, the receiver can make a short low to high swing and lean into the ball to produce an excellent return. If the serve is to the forehand, the receiver can make a very solid stretch forehand with the backhand grip. The only serve that would really make the receiver vulnerable would be the high kicker to the forehand, and it is unlikely that the server will try this on a first serve. However, most second serves are kick serves. If this is the case, the receiver can either wait with a forehand grip to move around and smack a forehand, or he can slice a backhand from high to low and follow it into the net. If the receiver is successful in reading his opponent's service delivery, he is able to bring the server out of his set pattern. The server then reacts to the receiver's pattern, thereby giving the receiver a better chance of controlling the tempo of the game.

Technique of the return of the serve: As the receiver waits for the serve, his lower body should be relaxed and held so that the center of gravity is high and he is ready to move a step to the right or left. For many years, players have thought that it was best to wait in a very low crouched position with the knees bent and the center of gravity very low. But the laws of physics show that whereas a lower center of gravity is better for stability (such as a three-point stance for a lineman in football or on all fours for a wrestler), a higher center of gravity is better for a quick movement in any direction. John McEnroe is a player who uses this stance effectively. The best technique for a player is to wait in a low position, come up on his toes for a higher center of gravity and readiness to react to the serve, and then lean in to the ball with a wide base that provides stability and allows weight transfer into the shot. The upper body movement is quite simple. As the server tosses the ball, the receiver comes up for a higher center of gravity and turns only his relaxed shoulders, to the forehand or backhand position, and then he flows forward along the path of the oncoming ball.

High to low or low to high: On a flat, hard first service, it is best for the stroke to flow in a low to high arc. Very often a player will try to slice (high to low) a hard, fast serve. Although this may feel comfortable and safe, it usually either produces a ball in the net or a weak, floating return. A low to high arc allows the racquet to hit along the plane of the ball and lift it to clear the net. However, on a high, kicking serve, the returner should try to hit the ball with a high to low arc to bring the ball down into the court. He may also want to move around and smack a forehand as well if he is able to do so.

Transition Shot Four: The First Volley

The first volley is considered a transition shot because of its similarity to the approach shot.

There are three rules to remember for the first volley:

Rule #1: After the server delivers the serve, his movement should allow him to get in as far as the service line. This will give him a good opportunity to make an effective first volley. Otherwise, a first ball popped up will make it very easy for the returner to pass the server unless the ball can be put away with a winner.

Rule #2: The first volley should be hit back to where it came from or to the middle of the court, and the finishing volley should be placed to the open court. This rule is very important because if a crosscourt volley is not put away, the whole court is left open for an easy passing shot by the opponent. In general, for any ball that can be put away, the player should go to the open court. If the ball cannot be put away, the court should be kept closed. A reminder to my team when we do serve and volley drills is to call them serve and volley-volley drills, which reminds the players that it takes two shots to volley.

Rule #3: The net should be closed off after the first volley. If the first volley is effective, then the server should be in control of the point. As the ball is in flight, the server should take three or four steps in to the net to close out the point. Not closing off the net is a mistake that gives the opponent an angle to hit a passing shot or a chance to get back into the point.

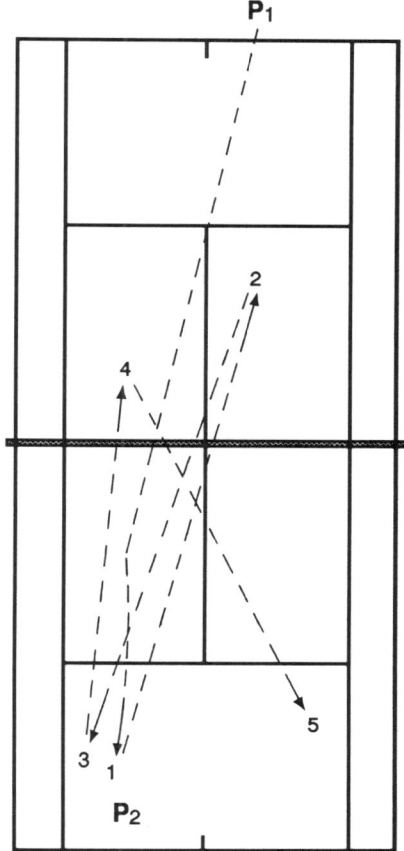

Figure 6-54. The perfect serve and volley point. The server (player 1) makes a first serve to the middle of the ad court (1), moves into the service line, volleys a low ball back to where it came from (2 and 3), closes off the net, and angles the second volley crosscourt (4 and 5).

JOB SEVEN: THE LOB

The lob is one of the best passing shots to use when the opponent comes to the net. There are two kinds of lobs: the defensive lob and the offensive lob. If the opponent's shot can be controlled, the player should hit an offensive lob as an alternative to a passing shot. If the opponent's shot stretches the player or the player is out of the play, he should hit a very high defensive lob.

The Defensive Lob (The Sky Lob)

The defensive lob should be used when a player is definitely out of position and needs time to set up. If the player can get the ball up high enough and back on the baseline, his opponent will virtually have to start the point over. The higher, the better on a defensive lob because there is nothing more difficult than hitting a ball that is falling rapidly. When a player is stretched out, it is a good idea to use a continental grip in order to keep a firm wrist to give leverage for a firm ball.

The Offensive Lob

The offensive lob should be used as an option to a passing shot—out of choice, not out of necessity. The player must have complete control of the ball and be able to disguise the shot until the last second. The arc of the ball's flight should be much lower than the arc of the defensive lob, and it is also a good idea to place the lob over the opponent's backhand side, where an overhead would be very difficult. Players today are quite adept at hitting the top spin lob, but this shot should be used only when the ball is sitting up enough to use a full swing and grip that allows a lot of top spin to be put on the ball.

JOB EIGHT: THE DROP SHOT

One principle for controlling the depth of a shot at strategic times is to hit balls short, thereby forcing the opponent to come to the net. A drop shot is an excellent shot to use to do this, but it must be well disguised and it should not be used as a defensive shot but only as an offensive tactic. Placement is very important, because a poor drop shot is disastrous in that it allows the opponent to take immediate charge of the point.

Three rules are important to remember when executing the drop shot:

Rule #1: If a player makes a drop shot from the baseline, he should make it crosscourt. This keeps the court closed so that if the opponent does get to the ball, the player will have a shot to pass him on the next ball.

Rule #2: If a player makes a drop shot from the forecourt, he should make it in front of himself, or down the line. This keeps the court closed and gives the player another play on the ball if his opponent runs the ball down.

Rule #3: A player should use the drop shot only as an offensive tactical shot, which makes the opponent react to him. As a desperation shot or a way out of the point, it is one of the worst shots a player can choose.

Figure 6-55. The flight paths of the offensive and defensive lobs.

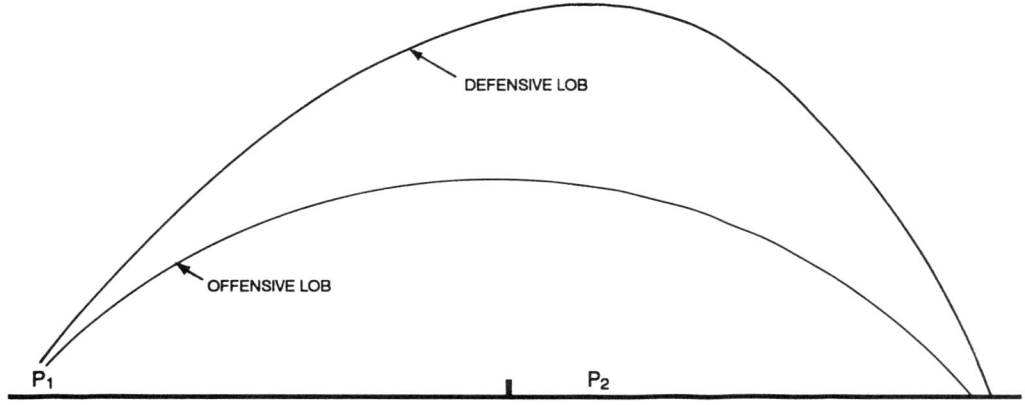

DEVELOP YOUR TECHNICAL SKILLS AND STROKE PRODUCTION

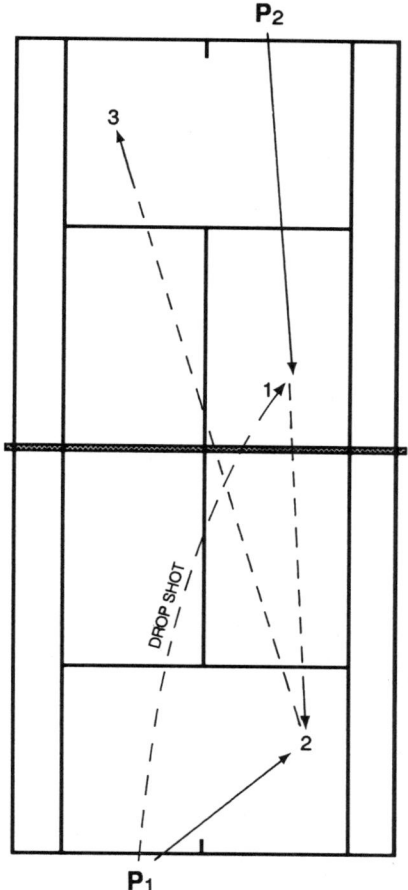

Figure 6-56. From the backcourt, hit drop shots cross-court.

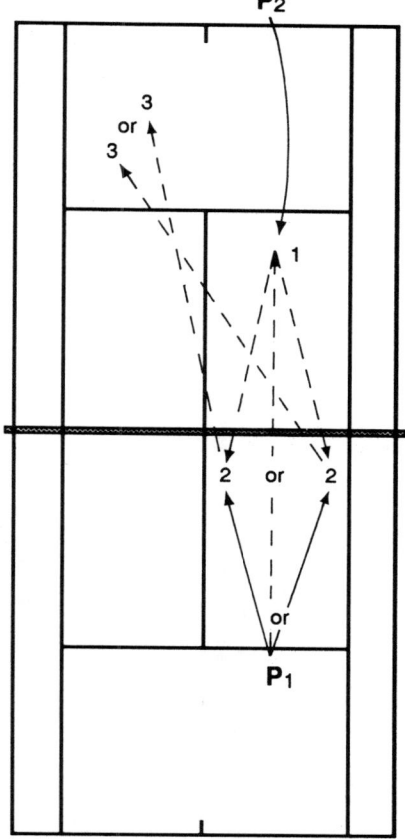

Figure 6-57. From the forecourt, hit drop shots down the line or in front of you.

NOTES

Figure 6-58. The continental grip works well when you are stretched, and for a forehand on the run.

Figure 6-59. Two-handed players should learn to use one-handed shots on the stretch backhand.

DEVELOP YOUR TECHNICAL SKILLS AND STROKE PRODUCTION

Figure 6-60. Good leverage for torque on ground strokes comes from the legs and hips.

Figure 6-61. Two-handed backhands are a deadly weapon for balls that sit up.

Figure 6-62. Legs should be bent well for effective half-volleys.

SUMMARY

Each tennis player's strokes are developed according to his personality, and it is important that each athlete be allowed to develop his strokes from the inside out so that he can reach his full potential. In the early stages of development, players must learn proper fundamentals—this includes the technical tools of grips, footwork and balance, preparation, contact point, and follow-through. These tools can be used to develop the skills of consistency, then placement, depth, spin, and power. Once these tools and skills are learned, players can put them to use in the strokes (jobs)—the forehand, one-handed and two-handed backhands, serve, volley, overhead smash, transition shots, lob, and drop shot. After these fundamentals are learned, each player will be able to further develop his individual style of play and shot delivery.

CHAPTER 7

PREVENT AND TREAT ATHLETIC INJURIES

"Whoever said, 'No pain, no gain,' wasn't talking about preventable injuries."
—Cheryl Martin, State Farm Insurance

Tennis players must compete more than any other athlete. Although a tennis player does not have to deal with bruises and contusions as do athletes in contact sports, the continuous periods of competition cause many stress-and-strain-related injuries. The body's connective tissues, such as the tendons and ligaments, can be affected, and muscle tissue, bursa, tendon sheaths, and other lubricating substances of the body are also at risk.

Tennis has become a year-round sport. Most other sports have an off-season when an athlete is able to completely rest and heal his body. But the constant chase of the next tournament or ranking often forces the tennis player back into competition before he is ready for full speed play, and this increases the chance for reinjury and a further setback. Since tennis players will most likely continue to put continuous excessive stress on their body, an understanding of injury prevention, management, and treatment is of critical importance for both the coach and the player.

INJURY PREVENTION

Injuries are very frustrating to the athlete because of the training time lost, and it is very important that a tennis player take action to prevent injuries. The following measures will help in injury prevention and should be part of a tennis player's daily ritual.

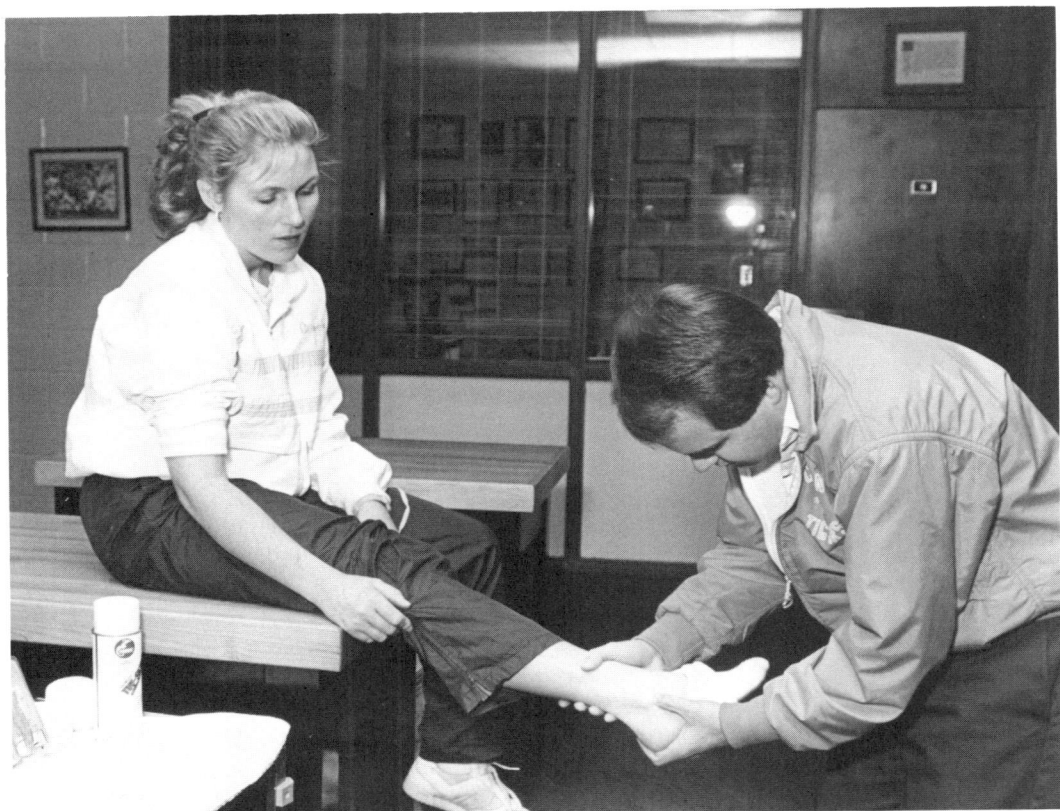

Figure 7-1

Raise the Body Temperature Before Practice

The athlete's muscle fibers and connective tissues can be compared to a rubber band. If a rubber band is cold and is jerked quickly in a ballistic manner, it may tear or break. If, however, the same rubber band is warmed and is then very slowly stretched without rapid and jerky moves, it will be elastic. Likewise, a cold muscle that is put through rapid flexing and stretching may also tear. Raising the temperature of the muscle and then slowly stretching it with nonmovement (static) stretching allows for effective flexions and extensions. When the body temperature is raised, the speed of contraction and relaxation of the muscles is increased. Light jogging, rope jumping, or calisthenics work well to raise the body temperature.

Use a Consistent Stretching Routine

Stretching allows the muscles to relax and allows for a good blood supply and oxygen transport to take place. Flexibility exercises also help in reducing muscle soreness by transport of lactic acid out of fatigued tissues.

However, overstretching may cause damage to ligaments and joints. Therefore, an athlete should follow a familiar program every day that includes solid static (nonmoving) fundamentals.

These guidelines should be followed in a stretching routine:

1. Warm up the body by one degree or until sweat breaks.
2. Use only static (nonmovement) and gradual exercises. Never use ballistic (movement or bouncing) exercises.
3. Stretch all muscle groups.
4. Do not overstretch, do not understretch.
5. Bring the body to a sweat once more before starting workout.

TREATMENT AND MANAGEMENT OF INJURIES

When an injury does occur, proper methods of treatment and rehabilitation should be used. There are three categories of injuries based on severity of the injury and recurrence. Athletes and coaches should know the proper treatment for each.

Acute Injury

An acute injury is an immediate injury, or an injury that occurs by accident during training. Examples are: ankle sprain, muscle tear, broken bone. The athlete cannot compete with this type of injury.

Treatment: Use ice compression and elevation for the first 24-48 hours. Never, never use heat or aspirin for the first 48-64 hours! Usually a three or four day layoff is required for rest.

Subacute Injury

A subacute injury is an injury that builds up over time to hamper play. Examples are: Osgood Slaughter knee disease and overtired strained muscle. These injuries cause great frustration because although the athlete can participate, his performance is usually hampered.

Treatment: Warm up slowly. Use ice after workout, and anti-inflamatory medications only by doctor's prescription.

Recurrent Injury

A recurrent injury is usually a joint injury such as tennis elbow, rotator cuff, and shoulder bursitis. Recurrent injuries can return very unpredictably.

Treatment: Warm up slowly. Use ice after workout, and aspirin and prescriptions only under a doctor's supervision.

Note: Ice constricts blood flow to tissue, therefore reducing swelling of an acute injury. Heat dilates blood vessels and speeds up blood flow and can make an injury much more severe. Aspirin tends to thin blood, thereby increasing swelling to an injured muscle or joint. When competing with an injury, the athlete should warm up gradually and use ice massage or compression immediately after competition.

REHABILITATION

Rest and treatment allow the healing process to take place. As pain subsides, athletes feel ready for full-scale competition again, but the most frequent mistake they make is to force themselves back into full speed before rehabilitation is completed. The major concern is that the very rapid atrophy and degeneration of the muscle tissue that takes place leaves the athlete extremely susceptible to reinjury. When reinjury occurs, the entire rest and treatment process must take place all over again. This can start a cycle that can be extremely frustrating for the competitive athlete.

As pain from an injury starts to subside, the athlete should gradually work himself back into practice. Most of the heavy exercise should be done with the stabilizer or support muscles close to the injury, with activity that that does not aggravate the ailment. As the injured area becomes stronger, more and more exercises should be done to make the muscle tissue strong and to prevent reinjury. Taping to restrict movement of the affected area can also be of great help during this rehabilitative period.

PART TWO
THE MENTAL THIRD

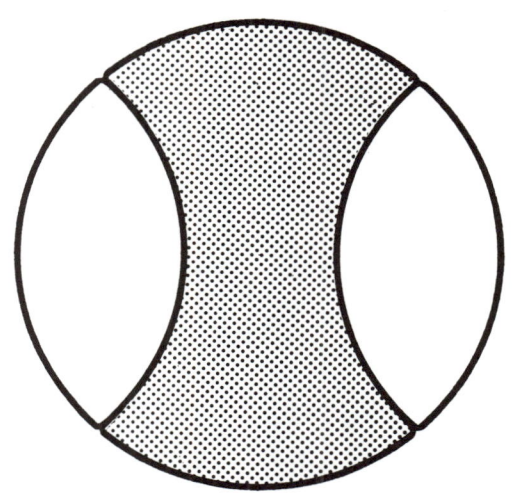

CHAPTER 8

BUILD YOUR BEST GAME

"Don't fit in, stand out!"

—Anonymous

SELECTING A GAME STYLE

One of the most important decisions the coach and player must make is choosing the style that best suits the ability and temperament of the player. Lessons and coaching can dramatically speed up the development of a player's technical skills, but it is critical that good judgment be used in developing a game that fits an individual physically, mentally, and emotionally. This can save months or even years in his development.

Very few people are gifted enough to do everything well, and it is important to understand a player's strengths so that they can be used to their fullest in the style selected. Even after a style is chosen, though, the critical ingredient that determines whether or not that style will be effective is how it fits the player's temperament. Bjorn Borg's very disciplined and methodical style would not have been successful if his temperament had been like that of Ile Nastase. Likewise, Nastase's flashy, aggressive game probably would not have been successful with Borg's even temperament. Nastase, McEnroe, and Laver are all creative learners. They are all champions, and they are all successful within their styles and their own mental and emotional framework. Borg, Wilander, and Rosewall are all seemingly repetitive learners, successful in their own way and special because of their unique makeup.

If a player had never had a lesson, had never been coached, and was simply asked to play sets for a period of time, his personality traits would eventually surface in his tennis game, and his style of play would inevitably become a mirror image of his

Figure 8-1. Stick with your game style.

personality. A tennis player with a game style that does not fit his personality is like Bob Cousy playing center for the Boston Celtics or William "Refrigerator" Perry calling the plays for the Chicago Bears.

A player should learn all the physical skills of stroke technique and fundamentals, but he may concentrate on one of three game styles: the counter punching game, the attacking game, or the all-court game.

STICK WITH YOUR GAME STYLE

Over the Christmas holidays of 1983, my team was participating in an indoor tournament in New Orleans. We were anxious to watch a match-up between two of the top collegiate players in the country. It promised to be a classic match-up between two players with completely contrasting styles. One was the aggressive serve and volleyer, and the other was the number two ranked player in the United States, Johnny Levine from the University of Texas.

When the match started it appeared as if we would not be disappointed. It reminded me of some of the exciting Wimbledon matches between John McEnroe and Bjorn Borg in the early 1980s.

Soon after the match began, though, I was disappointed. One point after another was won by Levine, and in a period of 35 minutes the match was over with Levine winning 6-1, 6-0. I wondered how a match with such great possibilities could end with such a lopsided score. The reaction of my team and other bystanders was that Levine was a great player, who was very physically and mentally tough. He definitely would be a great pro and no one in college tennis could touch him. I was disappointed by this very elementary reasoning.

Levine's opponent walked up to the lounge area with the rest of the players, and his reaction was pretty much the same as those who watched the match. He told his teammates and coach, "I don't really know what happened. I tried everything and nothing worked." As he said this, I turned to my players and asked, "Who in the world is good at everything?" I told them that I would have rather heard him say, "I played my game. I was hardheaded. I stuck to my serve and volley game, which is my natural style. He was just better at his style than I was at my style."

When a player's confidence cracks during a match, he will often revert to any other style to try to find a winning combination. As soon as this happens, the match is pretty much over. Players are never as good at other styles as they are at their own individual way of playing. I always tell my players, "You are number one in the world in the way you play. The best you can ever be at someone else's style is an imitation or number two. You're usually just grasping at straws when you try a lot of different styles. This does not mean you cannot make adjustments in playing different strategies within your style, but the strategy should always be to stick to the play that is most familiar to you. To try many different options usually only makes it easier for your opponent and further confuses you."

THE COUNTER PUNCHING GAME

The counter punching game style favors the athlete with limited ability. His temperament may be laid-back, but tough-minded athletes often fare well with this style. The main skills to learn are good passing shots and lobbing, a good return of serve, and good side-to-side movement on the baseline. Consistency, placement, and depth of the player's shots are the areas of concern during practice sessions.

The advantage of the counter punch game is that it is the easiest style to learn, and it gives the fastest results. A player has fewer decisions to make than he would with another style, since this style relies on reacting and countering rather than dictating the points with aggressive play. An adept counter puncher is extremely difficult for the intermediate player to beat, and results will be very consistent. Problems arise when the counter puncher faces an aggressive player who is a bit too good at his skills or another counter puncher who is a percent or two better than he is. For quick results for a player with limited athletic ability, this is the best style to play.

THE ATTACKING GAME

The attacking game style is suited to a good athlete with an aggressive temperament, or an athlete with a nonaggressive temperament if that athlete is excellent with details and takes care of routine matters.

The skills needed include a forcing serve, good approach shots, consistent first volleys, and a good overhead smash. Errors will be made with an attacking style, but the athlete should always remember to make them aggressively and decisively. Doubt and hesitation are the culprits for the attacking player, so controlled aggression is critical. Taking care of details is critical, as is taking time between points and being fully aware of momentum swings.

This style takes longer to develop, but it gives the player opportunities for big wins. Initially, the results will be more inconsistent, and patience is needed while taking some losses along with those big wins.

THE ALL-COURT GAME

The all-court game is the best style to teach if there is adequate time to train and if the athlete is versatile and well-equipped physically, mentally, and emotionally. All the skills that allow the counter puncher and the attacking player to be successful are needed to play the all-court game, so this style takes the longest time and requires the most patience in waiting for the best results.

Because consistency, placement, depth, spin, and power are needed with all the strokes, the player must have a disciplined temperament. Mastering this style produces the best results of any of the three, but because confusion may be caused by the number of decisions and choices, the player should be prepared for occasional bad results. It is also critical to master momentum control and understand the flow of the match to obtain the best results.

BUILD YOUR BEST GAME

SUMMARY

Table 8-1. Building your best game.

THE COUNTER-PUNCHING GAME	THE ATTACKING GAME	THE ALL-COURT GAME
• Best style for limited athlete • Easiest to learn • Fewest decisions to make • Fastest results • Hardest for intermediate player to play against	• For the good athlete • Minimal decisions to make • Somewhat longer to develop • Chance for bigger wins • More inconsistent results	• For the best and smartest athletes • Allows greatest flexibility against all types of players • Longest to learn • Gives widest base for long-range results • Best results if mastered — worst results if not mastered
SKILLS NEEDED • Consistency • Placement • Depth	**SKILLS NEEDED** • Placement • Power	**SKILLS NEEDED** • Consistency • Placement • Depth • Spin • Power
EMPHASIS AREA • Passing shots • Lobbing • Good movement • Good return of serve	**EMPHASIS AREA** • Good serve • Approach shots • First volleys • Overheads	**EMPHASIS AREA** • All skills and strokes

CHAPTER 9

CONCENTRATE ON YOUR PRE-MATCH PREPARATION

"The trouble with the future is that it usually arrives before we're ready for it."

—Anonymous

Preparation for a tennis match can and should start the day before the actual event, if not earlier. Because tennis is an individual sport and so many of the variables leading up to the start of a match can be controlled, consistent routines for pre-match preparation should be developed. Whatever the routine, it should fit the style and personality of the player, and the player should feel comfortable with it and have confidence in it. A team routine is much the same. It should fit the image and personality of the team, and the guidelines should be consistent in order to gain the trust and confidence of team members.

The body, the mind, and the emotions should all be prepared for a match: the body should be warmed up, strategy should be reviewed, and attention should be given to emotional balance. The day prior to competition, special attention should be paid to diet and rest routine. Tough workouts are stopped 48 hours before the match, and a light physical workout is done the day before. A routine for a team the day of the match might be to meet at the match site an hour before the start of the match. A 30-minute physical warm-up period is optimal. The next 15 minutes should be spent in a brief strategy session on what to expect from the match and the course of action to use against the opponent. The last few moments before the match should be spent in preparing the emotions for the battle ahead.

TOTAL TENNIS TRAINING

PHYSICAL, MENTAL, AND EMOTIONAL PREPARATION

The following checklist contains the important physical, mental, and emotional considerations to review before the match starts. It starts with the more fundamental and obvious and progresses to greater detail.

Take Care of All Details that are Controllable that may Affect Physical Performance

1. Follow a consistent routine before the match.
2. Be comfortable with a consistent routine that will be used during the match between points that have been won or lost.
3. Take care of all physical details:
   a. Eat right.
   b. Get enough sleep.
   c. Make sure to have the right equipment.
   d. Perform an adequate warm-up and stretching routine.

Understand Your Game Plans and Know What to Expect from Your Opponent

Understanding game styles of different players and how they affect your own performance is one of the most confusing aspects of planning strategies for a match. Knowing exactly what to do in all situations is nearly impossible; thus, it is critical for the player to have a set routine and guidelines to follow in various recognizable situations.

The two defining factors in a match are, very logically, your own play and your opponent's play. The relationship between these factors can be explained by a simple formula:

MY WINNERS minus MY ERRORS must be greater than MY OPPONENT'S WINNERS minus MY OPPONENT'S ERRORS

$$MW - ME > OW - OE$$

The applications of this formula are many, but it should be remembered that seldom can more than 50 percent of the outcome of a match be controlled. It is perhaps the last part of proficiency that a player learns which enables him to force his opponent to play poorly. Therefore, the first priority in a player's strategy is to control those things that he can control, namely his 50 percent. A player's confidence in his own tools will eventually be the factor that dents the confidence of his opponent. If a player's first priority of believing and trusting in his game and keeping his game intact cannot be accomplished, all other strategies are worthless. This does not mean that a player should bullheadedly play only one way, never making adjustments, but it does mean that he should control how he wants to play, forcing his opponent to react to his style. Winners act, and those who react do not win. No matter which style a player uses, this is always the determining factor in the match.

Playing Against a Player With a Different Game Style

What adjustments should be made when you are playing a player with a different game style? Mark Dickson, a former Clemson All-American, once explained a basic diagram to me that simplified many aspects of the technical considerations of strategy. Anyone who has ever played the game rock-scissors-paper will easily understand. His analogy was that just as rock beats scissors, scissors beats paper, and paper beats rock, in tennis, flat beats loop, loop beats net, and net beats flat.

Figure 9-1

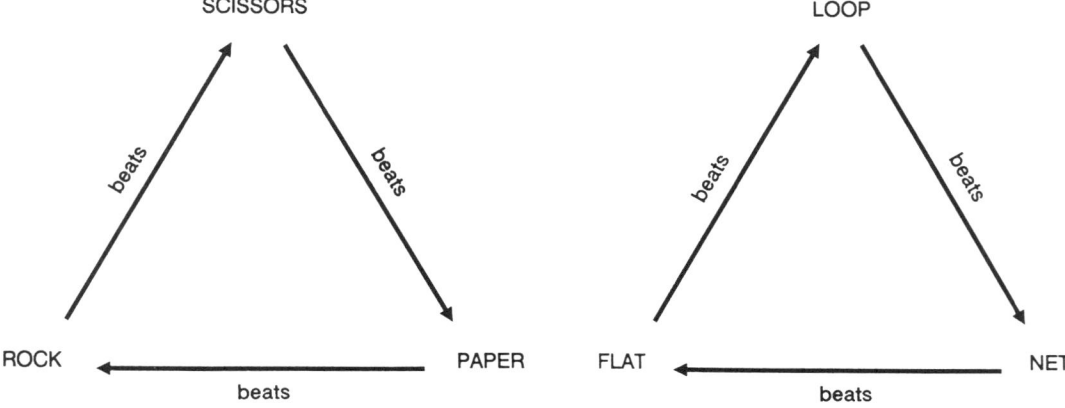

In the first instance, to beat a player who loops the ball, you must be able to catch the ball in the proper strike zone, hitting flat, which allows for an offensive ground stroke and which also forces the loopy player to hit low balls well out of his strike zone. An example of two players with these styles are Bjorn Borg and Jimmy Connors. In their matches, Borg would hit his high top spinning balls, but Connors had the technical advantage. It was always obvious that Connors's style was a problem for Borg, even during his peak. But, of course, Borg's adaptability was always one of his greatest strengths.

In the second instance, in order to beat a player who hits flat, it is critically important to attack the net. The flat player's margin of error on his passing shots is always very small, and often under pressure these flat passing shots will miss their target. Also, those passing shots that travel in a straight trajectory are much easier to volley than balls that dip at a player's feet as he comes in to the net. A good example of this would be John McEnroe with his aggressive net style versus Jimmy Connors with his flat style. Unless Connors can come to the net a lot himself against McEnroe or take balls early enough to prevent McEnroe from getting in close enough to the net, he is at a definite disadvantage.

In the third instance, a player like John McEnroe would have a lot of difficulty playing Bjorn Borg because of Borg's ability to loop balls at McEnroe's feet and out of his optimal volley strike zone. A net rusher's best play against a looping player is to gain a court position good enough to allow most of the volleying to be done with balls before they dip to his feet. This would mean, once again, hitting ground strokes early and flat enough to allow the superior court positioning. Perhaps a third triangle might be composed:

Figure 9-2

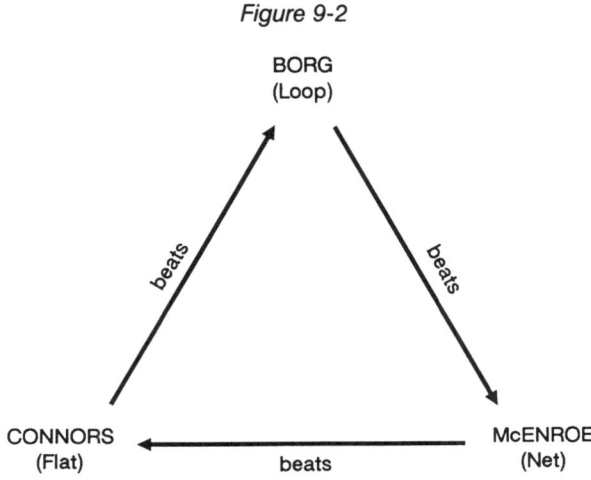

The combinations of styles are endless, but having this working procedure can surely be helpful in pre-match strategy planning against a different style. A strategy for a player to break serve and cause the server to lose confidence is to make the server come out of the style that he likes on his service game. A player can do this by playing the opponent's style when the opponent is serving. For example, the player would come to the net on returns against a server who is a serve and volley player. This may cause the opponent to stay back on his serve a few points at critical times. Or, it would mean making a baseline player play long and tedious games in order to hold service. This might cause him to get frustrated and rush to the net to try to finish points faster. The rule is: *On my serve I play like me, on his serve I play like him!* In any case, the objective of the return game is to force the opponent out of the style that he is comfortable with. Challenging him with his own style is a way of doing this.

Playing Against a Player With a Similar Style

What about players with similar styles? It was always amazing to see Bjorn Borg beat Guillermo Vilas so badly in almost all of their meetings. Because of the scoring system used in tennis, if two players have nearly identical styles of play, it takes only a slight edge, perhaps only one or two percent more proficiency, to cause very lopsided scores and results. When the styles are alike, the lesser player has no way at all to attack the superior game, and the player who is a little better will almost always win big. For years, Chris Evert won match after match against baseline players just slightly less adept than she. Her biggest threats were players like Evonne Goolagong, Martina Navratilova, and Hana Mandlikova. Against almost all other contenders who played the same type of baseline game, she played nearly flawlessly for years.

In playing a match against an opponent with the same style, you have two alternatives: you can stick with your style, or you can play another style. If you are favored, the choice is obvious. If you are the lesser player, abandoning your style violates the first law of strategy, and that is that you must trust your game. The best alternative is to be hardheaded and to stick with your game, remembering that although you may have a hard time hurting your opponent, your opponent may also have a hard time hurting you, and the difference between winning and losing may be only one percent. There may be opportunities to attack in a different manner effectively, but it is important for you to remember to stay with your style, for that is what you are best at. If you copy any of the best styles of the world to perfection, the best you can be is a good imitation. I always tell my players that they are ranked number one in the world in their unique style of play.

EVALUATE THE SITUATION THAT YOU HAVE TO FACE IN THE UPCOMING MATCH AND DEAL WITH THE PRESSURES OF YOUR ROLE

What is the situation? How might my opponent play? What should I expect? Can I handle it, and am I ready for a tough match? These are all good questions that are certainly worth asking before taking the court against any opponent. Different situations present different pressures and effects on performance. A huge mistake that coaches and athletes make is to either avoid their roles as they enter competition or to think that one situation is the same as all others. Players tend to begin playing without evaluating the situation, because of their doubts and their anxieties about dealing with those doubts. Or perhaps they do not want to deal with the job until they have to. The problem, though, with this approach, is that what happens may be totally different from what the player wants or is ready for. Automatically this places him in the role of the reactor in a competitive situation. Ironically, though, many great players take this attitude and prove to be excellent crisis managers. But it is not a good way of dealing with the situation. It leaves the player's coach unable to count on anything. It is better instead to recognize and prepare for the situation and job at hand.

Match Roles

There are very specific roles that a player can carry into a match. Either a player knows his opponent or he does not know his opponent. If you do not know your opponent, either:

1. You are favored.
2. The opponent is favored.
3. It is an even match-up.

If you know your opponent, either:

1. You have played him before and won.
2. You have played him before and lost.
3. You have never played him. If this is the case, either:
   a. You are favored.
   b. The opponent is favored.
   c. It is an even match-up.

WHAT IF YOU DO NOT KNOW YOUR OPPONENT AND YOU ARE FAVORED?

This is one of the hardest positions for a player to be in as he enters a match. Since you are favored, your opponent has something to gain, and you have something to lose. Since you and your opponent do not know each other, it is even more difficult because your advantage carries with it no more clout than hearsay. You should expect your opponent to play fearlessly and perhaps above his usual level of play. In fact, this is the situation in which most upsets occur, and often this happens when playing against players in their first year on the pro tour, their first year in college, or in the initial period after they move into a new environment. In all of these situations, the new kid on the block has an all-to-gain, nothing-to-lose situation. The established player has an all-to-lose, nothing-to-gain situation and, even tougher is that as the favored player he does not know anything about his opponent.

In preparing for a match in this role, the key is to expect a difficult task. If you have this expectation, you will be able to play close to your very best, thereby reducing the chances of being upset. It is also important to remember that in tennis the underdog plays with more enthusiasm and less fear, but the favorite usually wins. Upsets usually occur when the favorite either does not prepare properly for the tough match or just plain ducks the pressure of dealing with it. In this match, the lesser player will keep his game (confidence) intact for a long time, but the flow will usually turn against him with a missed opportunity about three-fourths of the way into the match. The favored player must keep his game intact and be ready to take advantage of the opening when it appears. Failure to do so allows the underdog another chance, and there is nothing that will give the underdog confidence faster than the favorite's hesitation when it comes time for him to take his rightful place as the leader. This work must be done decisively.

WHAT IF YOU DO NOT KNOW YOUR OPPONENT AND THE OPPONENT IS FAVORED?

This can and should be the role that is most fun of all to be in. There is much to gain and little to lose. The opponent does not know what to expect from you, and it is a great opportunity for you to catch him napping. But, even so, anything that appears so good always has its pitfalls.

Beware whenever someone says, "Have fun and play loose—you have nothing to lose!" What you lose is always the match. The balance of pressure that is critical to a good performance is extremely hard for the lesser player to maintain for an entire match. If the pressure is there only for a good showing, a good showing is all you will get. The underdog role is very enjoyable to play, but the underdog usually does not win. In order to win, a player must perform as if he were the favorite. Therefore, it is critical for a player to approach this match in the same way he would approach the favorite role: expecting the opponent to play well and expecting a tough match. It is essential to prevent a situation that is pressure-free. The right balance of pressure is critical in maximizing the opportunity and in getting full growth from a win.

WHAT IF YOU DO NOT KNOW YOUR OPPONENT AND NEITHER OF YOU IS FAVORED?

This is a match nearly free from pressure, because there are no expectations for either player. This match should be a test of pure physical and mental skills, nearly void of emotional factors.

Many times the player who gets ahead can stay ahead; therefore, it is important to display good initial body language and to appear supremely confident because your opponent does not know any difference. Sticking to fundamentals and a solid game plan is important. This is a role that also should be fun.

WHAT IF YOU KNOW YOUR OPPONENT AND YOU WON THE LAST TIME YOU PLAYED?

This is the hardest role to play but it can be the most reliable of any for a chance of a victory. In tennis, pecking order reigns supreme. The player who won the last time will usually win again if he takes care of the necessary pre-match details. Again, body language is critical before, during, and after the match. You must expect a tough, tough match because if you own just one win over an opponent, the revenge factor will allow your opponent to play with relentless aggression for much of the initial and middle part of the match. In recognizing this, it is critical for you as the favored player to also start out aggressively. You must try to take charge immediately, thus denting your opponent's confidence. Above all, you should never let your opponent dictate tempo for extended periods of time. This would allow him to play better and better until he becomes very confident in the role of the leader.

Usually if a player can beat the same opponent twice in a row, he will have dominance for some time to come. It then becomes a true matter of pecking order. Tennis players know their pecking order and although they may deny it, they eventually become subject to it until they make a concentrated effort in training and discipline to break out of it.

WHAT IF YOU KNOW YOUR OPPONENT AND LOST TO HIM WHEN YOU PLAYED HIM LAST?

Revenge is a negative emotion and a negative motive. A positive cannot be gained from a negative. The revenge factor, although it feels good, always leads to its own undoing. If you lost the match when you played last time, you will naturally be a bit more aggressive and determined this time. Your opponent will also naturally have a letdown and not care to face you again. The opponent's tendency will be to sit back and protect those territorial pecking order rites that he has over you. These factors, without the revenge factor, will be enough for a good chance of victory.

The real determining factor, though, will be how you perform in the clutch at many times. The real truth of your confidence, or lack of it, will show when you and your opponent are neck-and-neck at the end of the match. At this point, you will make errors and winners and your opponent will make errors and winners, so the key ingredient in winning will be maintaining your confidence and continuing to execute as if you were the favored player. The scary thing about the clutch part of the match is that both players fully recognize that they are only an inch away from cracking their opponent or having their own game crack.

WHAT IF YOU KNOW YOUR OPPONENT, YOU HAVE NEVER PLAYED, AND YOU ARE FAVORED?

This role also carries with it the pecking order advantages of being the favorite. There is also a greater advantage in having an element of mystery about you which in itself is somewhat intimidating to the underdog. Strong, confident body language is critical to allow this advantage to help you. "Familiarity breeds contempt" is a phrase for all favorites to remember. The favorite should also be aware that flaws an opponent sees in his personality, training, and work habits may be all the fuel that the underdog needs to beat him.

This is one of the most important lessons I learned by watching pro players during their off-court time in my travels as the U.S. Junior Davis Cup Coach. The phenomenon of pecking order permeated even the off-court activities. Players spent their time with those they viewed as equals on the court. The better players associated with the better players, and the lesser players stayed with their own. Bjorn Borg, who was dominating the world of tennis at the time, stayed nearly exclusively to himself and with his coach. This seemed to provide a mystery about Borg that put fear into the other players. Players would even spend time sitting around talking about Borg's greatness, which made him more invulnerable for any underdog who might be trying to challenge him. This mystique is part of the advantage McEnroe lost when he took his long break from the game in 1985. It was not so much that his game dropped off, but more that the other players did not fear him nearly as much.

The main point to be remembered is that the advantage of being the favorite is greatly enhanced if mystery is also kept. This goes for team concepts as well. Everyone fears the unknown. Once familiarity occurs, your opponent's fear can and may become courage.

A strong start in a match in the role of the favorite is again important. If you are behind, it is important to be confident with all play and actions on the court. Your opponent will always doubt himself at a critical time of the match, leaving an opening for you to take your rightful place as the leader. Your job is to keep your game intact until this opening appears.

WHAT IF YOU KNOW YOUR OPPONENT, YOU HAVE NEVER PLAYED HIM, AND HE IS FAVORED?

This is one of the more difficult roles because of many of the factors mentioned already. You may be intimidated even before you take the court. You may have placed your opponent on a pedestal at an earlier time and might feel uncomfortable beating him. You may enjoy the lack of pressure but it may keep you from competing the way you need to in the clutch. Most importantly, though, if you are aware of these things, you may also be aware that your opponent might not be prepared to play you.

Again, in this role, it is critical to control those things that you can control and to execute your own game. A tactic that can also work when you are in this role is to try to disarm the favorite either by acting beforehand as if you are not ready to play, or to make a statement or two to build up your opponent.

Often players play more for respect than out of a desire to win. A mistake college coaches often make is to try to help their teams win in this underdog role by storming in the front door and letting the favorite team know that the underdog team is ready to win. In most cases, all this does is to coax the favorite team into preparation of its own and to give it a reason to compete and win. Because of our Clemson team's image, we have always had a hard time sneaking up on the favorite team, and therefore we score infrequent upsets. But, on the positive side, because of our always-ready-to-play image, we have seldom been upset by a lesser team.

However, some coaches are masters at disarming the opponent. In 1985, our Clemson team was one of the favorites to win the NCAAs. We had a winning streak of 16 straight matches against the top teams in the country as we rolled into Athens, Georgia on a sunny April afternoon. We were heavy favorites to beat a rebuilding University of Georgia team, and we were resting on the laurels of our successful conquests. We arrived for our pre-match warm-up and were greeted by the Southern Gentleman coach, Dan Magill. His only words were, "Chuck, mighty good job your boys have done," and with a lower tone, "Hope my boys can stay on the court with them." Not much, less than 20 words, a very sincere statement from a very great coach, but it was enough, even for me. "Yes," I subconsciously felt, "how good that respect feels, how good it is to be recognized for the great job we are doing." My team members were happy and feeling good about themselves and the match that day. I had no doubt, or fear, or nervousness about the match.

Thirty minutes into the match, I could see the end. Forty-five minutes later, Georgia had won four straight set matches and our number three singles player was desperately trying to hang on for our last chance. "How can this be happening?" I thought as I frantically rushed from court to court trying to rally the team. It was too late, and it was over quickly. We suffered a stunning 5-1 loss in singles and, even worse, we had not ever been in the match.

Afterwards, I was so sick I could not go into the restaurant with my team. I went into the parking lot and did some wind sprints and push-ups instead. The pain of the loss would not go away. "How could we be so totally dominated? We were such a good team. Why did we play so badly? What did I do wrong? Was I such a bad coach?" Finally, one of my players, Craig Boynton, came out of the restaurant to find me. He looked me right in the eyes and said, "Coach, we needed that loss. It'll help us down the stretch when it really counts. We were fat." As he walked back into the restaurant, I suddenly remembered what Magill had said in such a kind, sincere way before the match and I started to laugh. "That old fox, I can't believe it. He did it again!" My mistake was not to recognize the situation. My mistake was not to acknowledge or deal with the role that my team had entering the match. My mistake was not wanting to deal with such a tough, dirty job. I sure had not prepared my team for the match. We were fat, and we needed to lose.

Dan Magill had just given me and my team a great lesson in sneaking in the back door and catching a team with its britches down. I would not forget what I had learned that day from one of the greatest coaches in the history of college tennis.

WHAT IF YOU KNOW YOUR OPPONENT, YOU HAVE NEVER PLAYED HIM, AND IT IS AN EVEN MATCH-UP?

This situation can produce either the most exciting or the most boring match possible. Both players know each other, and there has not been a pecking order established, hence, both players know fully the implications of winning the match. A win could establish true dominance for one of the players over the other, but at the same time, a loss could cause a serious setback. It is definitely a hinge match or a momentum match for both players. Unlike the pressures of the even match-up when two players do not know each other, this situation presents considerably more pressure because both players are forced to live with the outcome of the battle. If the opponents do not know each other before the match, both players go away less blemished. When the opponents know each other, and if everyone looks at it as an even match-up, it builds the suspense of any showdown. It's like the Ali-Frazier fight, or the Marvelous Marvin Hagler-Sugar Ray Leonard fight, or like many of the interstate collegiate football rivalries the weekend before Thanksgiving when both teams have had very good years. The winner is allowed "bragging rights for a year"—like USC versus UCLA, Purdue versus Indiana, and Clemson versus the University of South Carolina—and the loser has to take it.

With so much riding on the match, usually what happens is that the two very calculating and conservative performers each try not to make a mistake that would give the other player any kind of an advantage. The play remains conservative until a player takes the first lead, which forces his trailing opponent to play more aggressively. At that point, the player who is behind may get himself further into trouble but instead usually catches up with and often even overtakes his opponent. This forces the initial leader to raise his level of play and that usually brings him to the forefront once again. This seesawing of the lead usually occurs because of the lack of pecking order and because each player is uncomfortable being the front-runner or being very far behind. This pattern usually continues until one player is forced to play too well for his capabilities and cracks. There are situations in which a player gets ahead and stays ahead because of the other player's cracking early, but usually the pressure of the situation causes each player's game to rise together at the same rate.

Again, confident body language is critical because each player will have feelings of doubt, and it will be just a percent or two that pushes one player ahead. Being aware of this and dealing confidently with it will certainly improve a player's chances of winning the match. A player's best approach is to realize that he cannot control his opponent's ups and downs and to stick to his own game and trust his strengths completely.

UNDERSTANDING PRESSURE AND PEAK PERFORMANCE

Basic to understanding the highs and lows and extreme or subtle swings in performances is having a good understanding of pressure and how it relates to performance on the tennis court. This concept, spelled out to me while teaching health to college freshmen has become the presentation of understanding peak performance.

The right level of stress and the athlete's ability to manage the pressure caused by stress are both critical to optimal performance, and a balance of pressure must be maintained throughout the entire match. Being ahead creates a tendency to take pressure off yourself, and being behind creates a tendency to put too much pressure on. Learning to keep a balance requires an understanding of the benefits of optimal pressure on performance and practice in developing it.

As the stress curve in Figure 9-3 illustrates, a medial amount of pressure produces the best performance.

Figure 9-3. Pressure curve.

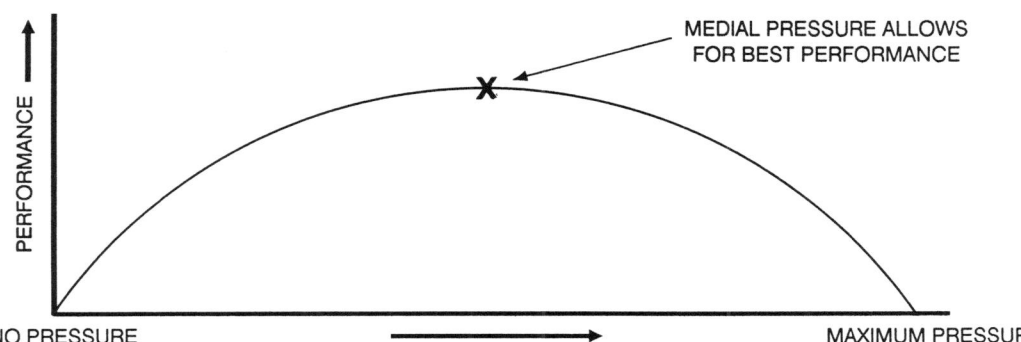

The Balance of Pressure

A coach can eventually read his players and recognize when they or the situation applies too much or too little pressure for the best performance. As a coach becomes more familiar with each athlete, he must develop tools to deal uniquely with him and help him feel the right balance of pressure. He should be able to recognize the critical point between too much and too little pressure. Pre-match preparation has a lot to do with finding this balance of pressure, but even after the match starts, it may still be possible to make adjustments.

Although better players play a bit better when they are behind, being behind, even by only a point, can sometimes lead a player into pressing. A good player will not make bad mistakes when he is behind unless he is cracking. The first bad mistake or unforced error that a player makes when he is behind should draw the coach's immediate attention, because this is almost always an indication that the player is either pressing or has lost confidence. It is usually easy for a coach to recognize when a player is trying too hard and putting too much pressure on himself, because he will be rushing, and he will appear frantic and desperate. At this stage, it is critical for the coach to try to help the player relax. I have always believed that when the player is going off the deep end, the coach has got to try anything to get him back on track.

I had to deal with this situation in a tournament in which one of my freshman players, Chris Munnerlyn, was playing a match against a player that he knew from his state. The situation probably provided a little too much pressure for the best play from Chris. As the match progressed, the harder he tried, the worse he played. The worse he played, the more negative energy he would put into the situation. It was obvious that Chris was not going to win the match if this cycle continued. I tried coaching him three or four times, and nothing seemed to work. Finally, realizing that I had to do something, I called him over to where I was sitting. Chris is a very strong, athletic person, and his body language always communicates extreme confidence. I thought that a humorous approach might loosen him up, and I thought he would be able to handle my attempt to come up with a joke. When he was close to me, I looked him straight in the eyes and said very plainly and distinctly in what I thought was a joking manner, "You stink!" I waited for a smile or laugh to cover his face, but instead he frowned and dropped his head six inches lower than it already was. I knew immediately that he had taken me seriously. As a freshman he had no clue that I was trying to say something to loosen him up. I returned to courtside. He looked at me with tears in his eyes and said, "My own coach thinks that I'm a terrible player." I sat there in total embarrassment and told him I thought he was a great person and I was only joking in trying to loosen him up. I told him I would stay with him during the match and try to help him through. But it was too late. He had lost his confidence, and he lost the match. As Chris walked out of the tennis center later that day, I made him look me right in the eyes and say, "Coach, you stink." We both laughed.

On the other hand, being ahead, often by only a point, tempts a player to take pressure off himself and to allow himself just a bit too much breathing room. This reaction creates a situation that allows careless errors, and even the best players make their bad mistakes when they are ahead. The statement, "When a player is behind, he will make his best shots, and when he is ahead he will usually produce careless play," is one of the most important that a coach can ever learn to help him understand match flow.

HAVE PROPER RESPECT FOR YOUR OPPONENT

A balance of respect is the key to consistent performances. It is the mistake and the downfall of any athlete to get too uppity or cocky but, likewise, underconfidence will prevent a talented athlete from ever getting in the ball game. The correct balance of respect for yourself and your opponent is critical for optimal performance. Confidence? cockiness? humility?—which is best?

Definitions I teach my players:

Confidence = belief in self and respect for opponent
Cockiness = belief in self minus respect for opponent

Four things can happen during a point to cause a possible reaction or mood swing: 1) you can make an error, 2) you can make a good shot, 3) your opponent can make an error, or 4) your opponent can make a good shot. A player's reaction to each of these is based mainly on his pre-match conception of himself in relation to his conception of his opponent.

SITUATION ONE: TOO LITTLE RESPECT FOR YOUR OPPONENT

You beat your opponent last time badly, or you are heavily favored (or at least you and everyone else thinks so). Players of individual sports often do not want to acknowledge the strengths or accomplishments of another competitor. There is an underlying feeling that this affects their own stature or confidence, but quite the opposite is true. It is the confident athlete who can give credit to another athlete and separate performance from feelings. Not having respect for an opponent is one of the easiest traps to fall into, though. Players tend to try to save their greatest concentration and energy for what they perceive as their toughest battles.

If a player has a lack of respect for his opponent, he is destined to play below his capabilities. His reactions to the four things he can react to are shown in Table 9-1.

The fact is that no matter who you are playing, all four of these situations will occur and will probably occur in the first game or two. A player may be able to react positively, even when bad things happen against an opponent who is not respected, but the main point is that rarely can anything good come from this attitude. This is true primarily because in not respecting your opponent, you have put yourself into an all-to-lose, nothing-to-gain situation. Having something to gain is a key ingredient to a good performance, and respect for your opponent is critical to prepare your mind for something to gain.

SITUATION TWO: TOO MUCH RESPECT FOR YOUR OPPONENT

Your opponent beat you last time, or he is heavily favored, or you hold your opponent somewhat in awe. In this situation, it is easy for a player to have too much respect for his opponent. Because of the pecking order in tennis, all players start in the underdog role. You almost always have to lose before you can win. The transition from being the underdog to being the favored player is a tough one, and this growth usually occurs in cycles. It is extremely difficult to win in the underdog role, especially if you have too much respect for your opponent. Table 9-2 shows the four situations that can occur.

The up-and-down play of the underdog role is what causes confidence lapses at critical times in the match. These highs and lows are caused by a player's reaction to what happens on the court and are difficult to keep in balance.

Table 9-1. Too little respect for your opponent.

POINT WON/LOST BY:	REACTION	COMMENTS OR THOUGHTS	LEVEL OF PLAY
My bad shot	Upset	How can I be playing so poorly against this player?	Down
My good shot	OK; no big deal	I'm supposed to make good shots against this player.	Same
Opponent's bad shot	OK; no big deal	This opponent is supposed to make errors against me.	Same
Opponent's good shot	Upset	This opponent is playing over his head; he's so lucky.	Down
State of mind	Upset/disappointed	I'm playing poorly and my opponent is playing above his head.	Down

Table 9-2. Too much respect for your opponent.

POINT WON/LOST BY:	REACTION	COMMENTS OR THOUGHTS	LEVEL OF PLAY
My bad shot	Slight disappointment	My opponent is really good—I'm supposed to make errors.	Down slightly
My good shot	Great!	What a shot—I didn't know I could make that one.	Up; zoning
Opponent's bad shot	Surprised	What a break!	Not reliable
Opponent's good shot	Slight disappointment	This player is really good—he's going to make great shots.	Down
State of mind	Ups and downs	What will happen next? I hope that I can hang in there...	Up and down

The underdog role is a fun and nonpressured role to play in a match. You as well as others do not really expect much, but, unfortunately, not much is what you get. In the underdog role, the player is destined to eventually react to the favorite. For long periods he may dictate tempo and play with authority, but late in the match or at critical stages, the opponent will take charge of the match, and the underdog will react to that. The winners of matches dictate action, and the losers react to their opponent's play.

THE PROPER BALANCE OF RESPECT FOR YOUR OPPONENT

The best attitude to have to maintain the proper balance of respect when entering a match should be: "I know I can win, but I know my opponent can win too if I'm not at my best." This attitude puts the athlete in a state of absolute readiness for a tough battle. Many athletes prefer to reject this attitude, though, because giving the opponent respect and recognizing the difficulty of the task at hand supposedly places them in a vulnerable position. Acknowledging this vulnerability makes an athlete uneasy, but it is this vulnerability and emotional readiness that allow an athlete to have his best possible performance, both mentally and physically.

If a player has the proper balance of respect for his opponent, his reactions to his good and bad shots and his opponent's good and bad shots are illustrated in Table 9-3.

The proper balance of respect between you and your opponent also prevents a rollercoaster effect from happening. The smart and experienced competitor is always aware that emotional balance is critical for his best play. The foolish player fails to respect his opponents, and the inexperienced player tends to respect some opponents too much. The best pre-match preparation is a matter of working to obtain the proper balance. This will enable you to give your opponent the credit if he wins, and to be a gracious winner if you win.

Table 9-3. The proper balance of respect for your opponent.

POINT WON/LOST BY:	REACTION	COMMENTS OR THOUGHTS	LEVEL OF PLAY
My bad shot	OK—stay tough	Stay tough; keep going.	Stable
My good shot	OK—keep it going	Fine, but I've got to stay tough.	Up and stable
Opponent's bad shot	OK—that helps	Fine, but he can still play well—stay ready.	Up and stable
Opponent's good shot	OK—stay tough	Good shot on his part—stay tough.	Stable
State of mind	OK—stay tough	I should win but so can he—I must be ready.	Up and stable

CONCENTRATE ON YOUR PRE-MATCH PREPARATION

Table 9-4. Pre-match state of mind (how I view myself, how I view my opponent).

	TOO LITTLE RESPECT (I'M GOOD, YOU'RE NOT)	TOO MUCH RESPECT (I'M NOT GOOD, YOU ARE)	BALANCE OF RESPECT (I'M GOOD, YOU'RE GOOD)
MY BAD SHOT	↓	— ↑	—
MY GOOD SHOT	—	ZONING	—
MY OPPONENT'S BAD SHOT	—	↑ OR ↓	— ↑
MY OPPONENT'S GOOD SHOT	↓	—	— ↑
MY STATE OF MIND	↓ = POOR PLAY	UP AND DOWN = UNRELIABLE PLAY	BEST & MOST RELIABLE PERFORMANCE

Figure 9-4 shows the flow and direction that a match will most likely take from the three different attitudes toward an opponent that can be taken before entering a match.

The best intensity to have to win a two-set match would be similar to the intensity a runner would have in running a two-mile race. He should start out quickly but settle soon into a comfortable stride. He should be solid for the biggest part of the race with few ups and downs and keep enough left over to finish the race.

Figure 9-4

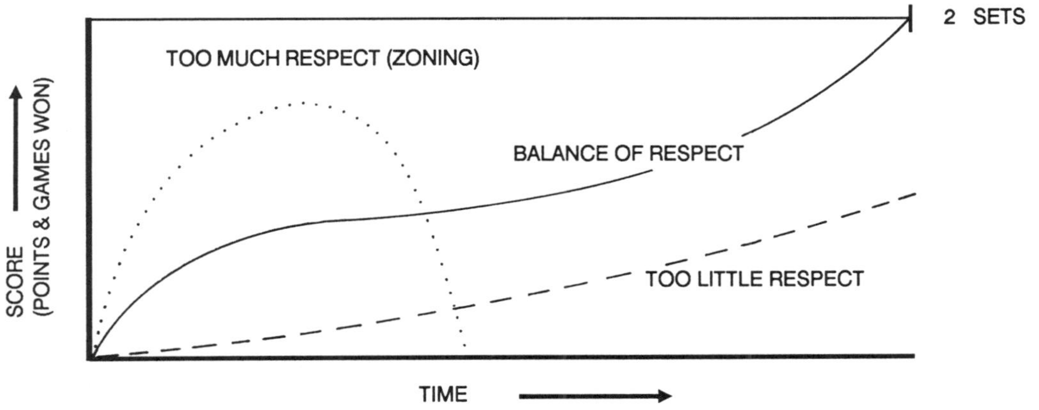

Respecting an opponent too much is like trying to run too well in this race. It is like a runner who goes out too fast and sprints off to an early lead but collapses quickly when things get close. Tennis players who assume this role often start off by playing all their best shots early in the match. A good opponent is not threatened by great shots early in the match, and often a player who starts this way will not have anything left when the points get critical.

Too little respect for an opponent would be much like a runner starting off the two-mile race in a jog and falsely reassuring himself that he can always catch up and that he does not have to run his best until later. This lack of readiness usually compounds his problems and most likely he will produce too little and too late.

SUMMARY

Correct and responsible pre-match preparation is a matter of knowing the toughness of the job and preparing to do it. It is a matter of physical, mental, and emotional preparation and the following areas should all be attended to:

1. Take care of the physical details that are controllable—understand the game style triangle.
2. Set a game plan and strategy to play.
3. Acknowledge the role in which you are entering the match.
4. Work to achieve the right emotional pressure as you enter the match.
5. Have proper balance of respect for your opponent.

Figure 9-5. Players should understand pressure and peak performance.

Figure 9-6. Players must maintain confident body language.

CHAPTER 10

OBSERVE IMPORTANT CHECKPOINTS FOR MATCH PLAY

"Far better to dare a mighty thing, to win glorious triumphs, even though checkered by failure, than to rank with those poor spirits who neither enjoy much nor suffer much, because they live in the grey twilight that knows neither victory nor defeat."
—Theodore Roosevelt

It can be confusing for coaches and players, even advanced players, to know exactly what to look for as a match develops. Often a player relies chiefly on his instincts, or he may have a tendency to concentrate on his stroke production. What are the areas that must be focused on? How much should a player rely on his natural instincts, and how much should he rely on a logical plan of action?

The three aspects of a match—the physical, the mental, and the emotional—provide the important checkpoints for match play. In the physical-technical area, game style match-ups and court positioning are the checkpoints; in the mental area, running the right play is the concern; and in the emotional area, the player must be able to keep a balance of pressure, and he must be aware of his emotional reactions to the good and bad things that happen during the match.

PHYSICAL CHECKPOINTS

What Are the Game Style Match-ups?

As discussed earlier, the variables in planning strategy for your particular game style against another's are many and can be quite complex. Pre-match preparation should be based on understanding the tools (skills) that are available to you and those available to your opponent. Your first and foremost responsibility is to be able to use your tools and to execute your game, because strategies against your opponent are totally useless unless your game is in operating order. Often a good strategy fails quickly because a player's tools were not sufficient for the strategy or because a player abandoned his tools early in the match to try an approach that was not within his skill level. A player should always lock in his style first and then work to derail his opponent. The game style triangle discussed in Chapter 9 is important to review and understand before taking the court. It can also be of value during a match to expose an opponent's weakness or to find the most effective way to exploit his style of play.

Am I Controlling Court Positioning?

Changes in a player's body language, intensity, and stroke production are usually obvious. But more subtle changes may occur in a player's court positioning, and this is an extremely important physical aspect to watch for. If two players were to rally and hit ground strokes on an open parking lot instead of on a tennis court with all its restrictive dimensions, they would probably discover that their normal shots would travel approximately the same distance every time, perhaps 65 or 70 feet. This is because the player's strokes have been developed within the normal court dimensions (a tennis court is 78 feet long). This rally delivers a ball that falls somewhere in the midcourt every time.

There are many advantages if a player is even one step closer to the net. Taking balls just a step earlier allows several things to happen. First, the ball delivered to the opponent is deeper, which forces his ball to be shorter. This allows the player to be offensive minded, and it forces the opponent into defensive play. In addition, as shown in Figure 10-1, the angles for court usage are much better. Good court positioning forces the opponent to make defensive shots, and it prevents the player from having to cover so much court. The greatest benefit, though, is that it rushes the opponent, preventing him from setting up, and thus preventing his ability to take charge of the point. To force the opponent, a player has two choices: he either hits the ball harder, or he takes the ball earlier. It is extremely difficult, if not impossible, for a player to force himself to hit harder instantly while still maintaining control. A much better approach for a player is to take his shots a bit earlier and to maintain his most confident stroke, which results in making the opponent rush.

The main disadvantage of taking balls early is that the player himself also has a little less time and should therefore hit the ball without changing the direction of its flight. He should hit the ball right back to where it came from, thereby cutting the margin for an error. The most obvious advantages of taking the ball early and of good court positioning are apparent in all transition shots, in which the benefit of forcing the opponent to rush is even greater.

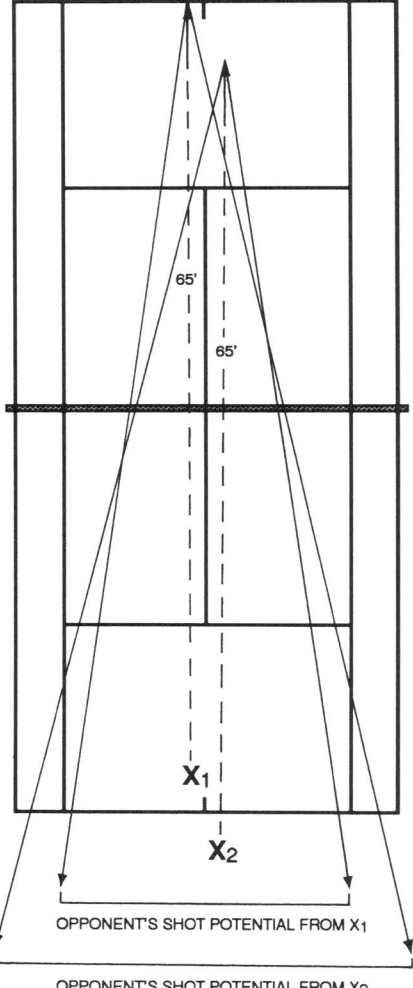

Figure 10-1

X_1 = SHOT MADE WITH GOOD COURT POSITIONING

X_2 = SHOT MADE FROM COURT POSITION BEHIND BASELINE

MENTAL CHECKPOINT

Am I Controlling the Momentum and Match Flow by Running the Right Play?

The physical checkpoints of game style match-ups and court positioning are the base for any other strategy, for without these fundamentals other efforts will fall short. Once these are in order, the next checkpoint is a mental or strategic procedure: Which play should be run? In all other sports, the answer to this question is more obvious than it is in tennis. Often, at the critical stages of a match, tennis players focus on their technical skills or on the trouble they are having with a stroke. This is wrong. Game time is not the time to worry whether or not your strokes are there—you have got to use whatever is in the tool box at the start of the match. Top basketball players do not worry about how their jump shot looks with a minute and a half to go in the game, and a quarterback does not think about his throwing release with the two-minute drill underway. In tennis, though, there is a tendency for players to overanalyze and pick out microscopic technical flaws in their games when they should be thinking only of which play they should run. "Paralysis by analysis" can be a fatal disease for the athlete in the heat of the battle.

EMOTIONAL CHECKPOINTS

Am I at my Optimal Balance of Emotional Pressure?

If a player has chosen the right technical way to play, has worked to control court positioning, and knows which play he wants to run, he has covered the checkpoints for playing a very solid match. The final, key ingredient that lets the whole thing run is making sure that he is in the right "emotional zone" or has the right balance of pressure, as discussed in Chapter 9. It is critical to note that although the physical and mental checkpoints should be taken care of first, this important emotional checkpoint allows everything else to flow and work together.

How Do I React to Points Won and Points Lost?

During the first two or three games of every match, a player will make winning shots and errors, and his opponent will make winning shots and errors. Often a player can judge his emotional state by noticing his reaction to these events.

Usually if a player is in a good frame of mind to compete, he will react positively to his good shots, and his poor shots will cause little or no reaction. His opponent's good shots will not bother him, and he will get a small lift from his opponent's bad shots. When this same player is in a poor state of emotion to compete, he will get upset and annoyed at his poor shots and at his opponent's winners. A poor emotional state will give him little or no satisfaction from the good things that happen. Once this cycle starts, it is difficult to reverse. This is a major checkpoint for emotional balance on the court.

Figure 10-2. Players must observe the physical, mental, and emotional checkpoints for match play.

Figure 10-3. Good returns like this result from attending to the emotional checkpoints of a match.

SUMMARY

Physical checkpoints:

1. What are the game style match-ups?
2. Am I controlling court positioning?

Mental checkpoint:

1. Am I controlling the momentum and match flow by running the right play?

Emotional checkpoints:

1. Am I at my optimal balance of emotional pressure?
2. How do I react to points won and points lost?

CHAPTER 11

USE THE POWER OF MOMENTUM TO CONTROL MATCH FLOW

> *"Momentum is the most awesome power in sports. If you could ever learn to can it when you've got it, and to shut it down when it belongs to your opponent, you've got the key to winning."*
> —Kent DeMars, men's tennis coach, University of South Carolina

In the sixth game of the 1985 World Series, less than an inning away from winning the world championship of baseball, it happened to the St. Louis Cardinals. They were virtually helpless in their attempt to turn back the almost magical power that the Kansas City Royals displayed for the remainder of the series. Likewise, in the sixth game of the 1986 World Series, the Boston Red Sox were only one strike away from winning their first world championship in years. A dramatic change of events occurred that resulted not only in the loss of their two-run lead and the game but, most unfortunately, the momentum for the series. The New York Mets were completely in control of the momentum and there was little the Red Sox could do to stop them. Having the opportunity to play the seventh game of the World Series would probably have been one of the highest expectations of the Red Sox on the opening day of spring training, but now they seemed disheartened about having to take part in the seventh game. In game five of the 1986 NBA Championship, a fight broke out and the championship series, which had seemed so obviously under control by the Boston Celtics, was now in jeopardy. The Houston Rockets now seemed to have a great chance to win the championship as the series moved back to Boston. In each of these situations, in a matter of moments, a single action reversed the flow of the championship series, and although the Celtics were able to recover in the next game, the Cardinals and the Red Sox were not. In the 1985 French Open finals, a similar thing happened to John McEnroe as he saw his two-set lead over Ivan Lendl and the championship slip away from him.

The power that allows these swings to occur seems almost magical, and no one has seemed to be able to harness it. Sportscasters refer to it on a regular basis, and sports competitors refer to it as if it is both their best friend and their worst enemy. This power is called "momentum" (I refer to it as "MO"), and it is the most awesome power in sports. All competitive tennis players have experienced the power of the MO. When the MO is with you, you feel as if the match is on the tip of your racquet and that you are dictating how each point is played. When the MO is against you, you feel like a puppet on a string as your opponent effortlessly puts together one powerfully played point after another.

Tennis, more than any other sport, is a game of momentum. The absence of a clock to do the dirty work of finishing off an opponent, and a scoring system based on units used makes the flow of the match much more important than any lead that has been established.

In sports other than tennis, momentum is also readily recognized and can sometimes be controlled. Basketball coaches are perhaps the most adept coaches at shutting the MO down. In tennis, coaches and players often focus a bit too much on stroke technique instead of being aware of match flow and sticking to a simple game plan that tells them when to attack and when not to. This is what the best basketball coaches learn to do in their coaching. At times they have their players put high pressure on their opponents and at strategic times they have the players let up on the pressure to frustrate their opponents into making mistakes. All too often in tennis, strategy is planned around an opponent's weakness, and too often the match tempo is dictated by how a player is feeling. This would be totally absurd in any other sport, but in tennis the very best players go into matches with the assumption that the outcome rests on their technical skills alone.

The most powerful skill that a singles or doubles tennis player can learn and apply during competition is the ability to manage momentum. Sometimes a drastic change of events can influence momentum, such as a rain delay, the fight in the Boston-Houston game, or perhaps an injury. These unplanned events can change momentum quickly and cannot often be controlled. But the athlete should understand that they do occur, and he should be ready to deal with the situation at hand in the best way he can. Some aspects of momentum can be controlled, however. These are based on two variables in the match: 1) the score, and 2) the events leading up to the score. In a tight match, pressure swings back and forth from player to player based on these two variables. During a match a player is either ahead, or behind, or even, and he will have a definite advantage if he knows exactly how to manage momentum in each of these situations.

MANAGING MOMENTUM BASED ON THE SCORE

Momentum management also includes a player's ability to: 1) maintain momentum once it has been created, 2) switch momentum once the opponent has it, and 3) create momentum when there is none.

The basis for momentum management in relation to the score is found in one simple truth: Players usually make bad mistakes when they are ahead in a game and their best shots when they are behind in a game. It is a natural tendency for people to do only as much as they have to do, and there is also a tendency for people to procrastinate when they find themselves in a situation that does not demand their direct attention. Thus, most unforced errors occur when a tennis player is ahead, because he does not have to win the points to stay in the game. When he is behind, he is forced into a crisis management situation in which he must concentrate and play his very best shots. Recognizing this can help dictate how to play the points in the ad court, where a player is always ahead or behind by one or three points. In the deuce court, three situations can occur: 1) you may be two points ahead, which may cause a greater tendency for you to let up, 2) you may be two points behind, which may cause a tendency to press, or 3) you may be tied, where the pressure is not so great either way. Regardless, more important than the tally of the points should be your momentum management. The following sections explain just how to do this.

MAINTAINING MOMENTUM —WHAT DO YOU DO WHEN YOU ARE AHEAD IN THE GAME?

When you are ahead by a point or two, some interesting things tend to happen. First of all, the pressure naturally slips. You do not have to win the point. Your opponent is the one who is in trouble, and you feel an opportunity to play a more recklessly aggressive point. After all, the worst you can do is be tied again. This is when you must guard against the danger of a possible momentum switch against you. When you are ahead, your opponent is behind. As you have a tendency to play a little looser, the opponent has a tendency to play a little better. His concentration picks up, he becomes a bit more aggressive, and if he is a good player, he surely will not make a bad mistake. The loss of momentum in this game usually occurs because your relaxed attitude and your opponent's aggressiveness cause the two things that actually change momentum: your sloppy mistake and your opponent's great shot. You find yourself at deuce in the score, but your confidence has slipped and your opponent's has taken a jump. Unless you now respond properly to this switch, your problems can quickly be compounded. As experienced tennis players know, even one improperly played point can start a snowball effect that changes the entire match.

Playing the Breakdown Point

When you are ahead by one point in the game (15-0, 30-15, 40-30), your objective should be to play a breakdown point. A breakdown point occurs when you break down your opponent's confidence and prevent him from making any great play that might switch the momentum against you.

There are two common tendencies that players have when they are ahead in a match and want to close it out. One is to rush or press for a reckless outright winner. It is like a basketball team, ahead by ten points, that comes across the 10-second line and shoots 25-footers. The other tendency is to play tentatively. Neither tendency is good, however. If you rush, or try for a "chain saw killing," as I call it, you will make mistakes. If you play safely and tentatively, you may give your opponent an opportunity to get back into the match and maybe even take charge himself. The object is to keep control, to keep your opponent's confidence low, and to try to win the point by forcing your opponent into an error. An error on your opponent's part not only wins the point and perhaps the game for you, but it further disarms your opponent's confidence.

A Chain Saw Killing

In 1985 we were playing Trinity University at Corpus Christi, Texas. Jay Berger, a freshman, was playing a match against a Trinity player who played a great serve and volley game. Jay knew he would have his work cut out for him.

Jay played excellent tennis for a set and a half by using his counter punching ability with tremendous accuracy and speed to keep his opponent off balance. The serve and volleyer was close to being defeated when all of a sudden, at 6-2, 4-1, Jay, who is a baseliner and rarely comes into the net, started serving and volleying on every point. The tide turned quickly and Jay lost two fast games, making the score 4-3.

My main concern was not the score, but rather the momentum that had changed because of Jay's impatience and failure to stay with his own game style. Jay's style was to peck away and work every point while trying to break down his opponent's game. As a serve and volleyer, he was just not effective.

At 4-3 I walked onto the court. Jay realized that the momentum had turned, but, as is typical of him, he was stubborn and did not want to hear any coaching advice that I might give him. I walked over to him, held out my arms, and said, "Okay, hand it over." He said, "What are you talking about?" I said, "Hand over the chain saw." Then he knew what I meant because we had talked so often during the season about the mistake of a chain saw killing when closing out a match. Jay knew that the correct way to close out a match is to do the dirty work meticulously and peck and peck away until the opponent's confidence in his game (his "dam") breaks. Jay said, "Okay," and pretended to give me an imaginary chain saw. I stumbled over to the trash can and pretended to dump it in. I walked back to where Jay was, reached in my pocket, and pretended to pull something out. I said to him, "All right, here's a chisel and ice pick. Pick away at your opponent and work the ball 10 to 15 rallies every point." Jay laughed and looked as me as if I were half crazy, but the point was made.

The next game was not an easy one, and it lasted a long time. Jay could not get back into his style of working the ball through his opponent, and he had to earn his points. Jay won that game, though, and he won the match. I learned that even the best players have a tendency to go for a chain saw killing when they are ahead. The simple chisel and ice pick method of pecking away is a tough one to master when a player wants to finish the match.

Playing Tentatively

The other common tendency of a player who is ahead is to play tentatively. There is nothing more frightening than closing out an opponent and nothing scarier than killing off a wounded opponent. A player can play a perfect match, but, in the closing moments, most players turn their head from the tough, dirty job of closing it out. An opponent who is behind is always going to play better, and the player who is ahead in the match realizes this.

One of the worst tendencies that becomes evident when a player becomes timid in closing out a match is poor court positioning, and it is court positioning that dictates the ability to control the points. If a player merely moves back one or two yards on the court on ground strokes, he gives his opponent the opportunity to take charge and possibly turn the momentum.

In 1987, in an excellently played match against the eventual National Champion Georgia Bulldogs, Craig Boynton, who has a counter punch game and usually plays long, drawn-out points, was playing against a player named John Boytim. These two players had almost identical game styles, and I felt they were in for an all-day affair unless one player played very well or very poorly.

Craig's strategy for the match was simple: He would maintain better court positioning than Boytim. If Craig could stay up in the court, his balls would fall deep, forcing Boytim's balls to fall short. Craig could then be in charge of most of the rallies, and it was critical that he maintain this control.

Craig played the first set very well and won 6-1. But at the beginning of the second set, I noticed a change. Craig, after a very, very long game which John Boytim won, stepped back from the baseline. He had been standing on the baseline or a foot inside the baseline to take all his ground strokes, but he was now a yard behind the baseline and was running from side to side, frantically trying to run down Boytim's fine-tuned shots. He was being jerked from side to side and dropped point after point. By the time I got down to the court, Craig was way down in the set that Boytim quickly won 6-2. Since the two players had identical games and were identical in just about every way, Boytim had won the set because of his better court positioning.

Before the third set, I again told Craig to stand inside the baseline and take balls as early as possible. He did so, and after a couple of very tough games, he was able to turn the momentum of the match to win the set 6-3.

The tendency for a player to play tentatively is hard for a coach to recognize. It has nothing to do with tentative shots or poor stroke production. Very subtle court positioning is usually the first tentativeness that is seen. The breaking down of strokes and the player's rushing the ball only come after court positioning is given up. There is nothing tougher than finishing off a tough opponent. It takes total concentration and coverage to meticulously do the right things at the end.

Getting Your Opponent to Play Poorly

Winning tennis matches is often not so much a matter of your great play, but more a matter of getting your opponent to play poorly. Tim Wilkison was unable to do this in his match against Boris Becker in the first round of the 1987 U.S. Open. Wilkison was ahead two sets to love and also a service break ahead in the third set. His style has always been to play with reckless abandon and to keep relentless pressure on his opponent until his opponent finally cracks. But this time his aggressive play only forced Becker to use his survival tactics of playing better and better. Wilkison would have been much better off if he could have manipulated Becker into playing a bit worse by using different styles of points mixed with his best style of relentless attacking. Some of the best basketball coaches succeed by using this method. At times they put high pressure on their opponents, and at strategic times they let up on the pressure to frustrate their opponents into making mistakes.

Playing the Breakdown Point When You are Ahead or Behind by Three Points

Breakdown points are also played at 40-0 and 0-40. With a three-point lead (40-0), the pressure on you can really let up. A long point allows you to keep concentration and prevent the possibility of a bad mistake on what seems to be a meaningless point. When you are behind by three points, take advantage of the fact that your opponent will probably relax. You can be sure he does not want to have to dig out a long, long point to win the game. He has probably already chalked the game up and is ready to move on to the next one. But if you can win a tough point and then an aggressive point at 15-40, you can turn the whole momentum of the game. Winning this game can turn the momentum for the whole match.

The breakdown point guidelines are as follows:

1. Your objective is to keep charge while preventing a MO switch.
2. Do not allow your opponent a quick winner in the point.
3. Force the error, stay in control of the tempo, hit through your opponent (no change of direction) and break him down.
4. Keep good fundamentals intact.
5. Keep confident and deliberate body language.
6. If your opponent makes a great shot when he is behind, realize that he did because he had to. Simply say "Good shot," and prepare to play the next point properly.

SWITCHING MOMENTUM— WHAT DO YOU DO IF YOU ARE BEHIND IN THE GAME?

Remembering your opponent's tendency to play a little sloppy when he is ahead is a big advantage. He may have periods of brilliance because of less pressure, but at some point he will worry about preserving his lead. His tendencies at this point will be either to rush or to play a bit tentatively. When you are behind, you should play tougher and put pressure back on your opponent.

Momentum is never turned by tentative play. All great competitors realize that they must attack or raise their level of play when they are behind. Unforced errors, though, will only put you in a deeper hole if you are behind, so it is essential to attack decisively and, if possible, without errors. There is also a tendency to lose confidence in your game when you are losing and to desperately try different things. This is wrong also. It is critical to believe in your game and to keep your "dam" of trust and confidence intact.

When behind in the game 0-15, 15-30, or 30-40, it is very important to run an aggressive play. If you are overly cautious, your confidence will decrease, and your opponent's confidence will increase. Playing aggressively to switch momentum does not mean taking unnecessary risks. Playing a bit more aggressively mentally and digging into a long point can sometimes also be effective.

Figure 11-1. Run an aggressive play when you are behind.

Playing the MO Switch Point

Whenever you are behind, your game plan should be executed within your own limitations. If you are a serve and volley player, be sure to get your first serve and first volley in. For a baseliner, it may again be a matter of being hardheaded and playing with more enthusiasm and emotion. Whatever your game style, be aggressive when you are behind.

When a player is behind, he may have a tendency to lie back and lick his wounds and try to pull some magic string that will get him back into the match. Often when he gives up hope he will come out of his natural game and play beyond his limitations. When a player is behind, his game plan should be executed within his limitations. If he is a serve and volley player, he should be sure to get his first serve and his first volley in. If he is a baseliner, it may be a matter of being hardheaded and playing with enthusiasm. But whatever a player's game style, when he is behind, he must play aggressively, making sure not to make unforced errors that would allow his opponent to gain even more momentum. He must be fearless, and he must dictate the tempo of the points played.

I learned this lesson at the 1985 NCAA Championships. Kelly Jones and Carlos Dilaura of Pepperdine were playing in the NCAA Doubles quarterfinals against a team from Harvard. The Harvard team had played flawless tennis for a set and a half and were ahead 6-3, 4-1. It seemed as if Jones and Dilaura could not get on track. Just when I thought the match was over, I saw Kelly Jones start hitting balls as hard as he could right at the opponents and start charging to the net with seemingly uncontrolled aggression. Kelly was famous for his "chain saw killer tennis" mentality, and he played this kind of tennis very well. But he seemed particularly reckless now and I wondered if he had completely lost control. He hit a couple of returns right at the net man and drilled one ball overhead so hard and with such enthusiasm that I thought he had broken the ball. It was amazing that a game later the Harvard team's every move seemed more calculated and more tentative. Jones's recklessness also picked up his partner, Dilaura, and they came back into the match winning a close second set and then a 6-2 third set decision as well.

After the match I asked Kelly, "What were you doing when you were behind 4-1 in the second set? You seemed almost wild in your play." He answered, "Well, I knew we were going to lose the match and I had to try something. All I did was play recklessly and try to scare them or throw them off their game." I looked at him and wondered if he recognized his genius as a competitor.

A player's ability to be reckless and fearless when he is behind is his ability to turn matches at any point.

Some players can never be taught this, and some are so afraid of losing that they will never let go even if they know that their style of game will lose. A player should win with fundamentals, but he should always lose dictating the action and being aggressive.

Jones and Dilaura went on to win not only the next match, but also the NCAA Championship. It was Jones's second NCAA Doubles Championship in a row. I never forgot that match, and I refer to it when my players are in a tight spot. The lesson is: *Be aggressive when you are behind.*

The MO switch guidelines to remember are:

1. You must attack—If you are going to lose, lose aggressively, dictating the tempo.
2. No unforced errors—stay within your limitations—keep your confidence intact and trust your shots.
3. Dictate the tempo between and during shots.

CREATING MOMENTUM— WHAT DO YOU DO WHEN THE SCORE IS TIED, OR YOU ARE AHEAD OR BEHIND BY TWO POINTS?

I often refer to these situations as take-charge situations or bread-and-butter situations. When the score is tied, the pressure on each player is about the same. The player who comes from behind to win the last point has a bit more momentum, but each player has the same objective—to take charge and create momentum.

Playing the MO Point

Momentum points are played in the deuce court, where you are either two points ahead (30-0, 40-15), two points behind (0-30, 15-40), or tied (0-0, 15-15, 30-30, 40-40, or deuce). Your objective when you are two points ahead is to keep the momentum. The odds are tremendously in your favor. In fact, the only way to lose the game is for a switch in momentum. Your opponent will definitely play aggressively in a nothing-to-lose manner. When you are two points ahead, it is more important to preserve momentum than to prevent the loss of a point (you are still up in the game). It is critical to try to take charge and dictate the flow. Do this by going with your strength or bread and butter. Even if your opponent wins the point, no harm is done because your game did not go down. There is only danger in letting a wounded opponent dictate the tempo and flow. Therefore, at 30-0 and 40-15, play a momentum (take charge) point.

Your objective if you are two points behind is to switch the momentum. The odds are definitely against you to win the game. You must be aggressive and dictate the flow. Tentative play will only bury you deeper in your hole. After you lose the point to go behind by two, it is important to take some time before playing the next point. Tie your shoe, or towel off, or do whatever is needed to slow your opponent's rhythm. Be deliberate, but as you line up to play the next point, think about playing aggressively.

Your objective when the score is tied is to create some momentum. Act, and force your opponent to react. Winning the point when you are tied means either shutting his momentum down, if he came from behind, or keeping your momentum on a roll when you came from behind. Matches are usually decided by the player who is comfortable taking charge when the score is tied.

To create momentum, these guidelines should be followed:

1. Take charge.
2. Go with your strengths (your bread and butter).
3. Dictate match flow.
4. Act, don't react.

FUNDAMENTALS OF MOMENTUM MANAGEMENT BASED ON THE SCORE

A story I often use to illustrate the basic rules of momentum control is about two men who are fighting at the top of a cliff. Both men are in a life-and-death situation and are desperately struggling to throw the other one over the cliff. The long fall and the jagged rocks below present thoughts of a terrible and painful death.

As the two men struggle, it is easy to see that there are three positions each man can be in: 1) the in-charge position trying to push his opponent off, 2) the desperate, losing position trying to prevent being pushed off, or 3) a neutral position, side by side, where neither has the advantage.

In the first position (maintaining momentum), the only obvious ways to mess things up are to rush, which could cause a stumble, sending you over the cliff, or to be tentative and turn away from the dirty job at hand, thereby allowing your opponent the chance to regroup and get back on steady ground. Neither the first (chain saw) method, nor the second (tentative) method will work. The decisive, clear-cut chisel and ice pick method of dissecting your opponent with your solid fundamentals is the way to finish him off. Remember that you have the better position, and you are in control. Peck away at the opponent, no matter how hard that may be, and stay with your game.

The second position (switching momentum) is a tough one. Your opponent is pushing you steadily back to the edge of the cliff. He is cold-blooded and tough and is neither rushing nor being tentative. You can play possum and act as if you are giving up, but this will work only temporarily. If you are tentative or afraid, you will go over the cliff quickly. You must square off, looking directly in his eyes, and attack him back. Smart aggression is the best, but reckless aggression is better than no aggression at all. You must dent your opponent's confidence. Once you can reverse the position, you must be ready to do your own dirty work quickly and without hesitation. Letting a wounded opponent survive is dangerous. If you do so, he will become fearless and it will be even more difficult to finish him off.

The third position (creating momentum), when neither fighter has an advantage, is one that tests your confidence and trust in your skills. Each fighter spars and trades blows. Back and forth it goes, each fighter trying to gain some kind of an advantage. You have two choices: You either go with your bread and butter and your best tools, or you try something else. Actually, there is no choice. In order to gain any advantage, even against a bigger, stronger, or more experienced opponent, you must go with your bread and butter, because that is the fight plan you know best.

MANAGING MOMENTUM BASED ON THE EVENTS LEADING UP TO A CERTAIN SCORE

Basketball coaches learn to manage momentum based on the score, but the main focus of their momentum control is on what has just happened and its effect on the flow of the game. They ask questions like, "Is the other team on a roll? Did my team just make some bad mistakes? Is the other team cracking? Is it time to speed up play? Is it time to slow down play? Should we play a zone defense? Is it time to fast break?"

Of course, in basketball and in other sports, the coach can slow down or speed up play by making substitutions, calling time-outs, and sending players in from the bench. In tennis, the coach cannot do this, and each player must have a good knowledge and understanding of how to manage this flow.

FLOW MANAGEMENT GUIDELINES

There are five situations that you as a player must respond to properly during a match:

1. Your opponent has just made a bad mistake.
2. Your opponent has just made a good shot.
3. You have just made a bad mistake.
4. You have just made a great shot.
5. You have just won a long point in which there was no dominance determined.

Figure 11-2. Momentum control guidelines.

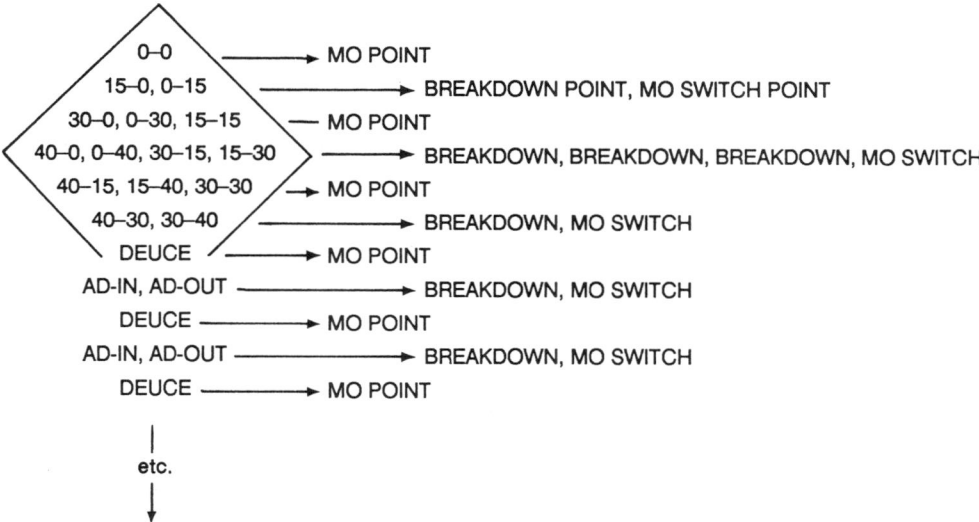

If Your Opponent Has Just Made a Bad Mistake

Bad mistakes at critical times of a match are not usually physical mistakes, but are often are related to nerves. This is especially true on fundamental shots. If your opponent makes a bad mistake when he is behind by a point or on a critical game point, this may be an indication that he is cracking. You should speed up your play a bit and squeeze him if you can. Even if it is early in the match, a show of confidence and taking charge at this time can cause your opponent's confidence to be damaged early.

If Your Opponent Has Just Made a Great Shot

The tendency here, of course, is to get a bit scared. You begin wondering if your opponent is really that good or if you can stay with him. Many players feel like retreating and licking their wounds, but this is definitely the wrong response.

After an opponent's basket, good basketball teams are trained to get the ball inbounds and down the floor as quickly as possible and attempt to score to negate their opponent's score. If they do not get the quick score, they then set up a calculated and well-planned play. In tennis, the proper response to an opponent's great play is to take the attack right back at the opponent. This prevents any confidence gain by the opponent and keeps your confidence from being damaged as well. If it does not work, you can then regroup and run a play based on the score to switch the momentum.

In the 1987 ACC Championship football game between Clemson and Maryland, the most important play of the ball game was just such a situation. Clemson was favored, but Maryland was a tough opponent. Clemson was ahead by three when the Maryland quarterback hit his tight end over the middle with a strong pass and a 78-yard touchdown. This put Maryland ahead 7-3. On the next series of downs, I sat in my seat watching with the hope that Clemson would try to hurt Maryland right back. This Clemson team was definitely a running football team and seldom used the pass. I was not quite sure what the Clemson coaching staff would do, and as I watched three consecutive running plays, I was disappointed. Although Clemson had gained a first down, trying for a long drive with Maryland in the lead could have dangerous repercussions. If they stopped Clemson's drive, they would be in control of the momentum, both offensively and defensively. Then it happened! On the first play of the second series, the Clemson quarterback faked a handoff up the middle and dropped back quickly to find his own tight end open across the middle. A well-delivered pass and a 65-yard run gave Clemson the lead and a major MO switch.

This dampened Maryland's confidence greatly and from then on Clemson dominated. It ended 45-10 in a blowout. I wondered as I left the ball game what might have happened if Clemson had played tentatively after they had been hurt by Maryland's great touchdown. In tennis and most other sports, countering your opponent's good play with a good play of your own is an important aspect of momentum management.

If You Have Just Made a Bad Mistake

Most athletes and coaches recognize this as a time to slow down, to call a time-out, to regroup, and to prevent things from snowballing against you. Even so, the human tendency is to want to make up for the mistake right away. Too often, however, this leads to another bad mistake and the start of the snowball effect that must be prevented.

A golf coach once told me that it is not your bad shot, but rather the shot after the bad shot that is critical. Sometimes a series of bad shots occurs because a player panics over a miscue. Knowledge of momentum and running the right play can help the athlete think instead of react to his emotions in this situation. The best thing to do after a bad shot, therefore, is to slow down and think about the play to run instead of following the emotions.

If You Have Just Made a Great Shot

Like tennis, golf has a way of keeping a person humble and helping him keep things in perspective. One day, after a year of practicing this game, I drove a ball from the second tee some 230 yards straight down the middle of the fairway. What a shot! It felt so good, I just knew that I could do it again, even though I was still 220 yards from the cup. I took out my three wood and lined up with the same stance I used for my great tee shot. Without hesitation or doubt, I lined up and let my swing rip toward the ball that I knew would carry to the green. The rest is obvious. The only green that my ball found was the forest of trees way to the right of the out of bounds. The next three shots were worse and my potential birdie turned into an eleven.

The lesson for tennis is the same. There are times during a match when your shots feel so good that you think you can do anything at all with the ball. The natural tendency is to try to play better, and better, and better, but instead your game collapses. It is interesting to note that the loser of a match often plays great shots right before he finally collapses. This is usually a result of his pressing to play above his limitations.

Good shots will be there during a tough match, but even so, it is solid fundamentals that wins tennis matches. Simply accept a great shot and run the next appropriate play. Staying within the limitations of your fundamentals is the way to achieve consistent results.

If You Have Just Won a Long, Tough Point, and Neither You nor Your Opponent Gained Momentum

After a long, tough point, you should expect another long, tough point. No dominance or momentum has been established, so running the right play based on the score is the best approach to take. These points are comparable to grinding out tough third down conversions in football or making a tough basket after seven or eight passes on the basketball court. No real momentum is established other than scoring the point. Many of these points must be won during the course of the match.

FUNDAMENTALS OF MOMENTUM MANAGEMENT BASED ON THE EVENTS LEADING UP TO A CERTAIN SCORE

The tennis player's response to how he arrives at a score and what happened last is an important factor in momentum. Your opponent's good and bad shots, as well as your good and bad shots, should be handled properly as well as the points where no dominance is gained.

After your opponent's:	Bad shot—put pressure on him
	Good shot—attack him right back
After your:	Bad shot—regroup
	Good shot—be content to win with your fundamentals
After a long point:	Run the right play according to the score

THE CONVERSION THEORY OF BOB LOVE: THE FINISHING TOUCH ON MOMENTUM CONTROL

An important concept in momentum management was taught to me by Bob Love, a good friend and one of the few people in America today to have done research on psychological momentum. When he learned of my work with momentum management and I of his, we got together to share notes and ideas. His conversion theory was an exciting concept to me because in nearly every case, it corrolated perfectly with my work on momentum control.

A conversion is defined as winning three consecutive points. Bob Love's conversion theory states that the key to winning tennis matches and controlling the flow of the match is to focus on two objectives: 1) make conversions for yourself, and 2) prevent your opponent from making conversions.

The scoring system in tennis dictates that whenever a player is behind by a point (15-30, 30-40, and ad out), he has to win three points in a row to win the game. The wisdom of this theory is far reaching. The most important aspect of the theory to me as a coach is that the favored player is usually very comfortable winning three points in succession at any time in the match. For the underdog, one point well played and won is very common, whereas two well-played points in a row usually satisfies his appetite, and winning three consecutive points is usually uncomfortable for him. The underdog always reaches his comfort level of achievement long before the favored player does. It is helpful to realize this to understand why the underdog usually does not win in tennis and in many other sports. With this realization, and the recognition of the importance of making and preventing conversions, the following two rules can be established.

1) To make a conversion: After the second point won in a row, do not slow down between the points, therefore preventing your opponent from regrouping. Win the third point with solid fundamentals and try to force the error from your opponent.

2) To prevent a conversion: After your opponent scores the second point in a row, take time between points to regroup. Tie your shoe, go back to the fence, or do whatever it takes to give you time to decide exactly which play you want to run. In trying to prevent the third point, play an aggressive MO switch point. You must regain confidence and try to dent your opponent. Above all, do not allow your opponent to stay on this upward flow.

Bob Love's conversion theory fits almost perfectly into the momentum control guidelines based on the score of the game. In using both concepts together, a player can see that when the conversion theory specifies the prevention of a conversion, the score dictates that an aggressive (momentum) point should be played (after losing two points in a row the score is either ad out, 15-40, or 0-30). The same is true when the conversion theory specifies to play a breakdown. (After winning two points in a row, the score is usually ad out if your opponent is serving, and ad in if you are serving. The only exception is at 30-0 and 40-15, where a momentum point is specified.)

The player who can use the momentum control concepts has an invaluable edge during competition. All three concepts—momentum control based on score, momentum control based on the events leading up to a certain score, and momentum control using the conversion theory—can be used independently or together. The more adept the player becomes at using all three, the greater the advantage he will have in controlling this seemingly magical power that greatly affects all sporting events.

POINTS TO REMEMBER ABOUT MOMENTUM MANAGEMENT

1. Winning the point is never more important than controlling momentum.

2. It is essential to manage momentum in each game, but be aware of momentum swings within each set and throughout the whole match. Major momentum swings are often a result of crisis situations, such as bad line calls, equipment problems, unnecessary delays, injuries, or rain. Take extra time when these things occur to regroup your thoughts.

3. When the momentum is definitely against you, take time to do whatever it takes to regroup your thoughts. When you start the point again, remember that your objective, more than winning the point, is to turn the momentum by dictating what should happen during that point.

4. Your opponent's great shot should never prevent you from executing your own game plan and dictating the flow, nor should your bad mistakes keep you from dictating your game plan as well. Run the right play, regardless of whether or not you are winning points by doing it early in the match. It will pay off late in the match.

5. Never let your confidence "dam" break when you are behind. Stay in the match mentally until the momentum swings back to you again.

6. Your opponent should never feel like he played well against you in victory or defeat. Controlling the momentum will prevent this.

7. Be able to recognize your opponent's checkout winners or checkout losers. Checking out of a point means his concentration is waning or that he feels too much pressure. It is a way of not dealing with the pressure and not taking care of the ball. The opponent just slaps the ball haphazardly. These checkouts should never worry you. It should only give you confidence in thinking that your opponent is about ready to crack.

8. The correct flow of the match is very much like running a three-mile race: Start swiftly, but then settle into your own pace and comfort zone. Finally, keep enough left to sprint or to play your very best at the finish line. Starting too fast is like sprinting the first one-half mile; you will fade at the end, whereas starting too slowly puts you so far behind that you will never generate the tempo to be in a position to win the race.

9. Breakdown break games: This type of game should be played when you are already ahead by a service break and working for the second break. Although you should be aggressive on the first point of the game to keep control, the rest of the game should be primarily made up of breakdown points to prevent your opponent from making any great shots and gaining momentum. The exception is to prevent a conversion if your opponent does get momentum.

FINAL MOMENTUM CONSIDERATIONS

In order of sequence for execution during a match, the conversion theory should be followed first, then the momentum based on the events leading up to a certain score, followed by the momentum based on the score. Following this sequence is the most practical way of learning how to control momentum.

The Tournament

You will seldom go through an entire tournament without poorly played matches and close escapes from disaster. Almost all tournament champions have to come from behind more than once during a tournament. Take your bad matches in stride. Kick the ball over to win if you have to when you are playing poorly. Remember, when you cannot be pretty, you need to play gritty.

The Match

Remember that you will always have to either get ahead and stay ahead, or come from behind to win matches. You must be comfortable and be able to execute in each role.

The Set

Regardless of the games you lose, always play the game point the way you want to play it. You dictate momentum. Never give up the momentum to win a point or game or set or match. It will haunt you later. Execute! Execute! Execute! No checkouts, no checkouts, no checkouts!

SUMMARY

1. Basic momentum guidelines. When you are even, two ahead, or two behind, play a MO point; when you are ahead, play a breakdown point; when you are behind, play a MO switch point.

2. Game score guidelines. The game score guidelines as illustrated in Figure 11-2 also tell you which type of play to run.

3. Flow management guidelines. How you arrive at a score is as important as the score. It is important to know what to do after your opponent's bad mistake or good shot, and after your bad mistake or good shot, or after winning a long point where no dominance has been established.

4. Bob Love's conversion theory. Try to win three consecutive points and prevent opponents from winning three consecutive points. Know how to prevent and make conversions.

CHAPTER 12

TAKE TIME TO EVALUATE YOUR MATCH

"If you make a mistake and do not correct it, you've made another mistake."

—Anonymous

What happens after a match can be just as important as the procedure before the match. Since a lot of time and preparation have gone into preparing for and playing the match, it is important for players to receive immediate and long-term feedback after wins and losses. The way the coach handles this situation can often hasten or delay the athlete's growth. In addition, the coach must address the player's physical, mental, and emotional needs. The right timing and approach to these areas is important. Chapter 19 includes a detailed description of the use of positive and negative feedback as well as a discussion of long-range affirmation guidelines.

POST-MATCH CONSIDERATIONS FOLLOWING A LOSS

Some losses are harder to take than others. The sting of some losses is just a little worse and lasts just a little longer. There is always a fine balance that a coach looks for in an athlete's reaction to a loss. The extreme reactions of discouragement and despair are not positive, whereas minimizing the loss and not dealing with it at all are also bad.

In some situations, in which the athlete has invested much in his training, the loss will hurt more than if he were casual about his preparation. The player who takes a loss hard may make the mistake of not training well or not making a full commitment to his preparation for his next match. Usually, the greater the commitment the greater the pain in losing, but without commitment the chance of succeeding is much less as well. Losing to an underdog can be painful, and in team match play, losses bear an added stigma because others rely on you to perform. Sometimes an athlete feels it is better not to try his hardest rather than to risk committed failure once again.

Whatever the reason, the coach must be aware if the athlete withdraws energy before, during, or after the competition and does less than his best. This is an obvious defense mechanism and must be dealt with. Lack of commitment to a match and/or to the game of tennis itself is common, especially in more talented athletes. The coach should always remember that the athlete does care, or he would not have spent hundreds of hours working at the sport. As a coach, though, you wonder, "Can I get this player to care and to make a commitment?"

Another situation is one in which the athlete takes his loss very hard and stays in a depressed state for a long time afterward. This reaction to a loss can be equally counterproductive. Some athletes always seem to take losses hard and will often replay the critical parts of the event over and over in their heads. As a coach, you want a player to care a lot, but you also recognize that this attitude may hurt later performances and could affect his whole concept of competition.

The coach wants the athlete to separate the match he has just lost from his feelings of self worth. A coach once said to me about Kent Kinnear, a player on my team, "When you win against Kent, you merely beat his tennis game, you never seem to beat him." Kent's approach to competition is very mature and is hard to learn, but it is one that the coach and athlete should strive for.

Figures 12-1 and 12-2 illustrate the effects of losing confidence, and I often show them to my players. Figure 12-1 shows the athlete whose confidence is totally determined by winning and losing and its upward/downward swing. Figure 12-2 shows the athlete whose confidence grows from a win, but stays the same in a loss. Winning should be a chance for confidence, and losing should be a chance for growth.

The physical, mental, and emotional aspects of the athlete must be dealt with after a loss, beginning with the emotional aspects. Usually the athlete needs a few moments to himself. Nothing concrete can be accomplished until the emotions have settled. The coach must be able to read the situation immediately and administer to the athlete's needs, with a scolding or with encouragement.

A scolding should be given only if the coach is certain that the athlete did not give his best effort. If, on the other hand, the athlete has given his best effort, a loss is the coach's opportunity to build him up. The coach should compliment the athlete on his effort and on the positive things that took place in

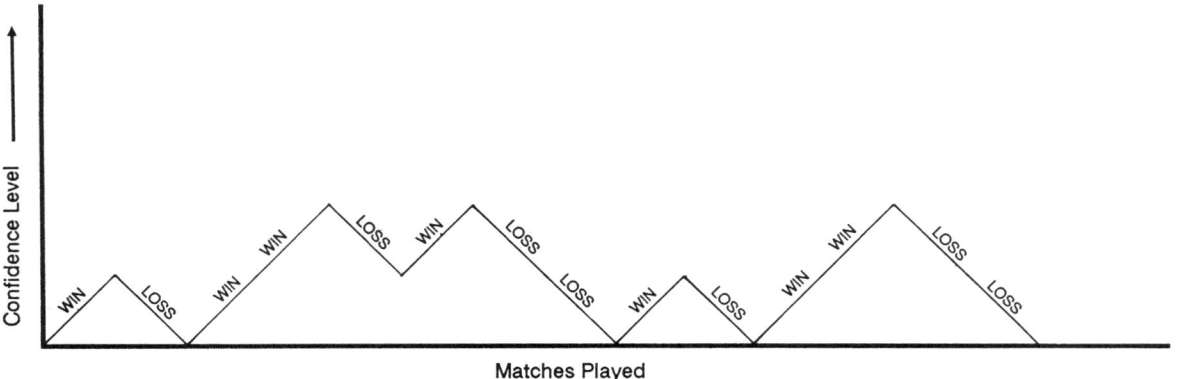

Figure 12-1. Poor response to wins and losses.

Figure 12-2. Best response to wins and losses.

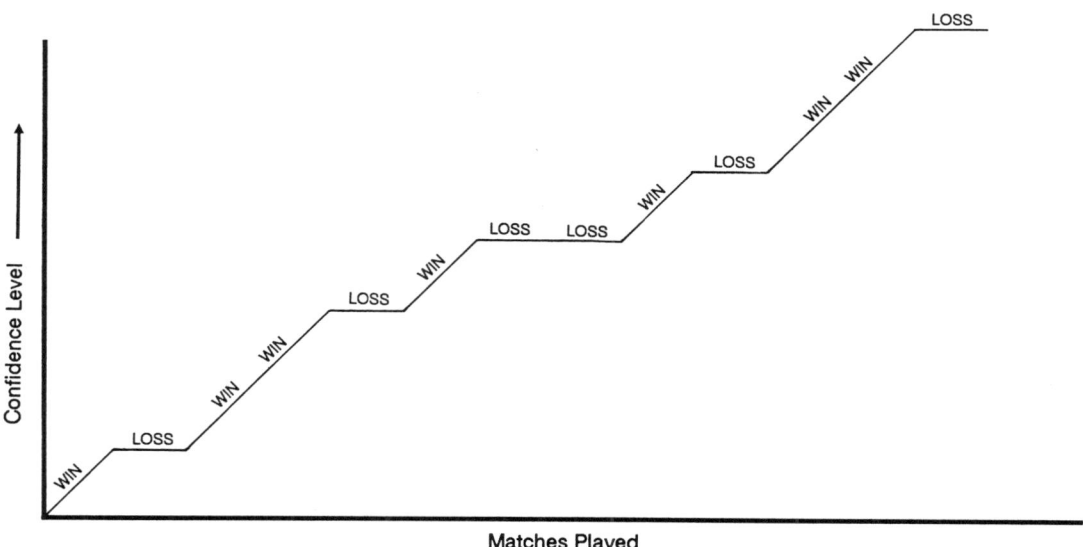

the match. The coach may appear disappointed, but he must not look as if he has doubts about his player. Another good practice is for the coach to help the athlete in giving credit to the victor, because this shows class and allows the player to get on with his own growth.

One of the best things to do after a tough loss is to go right back on the court and work out for a period of 20 to 30 minutes. Some of my team's best practice sessions have taken place immediately following a crushing defeat. This practice does two things. Primarily, it is a great way to release anger, aggression, and any negative emotion from the loss. Secondly, it allows the player to leave the tennis court that day in a positive frame of mind while putting an end to the possible negative effects of the loss. It is difficult to go right back to the court to practice after a loss. Both players and coaches alike would rather do anything than hit tennis balls. It is the best possible form of release, however, and should be considered a constructive alternative after a tough loss.

The mental perspective on what happened cannot be discussed until the emotional and the physical are first taken care of. It is always best for the coach to approach the strategic and technical part of the match after the player's emotions have calmed down and when what is discussed can be evaluated and of most help to the player. This might even be the next day. It is usually best for the coach to do this by asking questions so that the player himself has to search for the answers.

POST-MATCH CONSIDERATIONS FOLLOWING A WIN

Just as a loss sometimes needs to be treated as a win so that the coach can point out positive things in his player's game, so does a win give the coach an opportunity to point out the negative. In this way a player can always keep a proper perspective. In other words, after a loss the coach should help raise the player's spirits, and after a win the coach should help keep the player from flying too high. The key to a good performance time after time is to keep this balance, and never get too high or too low.

The coach's job is, and always should be, to help players perform to the best of their capabilities, and the coach's feedback is perhaps the most important of anyone's. Good judgment must be used to discern what each player needs in the way of positive and negative feedback. This is often difficult because the coach's own emotions will usually be high or low after a win or loss, especially if the match was an important one. It is important for the coach to remember that often the player will get a lot of praise from friends, parents, and fans, so he, then, can and should be the countering balance for the player.

GUIDELINES FOR THE COACH'S FEEDBACK

1. Deal with the physical, the mental, and the emotional after a win or loss.
2. Losses are good opportunities to reinforce the positive in a player's game.

3. The time following a loss can be a good time for a short and intense workout session.
4. Wins are a good time to be critical of a player.
5. Never reward a mediocre performance, regardless of its outcome.
6. Wait until the emotion of the match has settled for effective analysis.
7. The coach's job is to help the player keep perspective in both winning and losing.

CHARTING SYSTEMS FOR MATCH PLAY

Knowing what your objectives are before you chart a tennis match is critical to the effectiveness of a charting system. Charting a match, though, is one of the best ways possible for the coach and player to analyze the performance on the tennis court, since emotions can often prevent them from seeing what is really happening.

A match chart can:

1. Analyze the strokes used.
2. Identify the areas of the court that are producing missed shots.
3. Analyze the amount of aggressive or forcing play by a player in relation to his opponent.
4. Study match flow.

The following three charting systems can be used to study these areas.

Figure 12-3. Basketball shot tennis charting system tally sheet.

PLAYER 1'S ERRORS

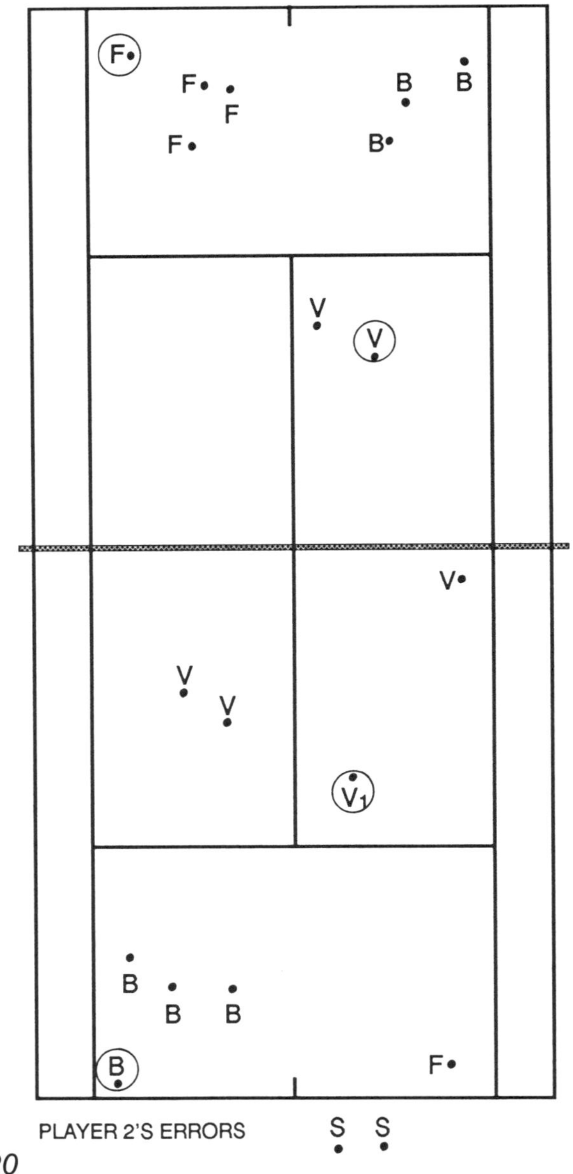

KEY

1. PLAYER'S POSITION AND STROKE USED:

   B = Backhand
   F = Forehand
   V = Volley
   S = Serve

2. WHERE AN ERROR WAS MADE:

   • = Where error was made; for example:

   B̥ = Backhand in net

   F• = Forehand wide to the right

   •V = Volley wide to the left

   S̥ = Double fault long

3. FORCED ERRORS:

   ◯ = Forced error; for example:

   Ⓕ = Forced error on forehand side

TALLY FOR SET

PLAYER 1

winners_____ vs. errors_____
double faults_____
service winners or forced errors_____

winners (   ) − errors (   ) = _____

PLAYER 2

winners_____ vs. errors_____
double faults_____
service winners or forced errors_____

winners (   ) − errors (   ) = _____

PLAYER 2'S ERRORS

TAKE TIME TO EVALUATE YOUR MATCH

The Basketball Shot Tennis Charting System

The basketball shot tennis charting system is similar to a charting system used in basketball. It shows three significant areas of importance: the shot that was missed, the part of the court the shot was tried from, and where the shot was missed. It is an error detection system, and it does not show winners that are hit by your player or the opponent. Tallies can be kept of the winner's double faults and other shots, and of the winner-error ratio. If a player's winners outnumber his errors, the match was well played. Figure 12-3 is a sample basketball shot tennis charting system tally sheet.

The Paul Scarpa Charting System

This charting system is an original system developed by Paul Scarpa, the tennis coach at Furman University. After charting hundreds of matches, Scarpa determined that in an average game, a player's game points were usually made by: 1) hitting one winner, 2) making one unforced error, 3) forcing one error from the opponent, and 4) accepting one error from the opponent. The fifth point and those thereafter pretty much tell the story. Hitting two winners in a game is good, and making two unforced errors is bad. This system can be used to show winners, errors, forced errors, opponent errors, the stroke used to win or lose the point, and the running score. The column that shows the forced errors is the most important, because the player who wins the match usually has a larger tally in this column. Figure 12-4 is a sample Scarpa charting system tally sheet.

Figure 12-4. Paul Scarpa charting system tally sheet.

Player 1 vs **Player 2**

ERRORS	WINNERS	FORCED ERRORS	COACH'S COMMENTS	SCORE	ERRORS	WINNERS	FORCED ERRORS	COACH'S COMMENTS
F	S	S B		1–0	F	V_1		
B BR	FA	F		2–0	B V B			
F B V_1 S				2–1		BR		
	FB			3–1	B B	S		
F S *		B	*Double fault-game point!	3–2	F		B F	
	V			4–2				
	V S	V V		5–2		FP		
F B F FR *			* Poor game	5–3				
S	S V1	V		6–3	FR BR	O		
14	9	7		TOTALS	12	5	2	
				SET 2				

KEY

F = Forehand
B = Backhand
V = Volley
V_1 = First Volley
O = Overhead

S = Serve
BR = Backhand Return
FP = Forehand Pass
FR = Forehand Return
FA = Forehand Approach

The Bob Love Flow Charting System

Bob Love's simplified flow charting system may be one of the easiest and most practical systems devised. Its main emphasis is the measurement of the flow and momentum of the match. In addition, it shows points won and lost, the stroke used to win or lose the point, conversions, and the running score. Figure 12-5 is a sample Bob Love charting system tally sheet.

SUMMARY

Post-match analysis is critical for the growth of the player. It is also critical for the coach to determine what actually happened during the match. The player's confidence and growth often depend on the method and system used for this analysis.

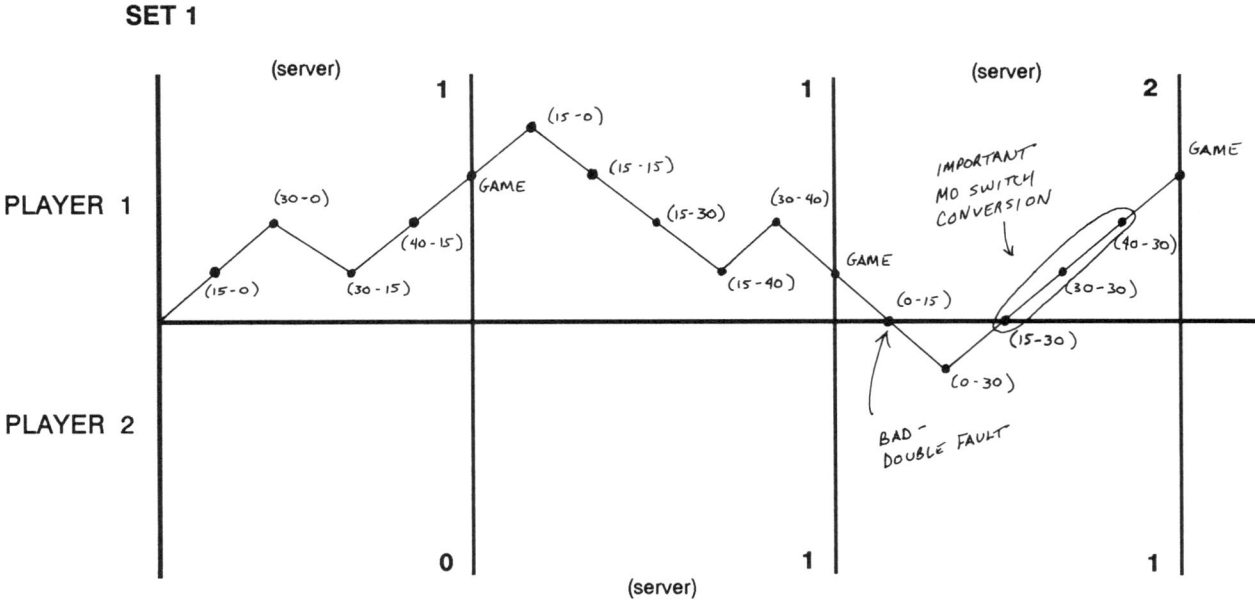

Figure 12-5. Bob Love flow charting system tally sheet.

PART THREE
THE EMOTIONAL THIRD

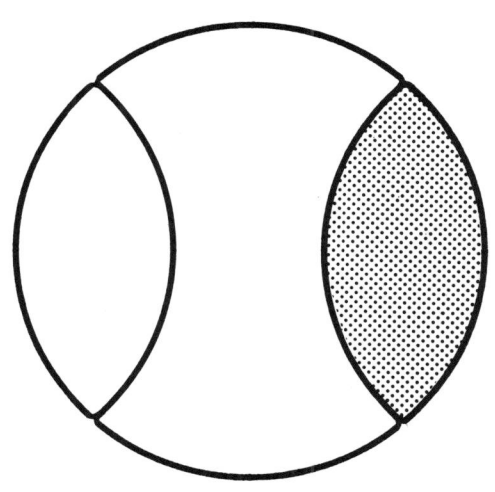

CHAPTER 13

USE YOUR ABILITY, DESIRE, AND OPPORTUNITY

"There is no heavier burden than a great opportunity."
—Naegele Outdoor Advertising Company

THE THREE INGREDIENTS OF THE SUCCESSFUL ATHLETE

You cannot do it on your own, but neither can anyone else do it for you. Three ingredients are necessary for success in tennis and in most other sports: ability, desire, and opportunity. Many unsuccessful athletes have had two of these ingredients, but all three are essential to reach peak performance in any endeavor.

Ability

Ability is the God-given part of an athlete's makeup. Basically, what you see is what you've got. If you are born with a four-cylinder engine, then you cannot run on six or eight cylinders. Your size, speed of movement, strength, coordination, and sport sense are some of the attributes you're born with, and each has a maximal capacity for development. These gifts may be great or small, but are usually somewhere in between. Their development is based on the factors of the athlete's desire and opportunity.

Desire

Desire is the athlete's job, for it is his choice whether to develop or to neglect the ability that has been given him. In the early stages of training, parents, teachers, coaches, or friends can coax the individual into developing some part of his skills, but ultimately, the athlete determines this development himself. Desire is the basis of motivation. How to instill desire is a mystery that is rarely solved, but in the end it is always up to the individual athlete.

Opportunity

Opportunity is relative but necessary for the tennis player. A tennis player needs to know how good he has to be. Tennis is so bound by the pecking order and ranking philosophy that, without opportunity and exposure, a player's growth can easily stagnate. Exposure keeps a player hungry by helping him answer the questions, "How good do I need to be? What do I need to work on? Who do I need to be able to beat? What do I do to get the necessary workouts and practice?" It may be detrimental that rankings carry such a heavy weight on the pecking order of tennis players. In other sports, athletes are usually rated on their athletic motor skills, rather than on how much exposure they have received. But in tennis, the player needs exposure, and his growth comes from knowing that he can perform. Without opportunity, this is impossible.

Opportunities are plentiful for tennis players in the U.S. Many of our young athletes have the not easily recognizable problem of too many opportunities available to them with little or no effort. Parents and coaches, aware that opportunity is an important element in the athlete's growth, often supply them freely before the athlete has paid his dues. Remember the story about the chick hatching from the egg. In America we are so enthusiastic about providing opportunities that we often prevent a person from making his own way, thus crippling our best talent. The following stories illustrate this point.

I got a tremendous amount of mileage out of the chick and egg story because it taught me the fundamental truth that there is no shortcut to developing as a tennis player and as an athlete. As a coach I would like to protect my players from the hardships they experience, but to do so would hurt their development. The self-reliance, inner strength, and pride they develop in knowing that they can do it is what makes them great athletes. After my mother explained the story to me, I told it in a team meeting. The reaction of the players was very ho hum, and I didn't think anyone had listened.

The very next week, our team was participating in a tournament that would qualify the two finalists for the National Indoors Tournament. That year, one of my players, Rick Rudeen, automatically got a tournament bid because he was a returning All-American. I also had an outstanding freshman player named Lawson Duncan, who later that year went to the finals of the NCAA Tournament. In the draw, though, my hope was that Richard Matuszewski, a blossoming sophomore, would have the opportunity to play well and perhaps even be in a position to make the finals. As the tournament progressed, he knocked off seed after seed en route to a semifinals meeting with Rick Rudeen. In the other bracket, Lawson Duncan had advanced to the finals and was waiting to play his next match. It then dawned on me that I might have three Clemson players in the National Indoors Championships. This would only be possible, of course, if my young sophomore could beat the All-American, Rick Rudeen. I thought about having Rick default or perhaps not play quite as hard as he should, giving the younger player a chance to go to the Nationals. After all, Rick was already assured of a spot in the tournament, so why should he have to win the match? Similar thoughts enter every coach's mind in the middle of a competitive situation. I guess it's a normal tendency to want an easier way for the players. But I realized that this would be a bad decision, and I dismissed these thoughts immediately. Obviously, it would be wrong to have Rick take a dive, and having him play less than his best would compromise his integrity as a player. Nor would this be fair to the promising young sophomore. He needed to open his own shell.

The match was played, and seniority and experience determined the outcome. When the match was tied at 5-5 in the first set, the younger player played tentatively and the older player took charge. The final score was 7-5, 6-4. Rick Rudeen won his spot in the Nationals, and the younger player was sent to the showers. On his way there, I tried to console him and tell him that his timing was just not there yet. I tried to make a joke and tell him that he was not ready to turn pro yet. This was small consolation. I saw tears forming in his eyes and heard his voice trembling as he talked to me.

It is a terrible feeling to see your players hurt when they don't accomplish something they want so badly. On the ride back from the tournament, I was still so upset that I pounded my fist on the dashboard, waking up Lawson Duncan who was in the back sleeping. He said, "Coach, what's the matter?" I said, "I don't know if I did the right thing. I could have had Rick default his match and we'd have had three players in the Nationals." Lawson said, "Oh, I never thought about that. You could have done that, I guess." Then he said, "Wait a minute! That would have been like opening Richard's shell for him." I threw my arms in the air, let out a yell, and said, "That's great! You guys really were listening the other day when I told that story."

Richard Matuszewski did not make Nationals that year. The next year, though, he played number one and number two on the team, making All-American the hard way by beating three tough players at the NCAA tournament and being selected, as a result, to the Junior Davis Cup squad. In addition, he won three tough qualifying matches as well as a main-draw victory at the U.S. Open and was ranked on the computer. He and his doubles partner, Brandon Walters, won the National Indoor Championships that year as well.

Richard's senior year was even better. He again made All-American and again went to the finals of the National Indoors Doubles. He is now well on his way to a fine professional career. He made the quarterfinals in the Stockholm Open in 1986 and was ranked as high as 81 in the world that year.

I know that if I had manipulated the situation and given Richard the shortcut of pushing him into the National Indoors, it would have hindered his growth as a player and as a man. By making him go the long haul and letting him earn his way, he ended up a far better player than he ever could have been if the situation had been manipulated for him. I'm glad I did not open his shell.

A similar situation occurred when I forced Lawson Duncan to go through a long qualifying event at the Nike All-American Championships as a freshman when he could have gotten into the tournament as a wild card. After four tough rounds, I told Lawson that I had indeed gotten him a wild card into the event, and he looked at me, eyes flashing with anger, and said, "Why did you make me go through those four tough rounds when I didn't have to?" I said, "Lawson, tomorrow you play the number two seed in the tournament's first round. How do you feel? Do you think you can win?" He said, "Shoot, yes! I know I can win!" I said, "Well, you just sweated through four tough rounds, and that's given you a lot of confidence. What if you had to play the number two seed in the tournament without having fought your way into this position? I know you'd be excited to play, but do you really think deep down that you would feel like you had an opportunity to win?" He looked at me and said, "No, I guess not. I really feel now that I have a chance to win this whole tournament." Lawson went into the tournament and won three tough rounds, making the semifinals, and finishing fourth in his first big national collegiate event. Once again, I think there's no way he would have gone on to have such a great freshman year and a chance to play professional tennis if I had given him the shortcut without making him earn his own way. That is the first great rule of coaching: Never open your players' shells. Make them bust out on their own and earn every step of the way.

SUMMARY

The coach and athlete should both recognize the critical ingredients to reaching potential. Ability, desire, and opportunity are all essential for the athlete's growth. But the responsibility of each comes from different sources. Ability is God's job, desire is the athlete's job, and opportunity is the parent's, teacher's, or coach's job.

Figure 13-1

CHAPTER 14

DEVELOP YOUR MOTIVATIONAL PROGRAM

"If you don't invest very much, defeat doesn't hurt very much, and winning is not very exciting."
—Dick Vermiel, former coach
of the Philadelphia Eagles

THE RISK OF COMMITMENT

The objective of any motivational program or technique is to help a person reach the point of making a commitment. Most people know that success is difficult to come by without a commitment, and it would seem that everyone would be eager to make one, but this this is not the case. Commitments are difficult to make, because making a commitment means taking a risk. Many competitive tennis players play the sport for years without ever making a commitment to the game or to themselves.

Taking the risk of commitment is like walking on thin ice. A 100 percent effort brings elation if the effort succeeds, but many athletes fear that failure after making a commitment will produce great damage to their self-esteem, and therefore they choose to make only a partial commitment. The athlete wants the elation of winning while risking only moderate disappointment in losing. A partial commitment seems to eliminate risk. Thus the athlete tries to preserve his self-image by settling for a mediocre job.

The most frustrating and difficult thing for a coach to do is to try to induce his athletes to make a total commitment. "Why doesn't he try harder?" or "He has so much talent, why doesn't he use it?" are questions every coach wishes he could answer. Teaching athletes the value of the risk of a commitment is often the greatest gift a coach can give his players. The ability to make a commitment will be with them throughout their lives on a job, in a marriage, or in adherence to a religion. In America today we can satisfy 70 to 80 percent of our needs and achieve 70 to 80 percent of our potential without a commitment. A prosperous society allows us hesitation in taking the risk of commitment, but the last 20 to 30 percent that brings total success cannot be possible without a commitment.

Often a player tries to delay making a commitment by relying more and more on his talent. The greater the natural ability of the player, the longer he will usually procrastinate. Less talented athletes make a commitment more easily. If they don't, they cannot succeed and cannot stay at the desired level of competition.

THE THREE D'S OF EVERY CHALLENGE

A method I use with tennis players to help them overcome the fear of commitment is to tell them, "There is no heavier burden than a great opportunity." I try to teach my players the 3 D's of every challenge: First, they must have the dream; following that there will usually be disappointment, and then comes either discovery or discouragement. For anything of value, "a *breakdown* usually occurs before a *breakthrough*." This is an important truth for an athlete. His job is to decide on the reaction that will give growth.

EXTERNAL AND INTERNAL MOTIVATION (OBSESSION AND INSPIRATION)

Indirect or external influences—such as coaches, parents, and peers—are usually prime motivating factors early in a player's development. Tennis is a difficult game to play, let alone to become proficient at. Many failures and setbacks occur, and every level of competition presents new and more frustrating obstacles. External motivation from parents, coaches, and friends is necessary, therefore, to help a player work through difficult times.

In order for maximum growth to take place, internal motivation is essential. As described by the learning curve in the introduction to the book, a player's growth in the initial stages of training is relative to his amount of work. At some point, however, growth slows, and a player reaches plateaus and barriers in his development. These may have a positive effect and bring about a commitment, or they may have a negative effect and cause frustration. Eventually, though, a commitment must be made or growth will stop.

When an athlete finally decides to make a commitment, he can make it either by obsession or by inspiration (externally or internally). A commitment made by obsession is final-result directed. This does not mean that the athlete's motives are wrong, nor does it mean that he will not be successful. But it does mean that his drive and determination are caused by a deep need that goes far beneath the surface.

The award-winning movie, *Chariots of Fire*, told the story of two quite different athletes as they prepared for the 1924 Olympics. One of the athletes was motivated by obsession. Each of his actions was well planned and goal directed, and he drove himself with one thought in mind—winning the gold. He was so obsessive about winning that, after all his planning and training, when the time came to compete, fear of both failure and success engulfed him. Only a very wise coach could help him perform his best to become an Olympic champion. The other athlete in the movie was motivated by inspiration. His drive came from within himself. For this athlete, running was not a mechanism for success, as it was for the other athlete, but rather, it was a way of expressing his inner self. Training and competing seemed to be joys instead of burdens, and success and medals seemed to be natural outcomes of his pursuit, not ends in themselves. He too became an Olympic champion.

A coach might learn from this great movie that athletes can be successfully motivated by either obsession or inspiration. When the athlete motivated by obsession is successful, he feels relieved and expects rest and relaxation until the next competition. His successes or wins are usually not as fulfilling as he had hoped. Competition presents anxiety and nervousness, and fear of a negative outcome is a constant threat. Defeats or setbacks produce anxiety and discouragement and, more importantly, tremendous fear of further competition. The athlete who is inspired from within, on the other hand, finds satisfaction and happiness in his successes. His fulfillment is magnified as the depth of his inner spirit is realized. A failure brings disappointment, but it also brings an eagerness to compete once again.

I thought of these two kinds of motivation as I searched for a way to help one of my team members. My number five singles player, a freshman, was just not playing up to his ability. I tried everything I possibly could to help. I felt that reasserting my confidence in him and explaining to him that things would come around if he kept trying were the best things to do. The longer I tried, the worse things got. It wasn't that he was not trying hard. He continually played close matches but would somehow find a way to lose. Whether out of fear or out of frustration, he was just not coming through. Every time he got close in the third set, he would miss balls for no apparent reason and come away losing.

The solution came from a conversation with my parents three days before a very tough match against the number three team in the country, SMU. I explained the situation to them and my father immediately said, "Son, have you told the boy how much you care for him and reminded him of all these things?" Before I could answer him, my mother said, "The hell with that stuff. Pull the rug out from under the kid and see if he can fly on his own." It sort of shocked me the way my mother talked, but trusting her as I did, I thought she could be right. I had tried everything I could think of and nothing had worked. Her idea could not have any worse results. So I resorted to the last straw—I decided to yank him from the lineup.

The next day I spent extra time with this talented freshman after practice to work on his volleys to make sure they were well tuned. Right after the workout, I walked up to him and said, "This is a tough decision, but you are not going to play tomorrow against SMU." He looked at me in disbelief. Before he could say anything, I said, "You're a good player, but you're not playing well. You're going to have to get it together if you want that starting position back." With this, I walked away from the tennis court. Fifteen minutes later I looked to the court from my office, and he was still sitting there. I thought to myself, "He's going to quit the team now. He's definitely going to give it up." The player got up and walked away. I knew that he had one of two choices to make: He could take the negative route and feel sorry for himself, or he could work to improve.

As coaches, we often hesitate to put a player in a position in which he has to fish or cut bait, because our feelings tell us to be gentle with the player's confidence. But if we don't let a player make his own decisions, we prevent his growth. In this player's case, he responded beyond my highest expectations. For two weeks straight, he worked out extra in the early morning. I've never seen a player more determined than this freshmen was during the next two weeks. Of the last eight matches of the year, he dropped only one and went on to have an exceptional summer. He came back in the fall and earned the number one position on the team. This growth spurt, I am convinced, was caused by putting the burden completely on his shoulders; it was his responsibility to improve or to stay out of the lineup. I truly feel that the smart move by the coach sometimes needs to be putting the more talented athlete in a failure position to spur his development and his commitment. Figure 14-1 illustrates an athlete's commitment making process.

Figure 14-1. Motivation and commitment.

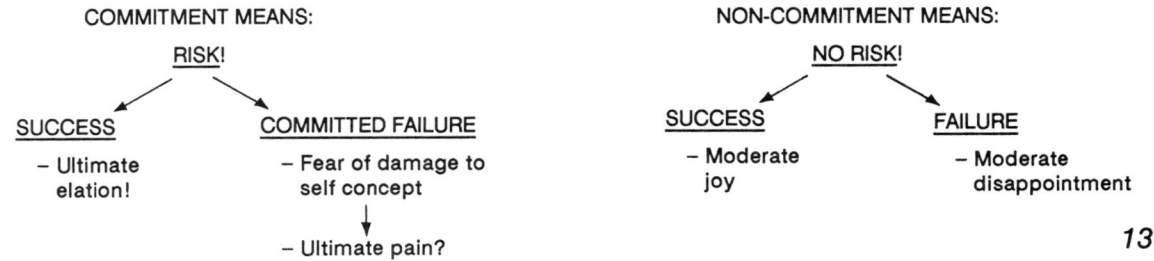

PUT P.E.P.P. INTO YOUR MOTIVATIONAL PROGRAM

In planning a motivational program, it is important for an athlete to construct a well thought out and specific plan of training and then stick to it. It should be thorough, and it should cover all bases of training. P.E.P.P. is a plan that can give direction and guidance to the athlete in his training. P.E.P.P. can be used as a plan for other jobs, whether it be in the training of an athlete for a specific event or the work of another occupation that takes discipline and direction. P.E.P.P. covers training from the planning phase through the actual execution and success.

P (PREPARATION): THE ATHLETE'S FIRST OBJECTIVE

Bob Knight, coach of three NCAA Basketball Championships at Indiana University, said it best in a television interview, "More important than an athlete needing the will to win, he or she needs the will to prepare to win." Without preparation and planning in both physical and mental areas, the athlete has little or no hope for success in his sport.

Preparation is the base that has to be laid before an athlete steps onto the court or playing field. An athlete's preparation must be detailed and thorough. It must include complete programs of training for the body, the mind, and the spirit so that at its conclusion the athlete is mentally, physically, and emotionally ready for the job he has to do. A well thought out plan of training gives tremendous confidence, but without a well-designed program of preparation, success on the playing field is almost totally left to chance or good fortune.

Preparation Step One: Have a Burning Desire

Nearly every person involved in athletics will say that he has a desire to be successful. But simple desire is very different from burning desire. It is the intangible difference that makes the difference between good and great, between okay and super, between just another day at the ball park and one that is remembered for years. A burning desire cannot be manufactured. It must come from within, and each person must obtain it on his own. The athlete who has a burning desire will endure his training and the hardships and setbacks that take place along the way.

Preparation Step Two: Set Specific Goals

Most coaches and athletes agree that setting goals is very important to the success of anyone in competitive sports. Nearly all athletes and coaches set goals. Some goals are never realized. Others are always reached. Some direct the athlete in maximizing his talent, and others never help an athlete reach anything more than what he or she would have done in the first place. What, then, is the key in the setting of goals?

Working toward an athlete's maximum success does not depend only on the setting of goals, but rather on the setting of the right goals. The conflict in goal setting is that when goals are set too idealistically, few are reached. But when goals are set too realistically, all may be reached while performance remains far below potential. Goals infrequently reached tend to make an athlete lose enthusiasm for his work and to forget about the objective. And, although it is important to dream, there is a danger that success will remain a dream and never become reality. The key, then, is to set goals that help an athlete strive for the maximum use of his gifts while still allowing him to reach a moderate amount of the objectives set. Goals that are set properly should be reached only about 50 or 60 percent of the time. Proper setting of goals can be done by a person comparing what might be his totally idealistic goals with what might be his totally realistic goals, and then finding the point midway between the two sets of goals.

Goals should constantly be reset and redirected. It is best to set three goals for an objective: a long-term goal that is the ultimate objective (the thought of which keeps the flame of desire bright), an intermediate goal that is a year or so away (to keep on course toward the main goal), and short-term goals that constantly provide smaller successes and failures (to keep enthusiasm and learning stimulated for the ultimate objective).

There is a high correlation between athletic success, intellectual success, and social success. Goals should, therefore, be set in other areas including academics, social areas, family areas, career planning, finance, and spiritual areas. Success in each of these areas supports and aids the development of the others.

Preparation Step Three: Make Your Work Constructive and Positive.

Working hard is necessary to achieve goals, but it is not a guarantee of success. Hard work increases the chances of success and gives one peace of mind in knowing that he has done everything in his power to ready himself for the task at hand. Thinking that hard work deserves success distorts motives for competing and can lead to frustration.

Many people work hard for the wrong reason: they are result-oriented and think only of the reward. I call this "outside-in" work. This work is not productive because it is not inspired or creative. It results in frustration, and the successes that are sometimes achieved may not be fulfilling. Athletes or coaches who do their jobs for the wrong reason find their successes more of a relief than an elation.

On the other hand, working for the love of one's work, or pursuing a calling as an expression of one's self (what I call "inside-out" work), will inspire countless successes. "Great athletes compete to express, not impress." Athletes should work hard, sacrifice, and pay the price, but they should do so positively and for the right reasons. Love of one's work and enjoyment of the accomplishments that might result from it are the keys to longevity in a career. Working from the inside out rather than outside in keeps the motivational fires burning for a long time.

Preparation Step Four: Take Care of Details

Often both athletes and coaches alike have thrown away months or even years of hard work by neglecting the simple process of taking care of details. An athlete may have a burning desire, may set the most specific and appropriate goals, and may work in a dedicated fashion to prepare for a match, but all can be wasted by neglecting seemingly insignificant details. An athlete should pay attention to simple items like eating properly, sleeping properly, having a sufficient supply of equipment in good condition at courtside, taking time to have a good warm-up, and starting the match mentally prepared.

Preparation Step Five: Acknowledge Fear and Nervousness and Their Benefits

One of the best things the athlete can do prior to his performance is to face the fact that he will probably have some fear and nervousness before and during the event. Fear can be looked at as a prelude to the positive emotion of courage, because courage occurs only when fear is first present. It is important that the athlete recognize this fact and, when fear is present, to acknowledge it so that it can be dealt with and used productively. To disregard fear allows it to grow, leading to the negative emotions of doubt, worry, anxiety, and frustration, which can prevent the athlete from having his best performance.

Figure 14-2. Compete to express, not impress.

There are instances when fear in competition does not exist. Children usually are not very susceptible to the negative effects of fear until they reach the age of 10 or 12. This is about the age when pressure starts to become noticeable and when children can start reasoning logically about the rewards or consequences of their behavior. Sometimes both direct and indirect outside pressures can create a situation that is more than the youngster is capable of handling. For this reason, the pressures involved in competitive sports should increase gradually along with the young athlete's ability to understand and deal with them.

Another no-fear situation occurs when the athlete completely ducks away from the pressure of the event and convinces himself that he doesn't much care about the outcome. But if the event truly were not important to him, then fear wouldn't exist. This is one reason why not all athletes who are greatly talented show commitment to their sport. They feel that if they don't risk, then they don't lose. But unfortunately, in most cases if an athlete does not risk, he does not gain either. It almost appears that many athletes would rather have success come their way by good fortune or chance than by taking an active role in making it happen. Insane people do not have fear of the task at hand, for they have eliminated those pressures from their psyche. Many diseases and illnesses today have been proven to be psychosomatic, and often they are the results of a threatening situation that the person has consciously or subconsciously chosen to avoid.

E (ENTHUSIASM): THE FORCE BEHIND PERFORMANCE.

The word "enthusiasm" comes from the Greek *en theos*, which means "the spirit of God within." The meaning of the word describes its importance to the athlete or anyone working in a creative field. Inside-out or true enthusiasm is inspired, whereas outside-in or false enthusiasm is forced. The latter is seldom helpful. The former should always benefit the performance.

Athletics is perhaps the purest and most expressive of all art forms. Through sports, the inner self can be totally released in a creative manner. Athletes often inhibit this inner creativity and hold back their opportunity to express the inner self through performance. The most outstanding benefits of enthusiasm are:

1. Enthusiasm projects the athlete's confidence in his own abilities, and true confidence in one's own skills will always overcome the fear that may exist in competition.

2. True enthusiasm often makes the opposition fearful. Most athletes will not counter with enthusiasm when confronting an enthusiastic opponent, but rather they will remain passive and not meet the challenge. Many matches are lost for this reason.

Enthusiasm is difficult to generate as a job becomes routine. Even the most exciting experience has a tendency to become drab and boring after it's done a number of times. The true test for an athlete, therefore, is his ability to keep enthusiasm for his job day in, day out, and long after the novelty has worn off. Great players and coaches are usually able to perform their jobs each year with the same eagerness and enthusiasm as they had during their first year, and consequently they are able to grow and attain higher levels of development. Enthusiasm coupled with the experience of a veteran makes a great combination.

P (POISE): THE QUALITY OF THE EXPERIENCED ATHLETE.

Poise is the ability to execute one's skills on the court or playing field regardless of the pressure of the situation. It is an important skill to have, and great athletes are able to execute under pressure time and time again. In fact, poise must be learned by experiencing many pressure situations in different athletic contests.

It is difficult to teach poise, but there are a few directives that will enable the athlete to develop poise in the heat of the battle:

1. The athlete should know that growth occurs only when there is adversity and tough competition, and athletes should even train themselves to look forward to these situations. Every pressure-filled situation can only better prepare the athlete to become less fearful in more important matches or games in the future.

2. The athlete should know that creativity in any area of life comes from within only when a person is in a relaxed state. Creative talents are never forced to the surface. Writers, artists, and musicians often retreat to a hideaway so that their creative talents can flow and surface within their work. Players should use adverse situations to bring their creative talents to the surface.

3. The key to continuous growth in athletics is to treat success and failure in the same manner. This helps an athlete develop poise and confidence. The normal tendency after a success is to let the emotions run sky high. Likewise, the tendency after a setback is for the emotions to bottom out in grief, anxiety, or discouragement. But the athlete should learn never to get too high over a win and never let the emotions run too low over a loss. This is not to say that one

should not be happy over a win or disappointed over a loss. Any athlete who cares will have these feelings, but a balance between the two is critical for development. If excuses are not made, if losses are accepted as the athlete's own responsibility, and if positive qualities are recognized, maximum growth occurs. "Winning is a chance for confidence; losing is a chance for growth."

An athlete must learn to maintain a balance between enthusiasm and poise to achieve his best performance. This balance can be obtained by practicing concentration. The optimal situation would be for the rookie to have the poise of a veteran and the veteran to have the enthusiasm of a rookie.

P (PERSEVERANCE): THE DURABILITY OF COMMITMENT

The greatest athletes in the history of sports, and some of the greatest people in the history of the world, became great for no other reason than the possession of this one trait. Perseverance in all situations, and the ability to face all adversity and to keep trying, is the final quality all great athletes must have.

Many people see only the glory and glamour of the successful star athlete. It is difficult to see the hardship and struggle they had to go through at every level to achieve that greatness. But actually, it is

Figure 14-3. Great athletes are able to execute under pressure.

the hardships and the setbacks that mold the great athletes. Through their determination to keep trying, they learn to conquer overwhelming odds along the way. The confidence that is obtained from those struggles is what propels them to greater and greater heights. They fear little because they have faced and conquered much.

Many people today give up after two or three unsuccessful attempts. They cannot see down the road any farther than the immediate reward they are supposed to have from their effort. What is not taught often enough today is that it is not the immediate reward from the effort that is important, but rather the wisdom and experience that is gained from the process of pursuing a goal. The growth of deferred gratification is the true reward that enables a person to take advantage of a much greater opportunity when it becomes available. One can only imagine Thomas Edison's perseverance as he failed and failed again in his attempt to make an electric light bulb. Each time a player has a setback on the tennis court, it is like Edison's light bulb that flickered and then went off again and again, until one day, after much perseverance, the player finds a way to keep the light bulb lit.

One of my favorite quotes in understanding the importance of growth through never quitting is one of Winston Churchill's that says, "To each man there comes a time when an opportunity presents itself that is specifically designed for those talents and gifts of the man. What a tragedy when this time comes and finds the man unprepared to take advantage of them."

In developing perseverance, a few reminders are helpful:

1. Remember that breakdowns always happen before breakthroughs.
2. Setbacks are the clay from which all great people are molded.
3. Each person has his own unique timetable for success. Never compare your own successes with another person's, for this leads only to frustration. Keep working at your own rate.
4. Another person's accomplishments never make you look bad. Jealousy is a negative emotion and nothing positive can be gained by it. Be happy for others' successes, and you will find all your creative talents working for you in a positive way.
5. Be disappointed but never discouraged.
6. Know the difference between quitting and changing directions. Quitting is running away from a threatening situation and avoiding the responsibility involved. Changing directions is moving in a new direction that will improve the situation and be a benefit for one's life. A person may change direction in a field a hundred times during his lifetime, but he should never quit.

SUMMARY

Athletes must be able to make a commitment to their sport, and they must play from the inside-out. Each athlete must devise a specific training program, and the P.E.P.P. program can help an athlete make a commitment and reach his goals.

DEVELOP YOUR MOTIVATIONAL PROGRAM

Table 14-1. The P.E.P.P. system.

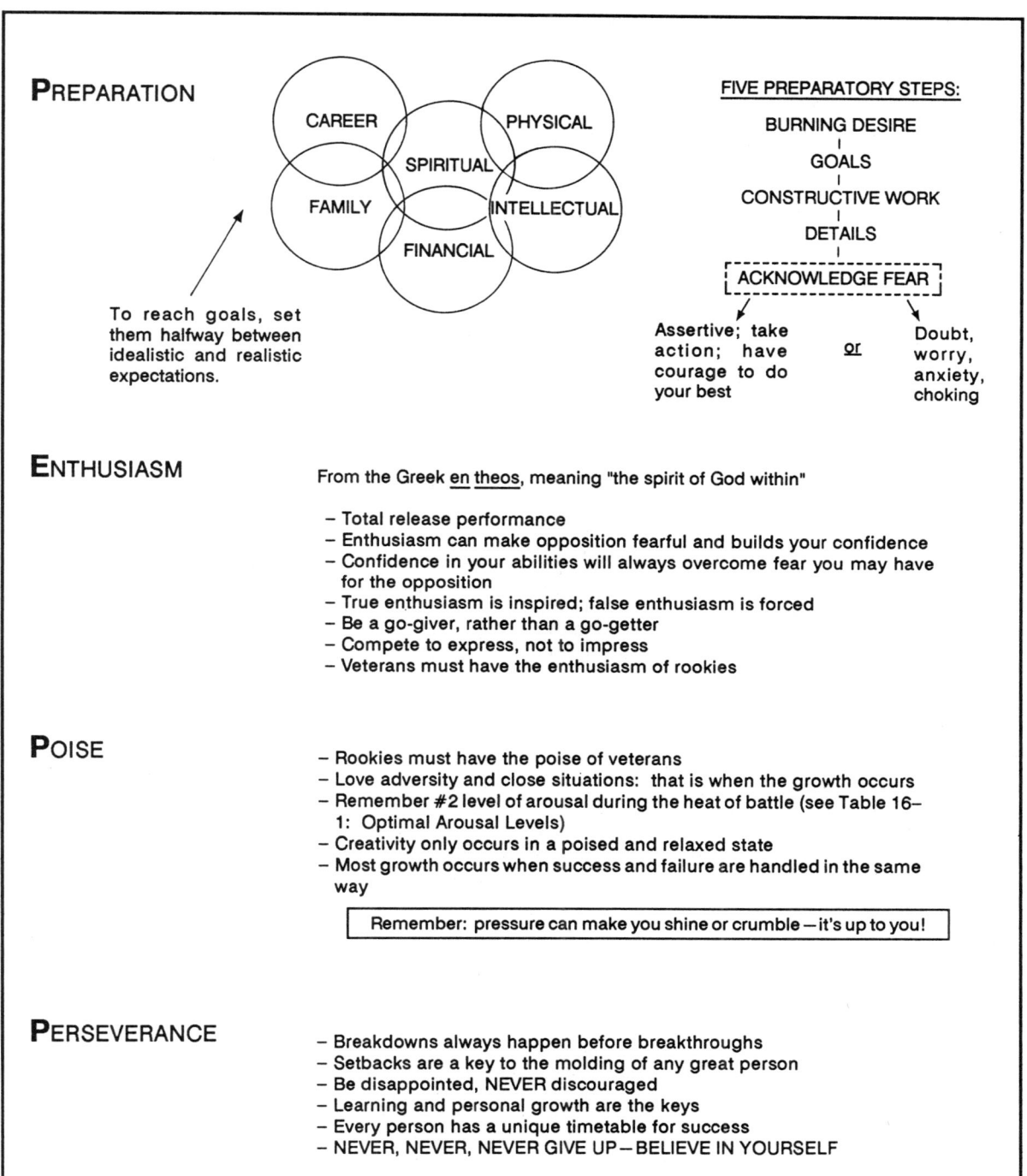

CHAPTER 15

SET HIGH EXPECTATIONS AND UNDERSTAND PECKING ORDER

"Seedings are what others think of you. Results are what you think of yourself."
—Chuck Kriese

WHAT YOU EXPECT IS WHAT YOU GET

In 1978, in my third year of coaching, I learned that the coach's expectations can easily become the player's expectations if the coach does not let the players know the difference. We should never have won the state collegiate tournament that year. My number one player, Mike Gandolfo, had a shoulder injury and was unable to compete. To make matters worse, our top freshman player was unable to play because of a disciplinary action. I was left with a much weaker team, and we had to face very strong opposition from the best teams in South Carolina. The team that I would field for the tournament consisted of three freshmen, two sophomores, and only one player who had much playing experience at all. As I evaluated the situation, I knew that we were going to get killed. There was no way in the world that I could expect this team to finish in the top three, and to think they could win the tournament was out of the question.

I realized that I had two options. First, I could expect nothing out of my team and be pleasantly surprised if they did well. My second option was to flat-out lie to my players and explain to them that we had our best chance to win the tournament anyhow. The tournament would be held on the clay courts of The Citadel in Charleston. I rationalized to the team that the two players who had to sit out were hard court players and we now had our best clay court team entering the tournament.

I told my players that champions are made from adversity and that because we had this adversity we would be in a prime position to win the championship. I explained to them, though, that the job was going to be very tough. I set a specific goal for the first day of winning at least eight matches out of the nine flights. Regardless of how our team did, though, I told my players that one other team would play great the first day and win all nine flights. Our goal for the second day would be to have another solid day. Another team would also play great the second day; we would be on the money rounds, and on the third day the best-conditioned team would win. Because our training had been tough, this was the day that our conditioning would have a chance to pay off. As I told the guys this, I thought to myself, "This is the biggest lie I have ever told in my life. There is no way in the world that these guys can win." But then again, I thought about my two options and I felt this was the best one.

My players actually believed me, and that fact taught me how important my expectations for them were. It also taught me that young people trust a person who is in a position of authority, especially if they respect that person. I learned that my job as a coach and a role model was a very important one.

The team meeting the night before the tournament was much the same as previous meetings. I told the players what they would be up against the next day and that one team would play great. We would have to fight through some very tough matches and accomplish our goal of having a very solid first day. To my disbelief, a few of the players who should never have won matches came through in the clutch, and we ended up winning eight matches the first day. South Carolina had a day equal to ours, and Furman won all nine of their matches and took an early lead in the tournament. That night, I told my players that we had accomplished our goal for the day. I told them that the second day would be a very tough day, and our goal for the second day was to have another solid performance. Once again, I looked at my team in disbelief, and wondered how I could tell them that we were going to do such unrealistic things.

The second day, the Furman team had a poor day, the South Carolina team won eight matches, and our team won seven matches. Once again, I was surprised to have so many wins. That night in the meeting, I congratulated the players on reaching their goal for the day and explained to them that this was the way it was supposed to be. We were now in a position to win on the last day, and that had been our goal all along. I told them that we had worked hard enough to be in better condition than anybody else and that the long matches on the clay had worn out a lot of the other players. I also told my players that none of the matches would be easy and that it would be clutch play from this point on.

Even after two days of performances like we had had, I still felt as if I were lying, and I did not really give my team much chance of winning on the last day. My expectations for my team were low, but somehow I faked my positive comments and actions. All of the matches were tough. In fact, five of them were three-setters, and three of those ended up 7-5 in the third. But the players came through in the clutch every time and when they walked off, instead of happy jubilation, they took the wins with a matter-of-fact attitude as if they were supposed to win. As we won the deciding point to win the championship, I caught myself before I could let out a yell. I immediately walked a hundred yards away, stood behind a tree, and let out a scream. I thought about how I had lied to my players and how I had so much less confidence in them than they had in themselves. We were certainly not the best team in the state tournament that year, and their confidence had merely come from the expectations that I had expressed to them. The bottom line, though, was that my players thought they were the best team, and that is why they won. I walked back onto the courts and did everything I could to contain my happiness, because I realized that if I were to celebrate outwardly too much, I could kill the momentum that we could develop as a team from that point on.

THE PECKING ORDER AND EXPECTATIONS

Tennis is a tough sport because of its ranking system. The pecking order is quickly established, and players discover what achievements they are comfortable with. The pecking order is so rigid that I firmly believe if a player is not favored to win at least in his own mind, he usually cannot and will not win. On the other hand, it is fun to play the underdog role because it poses the unthreatening situation of having something to gain and nothing to lose. But it has been my experience that when a player plays a match with nothing to lose, he usually loses the match.

A tennis player playing a match with an absence of pressure usually begins by making many great shots and points. The problem with this overextended play early in the match is that it usually cannot be kept up for long. The favored player usually catches up to the underdog late in the first set and then cruises for an easy second-set victory. It's as if the player who plays above his head uses all the shots in his tool box early on, and when he does not have anything else to use, he collapses.

SET HIGH EXPECTATIONS AND UNDERSTAND PECKING ORDER

The scoring system in tennis dictates that a player has to win a minimum of 48 "battles" or points to win one match. To close out the other player, a player must be better by two points every game. It does not matter whether a player is a whole lot better or more spectacular on point 21 or on point 37. The bottom line is that unless a player's great shots scare his opponent and dent his confidence, he still has to play better than his opponent on the last two points of the match to finish him off. The ingenious scoring system of tennis makes it difficult indeed to score upsets.

A match is lost when a player is challenged time after time and has opportunity after opportunity stripped away. This player's positive reactions when he made good shots early in the match turn neutral, and his neutral reactions to his early errors turn to discouragement. He has already thrown everything he can at his opponent, but the opponent still has not cracked. This up and down swing in emotions usually cracks the lesser player. Upsets can occur, but the favorite player usually wins.

Because playing as a favorite is so critical, it is important for a coach to help a player believe that he *should* win, not just that he *could* win. One attitude produces a win; the other produces a good chance to play close before losing. In nearly every endeavor in life, people will not achieve more than they expect to achieve. Many books have been written about positive self-concepts, positive thinking, and success attitudes, and they all have a similar message: How a person perceives himself and how comfortable he is with that perception determine what he will be.

Academic endeavors provide good examples of the effects of expectations on performance. For example, one student is and has been an A student for quite some time. He makes A's again and again with little or no surprise or excitement from teachers, parents, or himself. His success is expected and accepted, so his reward is also sometimes neglected. However, it takes the same work and dedication as always to get the A's. When a B is made, it is a tremendous disappointment to the student, his teachers, and his parents. The student's feeling of failure is great.

Another student has a C average. He is quite comfortable in his role as a C student, and his expectations are to make more C's. On one grading report this student makes two or three B's, and everyone sings the praises of the great job done. What different reactions for the same job done by two different people, and all because of the expectations placed on each of them.

One semester the C student changes his behavior and studies more diligently than ever before and makes straight A's. Everyone is thrilled; he is praised by all and is the most elated he has ever been as a student. The next semester he makes straight C's again. He and everyone else wonder what happened. Expectations are an indication of what a person is comfortable and is not comfortable doing or achieving. If someone achieves beyond his own expectations, he may retreat to the level that he is comfortable with.

A coach can have a tremendous impact on a player's self concept by helping the player feel comfortable with higher expectations. The scary thing is that along with achievement and higher expectations come a harder job and more responsibility, and it is obvious why many players remain mediocre.

OVERCOMING THE PECKING ORDER

The role of the favorite has definite advantages in a tennis match. The problem is that no matter how well a player is prepared mentally, physically, and emotionally, the opponent may be better and he may be the underdog. What are a player's options in this case? Not to play? Concede that he will probably lose, but play the match for experience anyway? To go for broke and hope that magic happens?

Figure 15-1 gives some guidelines for overcoming the pecking order of tennis. A player should remember that 50 percent of the match outcome has to do with how his opponent plays. It is critical for a player to try to maintain his best play while staying within his limitations and using the tools in his tool box. A player's goal then is to get his opponent to play at his lower limitations.

Follow the guidelines given and stick to a basic game plan:

1. Use only your tool box of skills.
2. Keep good court positioning.
3. Run the right plays (use the momentum control system).
4. Keep emotional balance and proper reactions to the ups and downs in the match.

TOTAL TENNIS TRAINING

Figure 15-1. Overcoming the pecking order.

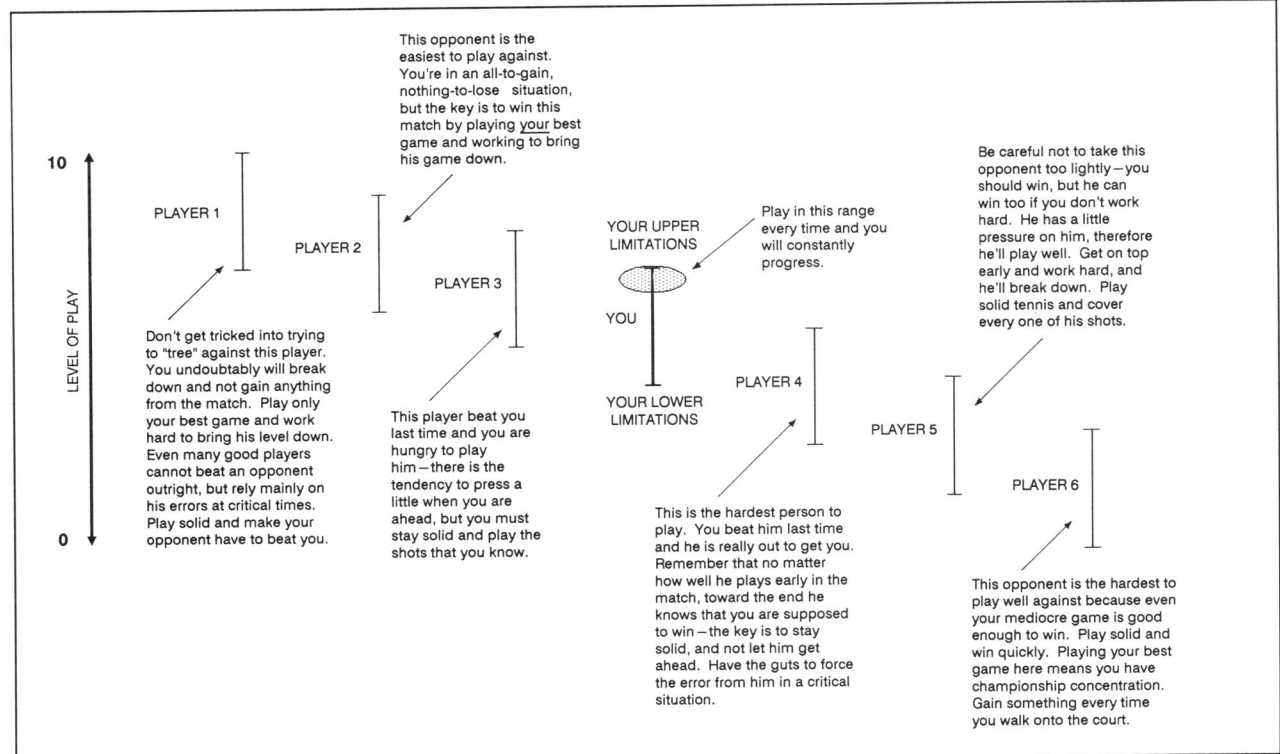

HAVE A METHOD FOR SETTING GOALS

"The person without a goal is like a ship without a rudder," as the saying goes. Every athlete and coach understands the importance of goal setting in trying to achieve potential. It is critical to set proper individual and team goals and work toward them. It may be easier to accomplish tasks in a group situation.

As discussed in Chapter 14, long-term, intermediate, and short-term goals should be made by both the team and the individual. The long-term goal might be two to four years in the future; the intermediate goal might be six months to one year ahead, and short-term goals might be one week to three or four months ahead. These goals should be constantly evaluated and reset as they are accomplished. The athlete should write down and post his goals in a place where he will look at them regularly.

Figure 15-2. Setting goals will help you reach your potential.

PLAYING ABOVE YOUR HEAD

In all sports, it sometimes happens that an athlete performs better than he usually does. This phenomenon is not the norm for competition or training, but players should recognize it as something that may have to be dealt with in playing an opponent. In tennis, "zoning," "treeing," "playing out of your mind," and "playing above your head" are all terms used to describe this phenomenon, and in other sports, the terms "the Cinderella team," "the home court advantage," and the "rookie sensation" are used to describe the same phenomenon. Whatever the label, in no other sport is this phenomenon seen more than in tennis.

When a player plays above his head, he is not playing above his physical abilities, because he must possess these abilities to do what he does. Rather, he is merely playing above his mental expectations because he is involved in an emotional situation. Most athletes have experienced the emotional high that allows such a performance to take place, and most athletes have also played an opponent who is going through such an experience. To compete against someone who is zoning is frustrating, and sometimes the usual pecking order falls apart. Physical educators and sports psychologists have recognized and labeled three distinct situations in which this emotional phenomenon takes place. They are: the novelty effect, the experimental effect, and reminiscence.

The Novelty Effect

The freshman year, the first year of the tour, playing up an age division—in each of these situations there is a good chance for an above-average performance. Perhaps the enthusiasm level has a great deal to do with it. Perhaps the lack of pressure in an all-to-gain and nothing-to-lose-situation allows it. It may have a lot to do with the fact that the veteran opponent who plays the newcomer plays poorly in this more-to-lose-than-to-gain situation. This is called "the novelty effect," and it has been the reason for many great performances by newcomers at every level of tennis.

The Professional Tour is marked by many cases of first-year players who have zoomed to a high first year ranking only to drastically drop in their second year after the novelty wore off. In college the second year is often referred to as the "sophomore blues" year, describing the deflating of the high-flying freshman year.

If a player is competing against a rookie or a first-time performer, it is important for him to be aware that his opponent will compete without fear and will make some above average shots. He should be ready for a tough, emotional match, and he should be aggressive and enthusiastic. If he can get ahead early and dent the rookie's confidence, he should be able to win comfortably. The longer the newcomer stays in the match, the better he will play and the greater will be the pressure on the favorite.

The rookie should use this situation to his advantage, but he should remember that initial good results do not necessarily mean that he has arrived as a player. The player who makes it is the one who keeps working hard after the initial enthusiasm has worn off.

The Experimental Effect

The home court advantage; a one-chance tryout; mom, dad, and girlfriend in the stands watching—all these situations provide what is called "the experimental effect" that can allow a person to play above his assumed capabilities.

The experimental effect presents a situation that allows the home team to play at a consistently high level in which bad play does not dent confidence, and good play creates momentum. The opposing team is put into a situation in which good play provides very little or no upswing in momentum, and poor play provides a definite downward cycle. It takes a very disciplined and well-trained athlete to win against this phenomenon of experimental effect.

The experimental effect situation means that a player and a team are on display. A player who is competing against the home favorite should be ready for and expect the opponent's great play. He should expect the home team's confidence to stay intact regardless of the score, because even when the home team is behind, there is a chance of them coming back. In addition, he must maintain his confidence in his skills throughout the entire contest. This is one of the toughest situations to win in. In many cases the fine motor physical skills, as well as the mental processes so necessary for playing tennis effectively, are overridden by the emotional effect of this situation.

There are many examples of the experimental effect in collegiate and professional sports. In the 1987 NCAA Tennis Championships, a major issue was made out of the fact that the University of Georgia had used its home court advantage to score major upsets on the way to its second championship in three years on its campus. The situation prompted a movement by coaches and NCAA officials to consider neutral or rotating sites for future championships. The 1987 NCAA Soccer Championships saw nineteenth ranked Clemson come from the bottom of a tough field to win that National Championship at its home site. The Boston Celtics' phenomenal record at the Boston Garden is an example of how experimental effect plays a big factor in professional sports. The examples are many. The advantages of experimental effect need to be recognized by both the athlete it helps and the athlete it hinders. It is truly a powerful force.

Reminiscence

A golfer plays three days a week for a year and averages in the low 80's. He does not play for three months during the winter months, and he shoots his best ever 75 on his first time out following the layoff. The basketball player who has been out for five weeks with an injury amazes everyone as he scores 25 points in his first game back. The tennis player lays off two months only to win his first tournament outing.

Perhaps it is the fresh enthusiasm and eagerness to compete, or perhaps it is the low expectation placed on the competitor that caused these above normal results. This phenomenon of superior physical performance immediately following a period of non-participation is called "reminiscence." It happens often, and it can sometimes fool the athlete into thinking that a program of steady and consistent practice is not important.

The problem is that the effects of reminiscence usually last for only a very short time. The elated golfer finds that his second and third rounds drop from that 75 to 95 and 96. The basketball and tennis players experience similar crashes in performance. Usually, though, their performance improves in each subsequent outing until they get back to their normal results. Because of its inconsistency, reminiscence should never be counted on for consistent performances, nor should it be a substitute for a solid training routine.

SUMMARY

Players should be familiar with the phenomenon of playing above their usual level, but this phenomenon should be recognized for its fleetingness and unreliability. Players should also be aware of the three situations in which this phenomenon takes place—the novelty effect, the experimental effect, and reminiscence. An understanding of each of these three situations allows the athlete to better plan for and deal with the up and down performance swings that can be caused by them.

CHAPTER 16

DEVELOP YOUR OPTIMAL LEVEL OF EMOTIONAL AROUSAL FOR COMPETITION

"The virtue of all achievement is victory over oneself. Those who know this victory can never know defeat."

—Anonymous

As I grew up and competed in tennis and other sports, I believed that the harder I tried, the more successful I would be. If I lost, I felt guilty that maybe I had not tried hard enough. Sadly, many athletes feel the same way and constantly berate themselves for being lazy when things are going poorly, often until their self-image and confidence are torn down.

Can someone try too hard? As a youngster, I used to play my best friend, Lester, in match after match. I tried so hard and got very fired up for each attempt at beating him. But, even so, each of our 15 or more meetings in the junior rankings turned out the same—close straight set losses to Les. The thing that always got to me was that he always appeared not to be trying. In a relaxed way he would move smoothly from corner to corner threading passing shots, always getting one more ball back until I would crack. I always responded by saying to myself, "I'll just work harder and try harder." My level of arousal when I competed was about the same as that of a pro football lineman, and Les always acted as nonchalant as someone sunbathing on the beach.

It was not until I was 24 years old and taking a course in graduate school that I learned about optimal levels of arousal for different sports. Was I really trying too hard? I had not thought that was possible.

I thought an athlete should always try 110 percent. My emotional level was so high when I competed that I would physically tie up and choke. This high level of arousal also hampered my mental processes, and I was unable to think clearly, making myself subject to the roller-coaster ride of my emotions.

Table 16-1 is a listing that was shown to me in a graduate school class, and I have kept it to help athletes who do not focus their concentration properly in the heat of the battle. It is from an article by Joseph B. O'Xendine, called "Emotional Arousal and Motor Performance."[1] It has been invaluable to me as a coach of such a delicately balanced sport.

DIFFERENT AROUSAL LEVELS AT DIFFERENT TIMES

Two different personalities prevail in competitive sports: the diligent hard worker, and the person who is loose-as-a-goose. The former is obsessive and driven, and he practices skills again and again until he does them correctly. The latter is a cocky competitor who thinks he can do it all.

The athlete with the driven temperament has obvious advantages, and most coaches love to work with this athlete. The problem is that on game day this athlete usually tries too hard and often chokes. The cocky

Table 16-1. Optimal arousal levels for some typical sports skills.

LEVEL OF AROUSAL	SPORTS SKILLS
5 (EXTREMELY EXCITED)	Football (blocking and tackling) Performance on the Rogers' PFI Test Running (220 yards to 440 yards) Sit up, push up, or bent arm hang test Weight lifting
4	Running long jump Running very short and long races Shot put Swimming races Wrestling and judo
3	Basketball skills Boxing High jumping Most gymnastic skills Soccer skills
2	Baseball (pitching and batting) Fancy dives Fencing Football (quarterback) Tennis
1 (SLIGHT)	Archery and bowling Basketball (free throws) Field goal kicking Golf (putting and short irons) Skating (figure eights)
0 (NORMAL STATE: NO EMOTION)	

athlete does a lot of good things on game day and always appears as if he can and will pull it off, but because of his lack of repetitive work, he often does not come through in the clutch and cannot be counted on for consistent performances.

Figure 16-1. Athletes should focus their concentration properly in the heat of the battle.

Bill Moore, a sports psychologist, helped our team by explaining that levels of arousal for practice day and match day should not be the same. It would be best if a player's personality were a combination of the two personalities—someone who is driven on practice day to do everything possible to polish his skills and who on game day is able to approach the competition with a confident or even cocky attitude. But athletes tend to be one way or the other and find it difficult to change arousal levels from practice day to game day.

There are exceptions in every sport to the optimal level of arousal theory. Even if an athlete knows what level of emotional arousal produces the best performance, he may not be able to compete comfortably at that level. Each athlete must find his own individual level of arousal and work to find that zone of emotional balance for competition.

SUMMARY

It is important for tennis players to find their optimal level of emotional arousal for competition and for practice. Athletes should be familiar with the optimal arousal levels for various sports.

Figure 16-2. Each tennis player must find his optimal level of emotional arousal.

Figure 16-3. Levels of emotional arousal for practice and competition should be different.

CHAPTER 17

ELIMINATE EXCUSES AND DEFENSE MECHANISMS

"The day you take complete responsibility for yourself, the day you stop making excuses—that's the day you start to the top."

—O. J. Simpson

One January evening, after wishing my mother a happy birthday, I told her that I was upset with my team for making excuses and failing to accept responsibility. "Young people nowadays," I said, "have the brashness to take a stand on anything, but few have the guts to accept responsibility. Why can't people just say, 'I screwed up, I'm sorry'? Why are there always 40 reasons why it happened?" My mother calmed me and said, "Human nature is the same as it's always been. The only difference now is that society has provided people with reasons. Let me put it this way: Mrs. Brown who lives next door is an old battle-ax. Nowadays we look at Mrs. Brown and say, 'Poor Mrs. Brown, isn't it sad that her husband is an alcoholic, her daughter ran off with her teenage boyfriend, and her son is taking drugs? Poor Mrs. Brown. She's upset. She's nervous. She's got troubles.' But, hey! The bottom line is that *Mrs. Brown is an old battle-ax* whatever the reasons!"

I thought of the old woman who lived next door to our house when I was a child. There were six kids in our family, and the old woman would yell at us and steal our ball whenever it went into her yard. I knew what my mother was talking about. Perhaps today we might have found an elaborate way of giving this old woman some excuse for her behavior. I remembered thinking, though, "Wouldn't that be the wrong thing to do?" After all, it seemed that the role of battle-ax was something she was good at and almost enjoyed. Why rob her of it by giving her excuses for her actions? I also thought, "Hey! If we had looked hard enough, we could have found reasons for a lot of old women on the block to be battle-axes."

This story made me understand that one of the toughest jobs in coaching today is to get young players to take responsibility for their actions. Tennis is a difficult game to play. It is even more difficult to play well, and it is one of the hardest games to learn to win. But the biggest frustration that I have as a coach is not that the physical and mental parts of the game are so difficult to learn, but that it is so difficult for the players to take the responsibility for their own play. It seems that usually the better the player, the more sophisticated is his excuse for coming up on the short side in a match. The temptation to make an excuse will always be with a player, because tennis is such a hard game to play. Another coach once told me, "Excuses are like people's rear ends—everyone has one."

DEFENSE MECHANISMS

Sigmund Freud stated that sometimes a failure situation is so painful for a person that he may need a defense mechanism in order to preserve his self-esteem. Unfortunately, though, a defense mechanism can seriously hinder an athlete's growth because it keeps him from working to improve his skill level. I tell my players that once they take the court, there is no reason for a loss other than, "He played better than I did." Once you take the court, that's all there is to say. If something is bothering you, don't take the court.

A player should be humble in victory and give full credit to his opponent in defeat, no matter how tough that may be. If, however, the loss is just too unbearable, I tell my players that they should at least know the clinical names for their excuses. Each year I give each of my team members a list that is taken from the book, *Life and Health*, by Grawunder and Steinmann.[1]

1. Repression is "forgetting on purpose"—pushing a shameful or distasteful experience or thought out of one's consciousness and pretending that it does not exist. Repression, which is usually an un-

Figure 17-1. If something is bothering you, don't take the court.

conscious process, is the most fundamental of the defense mechanisms.

2. Compensation is trying to make up for failure in one area by success in another area. For example, a person who is in sports may become a successful team member or sports writer.

3. Displacement is discharging an emotion on something other than the situation that caused it. For example, a teenager questioned by police for being out at 5:00 A.M. might kick a neighbor's trash can in lieu of kicking the police officers.

4. Sublimation is transforming "unacceptable" impulses into acceptable ones. For example, a person who feels the socially unacceptable desire to be aggressive may enter a highly competitive career field.

5. Escape is running away from problems through daydreaming, fantasy, books, movies, or even excessive sleep. Children who have intolerable home conditions, for example, have been known to construct elaborate fantasy worlds.

6. Regression is reverting to behavior more appropriate to an earlier stage of life. A woman whose husband yells at her for breaking something might revert to baby talk and call her husband "Daddy" as a way of avoiding responsibility for her actions.

7. Reaction formation is replacing a negative feeling with its opposite. For example, a parent who feels hostility toward a child may react to that unacceptable feeling by being overly nice to the child.

8. Identification is choosing another person as an ideal and then trying to emulate that person. A teenager might identify with a famous rock star in order to share vicariously in the star's successes, even to the point of dressing like the star and keeping a scrapbook of his career.

9. Rationalization is providing a substitute reason for an occurrence. It is an attempt to cover up one's failures or mistakes, to soften the blow. Common rationalizations include: "I would have done better if only I had more time," "The game was rigged," "There were too many distractions," "That professor doesn't like me," or "I was just testing you to see if you were listening."

10. Projection is shifting one's negative emotions or problems to someone else in order to maintain self-esteem. A person who accuses others of lying, cheating, or bigotry is often projecting.

11. Avoidance is staying away from situations that produce anxiety or bring repressed feelings to the surface. An insecure person may avoid demanding tasks. A person who is unsure of his sexual identity may avoid the opposite sex. A person whose self-concept is tied to family life may avoid traveling or other situations that bring separation.

12. Denial is refusing to perceive or accept some aspect of reality. A heavy smoker will deny scientific reports on the dangers of cigarette smoking. People who are vain about their appearance may deny that they are growing old.

The point about excuses is well understood and usually ends up being a lot of fun for the players. They are quick to pick up on another team member's attempt to make an excuse, even if it is a valid one, and to label it with the clinical name. In nearly all these cases, it makes a positive situation out of a painful loss.

On the more humorous side, Bill Bos, a former collegiate coach and currently a tennis pro in Dallas, wrote this list of excuses used by tennis players. I remember this list was a big help to me as a college athlete.

For the Tennis Player Who Runs Out of Excuses

1. Ate too much lunch.
2. Did not eat enough.
3. Drank too much water.
4. Favorite racquet broke.
5. Needed new balls.
6. Balls too light.
7. Balls too heavy.
8. Balls too fuzzy.
9. Net was too high.
10. Net was too low.
11. The racquet slipped in my hand.
12. Other player was better than I because he was ranked.
13. He beat a buddy of mine, so he should beat me.
14. He didn't play tennis—all he did was hit the ball back.
15. He was so bad I couldn't play tennis against him.

My dying brother-in-law once read to me "Rockne's Prayer" by Knute Rockne as I fretted and hurt during an impending defeat. Now, the words of the prayer are with me always as I go into competition. It reads:

Lord, in the struggle that goes on through life,
We ask for a field that is fair,
A chance that is equal,
With all this strife,
And the courage to strive and to dare.

But, if we should win,
Let it be by the code,
With our honor held high.
And if we should lose,
Let us stand by the road,
And cheer as the winners go by.

SUMMARY

Proper perspective in winning, losing, or competing is a must in being able to handle the emotions that accompany each. Growth can only occur for the athlete if he faces up to the responsibility of his performance and does not look to any reason other than his and his opponent's performance and credits his opponent's performance in losing or winning.

CHAPTER 18

BUILD A TEAM IN AN INDIVIDUAL SPORT

"Often our strengths are our weaknesses, and our weaknesses are our strengths."
—Anonymous

Coaching team tennis may be the most complex and unusual coaching there is. The paradox is that tennis is an individual sport and each player's game must be developed at an individual rate. It is the coach's job to develop a plan for each player's growth that is specifically designed for the needs and talents of that player.

At the same time, these individuals, who are all growing at independent rates, must mesh their skills, talents, and interests into the common goal of team direction and unity. Although this contradiction can make team tennis coaching very difficult, the situation usually allows great growth for all members involved with the team family.

THE ANALOGY OF THE TEAM WHEEL

It was mid-season in the spring of 1987, and our team had suffered more losses than in any previous year since 1978. We had done very well early in the season by reaching the finals of the National Team Indoor Championships, but that was about it. We were in a mid-season slump. A few of the team members were starting to get down on themselves, and I feared a snowball effect. We still had fourteen tough matches ahead of us including our conference season and the NCAA Championships.

I called a team meeting in hopes of reversing the momentum. I spoke briefly about where we were in the season, the job that was ahead of us as a team, and some goals that we needed to make in following through for a strong season. The players seemed bored and unfocused. Then, instead of saying anything more, I walked to the chalkboard and drew the following picture:

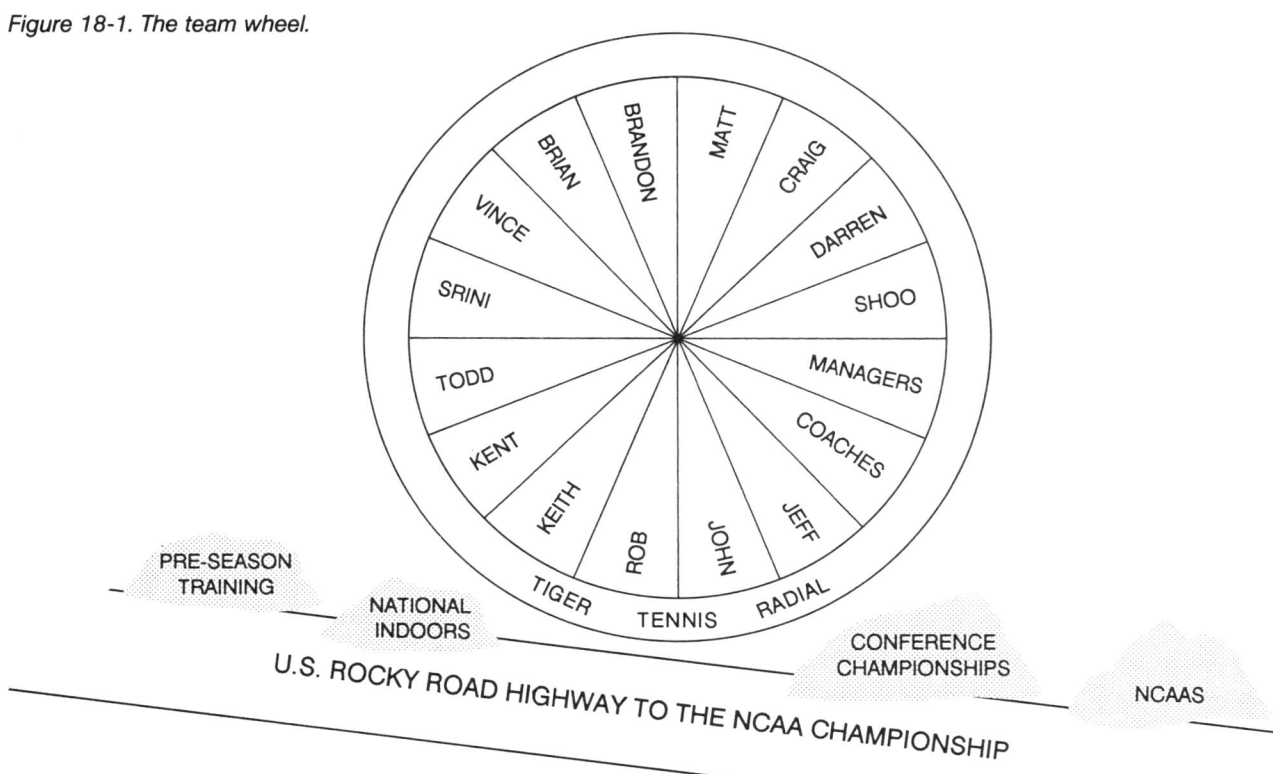

Figure 18-1. The team wheel.

I told my players that each one of them was a spoke in our team wheel. When the road is smooth the wheel can get by, even if a few of the spokes are not strong and are not doing their part. But on a rocky road, like the one that was ahead of us, a weak spoke may allow the road to bend the wheel and cause a breakdown. The team wheel is only as strong as its weakest spoke or member, and each spoke must do its part, no matter how insignificant that may seem.

A basketball coach once told me early in my career that it does not matter how small or large a team member's role is. What is important is that each person involved in the organization has a role and knows that it is important to the team. The coach should remember that the number 14 player's life is just as important as the number one player's life. In 10 years' time, the significant thing will be that the two players worked side by side to reach a common goal and that they learned about themselves and about life.

DIFFERENT PERSONALITIES FOR TEAM STRUCTURE

It is important to have a variety of personalities on a team. When I first started coaching, I felt it would be best to have a team made up only of self-motivated, hard-working members. I thought this would produce a team with few discipline problems that would always be a contender. I am now convinced that the team should be a melting pot of different personality types. Each personality type contributes in his own way and grows because he is surrounded by different ideas, different ways of doing things, and the unique styles of the other team members. More importantly, a team made up of a variety of different personalities allows each team member to grow independently, without having to compete for his own personal space on the team. I have also come to realize that 20 different personalities can easily work together for a common goal, and that when all the parts work together, there are few things more exciting to experience as a coach.

BUILD A TEAM IN AN INDIVIDUAL SPORT

A weekend seminar for my team with Bryce Young, a former coach, college administrator, and trainer of young people, gave tremendous support to this belief. He explained that a person's personality is formed very early in life and that each personality has strengths and weaknesses, and each is needed for a strong team structure. Table 18-1 lists six different personality types, and is taken from work by Taibi Kohler.[1]

Most people display two or three of these personality types, but usually one is dominant. If a coach understands these personality types and knows how to handle them, he can help each player develop at his best rate. The role played by each team member usually fulfills many of the needs of his personality.

Table 18-1. Personality types.

PERSONALITY TYPE	NEED	HOW HE RELATES ON THE TEAM
THE REBEL	Need for fun, attention, contact	Will be the team's leader or troublemaker
THE PROMOTER	Need for fun, likes to get reaction	Lots of fun to have on a team but often causes controversy
THE PERSISTER	Driven by a purpose—total direction	Totally goal- and purpose-oriented
THE WORKAHOLIC	Likes structure	Likes schedules and having everything laid out for every part of the day
THE REACTOR	Likes to blend in	Like a chameleon, he blends in well in any situation; very few ever find fault with him or fail to get along with him
THE DREAMER	Is always somewhere else	Hard to understand because he always seems to be daydreaming

I have discovered that each team has many of the following roles taken by its members.

The quiet leader: Usually a persister-reactor with some workaholic tendencies.

The loud aggressive leader: Usually a rebel-persister with some promoter tendencies.

The sidekick: Usually a reactor.

The flamboyant showoff: Usually a rebel-promoter (this can be a dangerous combination).

The strange one: Usually a dreamer, sometimes also a rebel, sometimes a persister.

The obsessive worker: A persister-workaholic.

The scapegoat: Can be many combinations, but usually has not gained the respect of the group and does not have a strong self-concept.

Of course, there are many other roles team members can take on. In addition, each team takes on a unique personality of its own.

NICKNAMES FOR TEAM MEMBERS

Many great coaches and athletes have been known and called by their nicknames more often than by their birth names. There is something very special and important about the confidence and identity that a nickname can give an athlete.

It seems that a team structure provides an appropriate setting for nicknames to emerge and be used. Even if team members act as if they do not enjoy a nickname, they probably do. Nicknames provide many positives in a team structure—but the coach should make sure that positive names such as Warrior, Thunder, Terminator, Scrappy, and Rocket are used instead of negative, derogatory names like Stinky and Porky.

THE FOUR-YEAR DEVELOPMENT OF A TEAM MEMBER

The development of a team member in his four-year high school or college career can be compared to a person's development from birth until he is 18 years old.

The Freshman Year: The Year of High Enthusiasm and Fast Learning

As the young child needs the constant caring and direction of the parent, so a freshman responds to and needs the same from the coach and the team. Most of the successes that come to a freshman are based on the combination of high enthusiasm and very little pressure, but always with much support from his new family of team members.

Often a player starts his career in a blaze of glory. It is good for an athlete to have early successes as long as he keeps a proper perspective and builds a strong foundation of fundamentals. The lack of proper fundamentals makes for a quick rise and a quick fall, and this scenario is all too common in American society. An athlete's career must be built on a foundation that will enable growth to continue after the initial enthusiasm has worn off. The coach must remember that the late show is always the great show in an athlete's career, and he must plan for the long term and not for the immediate rewards that seem to be fast-coming initially.

The Sophomore Year: The Sophomore Blues or the "What-am-I-Doing-This-For?" Year

Like the second lap of the mile run, the sophomore's initial enthusiasm is just not there any more, but his destination is not yet in sight. Sometimes the sophomore year goes very smoothly and the athlete is able to make steady growth, but more often it is a year of confusion and questioning. The coach should try to spend as much time as possible with a player during this year to help keep him focused on his goals. Individual workouts and frequent feedback are helpful.

The Junior Year: The Year of "I Can Do it on my Own"

Just as the 15-year-old reaches the stage when he rebels to some extent against his parents, so too the athlete will usually go through a similar period of rebellion against the coach or the team structure. Team meetings and the coach's structure and guidance were exciting for the freshman, but during the rebellious junior year, what the coach has to say does not seem to carry much weight with the player. Much of this simple rebellion comes from the first glimpses of seeing the end. This rebellion is very natural and should be taken as a positive part of the athlete's maturing process. It usually passes quickly as the player finds and better understands the direction he wants to take with his tennis and his life.

The Senior Year: The Year of Leadership and Direction

The reality of the approaching end is all that most seniors need to help them focus on what they really want to do. The realization that it is the last time around is usually a tremendous motivator. Senior team members, the same team members who were rebelling a year before, often take charge of the younger players on the team. Those players who do not take a leadership role usually become very focused and goal oriented. A team composed largely of seniors will almost always be successful because of its members' maturity level and because of the concentrated focus on what must be done for success.

If the coach recognizes these stages in the four-year evolution that his players go through, he has a great help in handling problems and in making players aware of the things to expect along the way.

DEVELOPING STRONG TEAM UNITY AND PRIDE

Although a coach can help his team develop unity and pride, they are primarily developed as team members share common goals and experience the struggles, hardships and disappointments of working toward these goals. Unity can be developed only through the ups and downs that people experience together. Pride comes only from successes that are earned by paying the price for achievement. The bonding that a team needs cannot be forced—it comes in its own time and only after enough interaction occurs between the team members.

The Coach's Job in Developing Team Unity and Pride

The coach's work with a team in developing unity and pride must begin on the very first day of practice. The coach should make practices tough, and he should challenge the members of the team daily. He should set a standard that requires physical, mental, and emotional strength. Often a coach can be misled by an athlete's talent or by his own expectations for promising young athletes.

Our armed forces have a tremendous concept in developing pride and group unity. Young people enter the service from every walk of life. Whatever a recruit may be—rich, poor, tall, short, black, or white—each and every one starts at base zero. The young men's heads are shaved, and the recruits are forced to go through six strenuous weeks of boot camp where they are pushed mentally, physically, and emotionally. In a sense, they are isolated from the rest of the world. They share common oppositions, and they have one common goal—to make it through boot camp. By the time boot camp is finished, this group of young people that was so diverse has become a unit bonded by pride and respect for each other and for themselves. Under totally adverse condition, they have overcome the obstacles put before them, and they have learned a lot about themselves and each other.

In a team structure, or in any group of people that has to work together, the same concepts apply. If they go through a struggle together, they will create a bond. A friend of mine related a story that illustrates how this bonding takes place. At girl scout camp there was an obstacle course, and on it was a wall that had to be climbed. As a girl scout arrived at the wall, she realized that there was no way to get over it alone. She had to have other campers boost her, and then once on top she had to help the last girl over from the bottom. What a great way to learn how to deal with the obstacles that occur in life.

When I started coaching I made a vow never to cut a player because of his playing ability. My feeling was that in winning or in losing, I wanted players who would build a strong team spirit through hard work, loyalty, and pride.

I set up a program that the team and all involved with the program now refer to as "Morning Madness." No matter whether he is ranked or unranked, recruited or not recruited, each new player has to meet at the track at 5:45 A.M. for a workout. The workout lasts about one hour and consists mainly of 440 and 880 yard intervals with some exercises in between. The main goal is that a person finish the workout. The players are encouraged to quit if they want to, and many do. A tryout squad of 40 or 50 is reduced to 10 or 11 after the first two or three days. After a week, usually everyone has quit except those individuals who have a burning desire to be a member of the team. These few people grow more determined every day until they reach a point where nothing in the world would make them quit.

One of the highlights of my coaching year comes on the day that I walk up to the athletes at the start of a workout and say, "I would be very proud to have you as a member of this great team. Congratulations!" It is breathtaking to see the elation of the new team

Figure 18-2. The 1980 U.S. Junior Davis Cup Team

members as they walk back to the dormitory arm in arm. I usually give them an inscribed T-shirt that says "Morning Madness Survivor."

From that day forward the struggles that those players have will seem very controllable, especially with the help of the other team members. After that it does not matter whether or not they are good tennis players. They will make a contribution to the team, and they will have respect for each other and for themselves.

HAVE ORGANIZED TEAM PRACTICE

Tennis team workouts are difficult to structure because of the multiple variables that are involved with each player, whereas the team as a whole needs work on doubles, conditioning, and match situations. Meeting these needs is critical to running a complete and very thorough practice.

In the daily routine, the more boring and repetitive work should be done early in the practice. Then the intensity should build in the practice with drill work that simulates match situations (see Chapter 21). Competition is best at the end of a workout because it allows the concentration and intensity to stay at a high until the end. Sprints or agility and movement drills at three or four different intervals throughout the workout help to keep a high intensity as well. Below are two sample practice schedules that incorporate these concepts.

Drill Day: Two-Hour Workout

15 Minutes:	Total body warm-up, flexibility work, and light hitting
3 Minutes:	Movement drills and agility work
30 Minutes:	Individual weaknesses and fundamental training
3 Minutes:	Movement drills and agility work
45 Minutes:	Match simulation and intensity drills
3 Minutes:	Conditioning sprints and agility work
20 Minutes:	Competition and match situations Optional individual work

Drill Day: Three-Hour Workout

15 Minutes:	Total body warm-up and flexibility work, light hitting
5 Minutes:	Agility and movement drills
40 Minutes:	Fundamentals and individual weakness work
3 Minutes:	Agility and movement drills
1 Hour:	Match simulation and intensity drills or station drill work
50 Minutes:	Competition and match situations
10 Minutes:	Conditioning work Optional individual work

On some days it is recognized that a practice schedule may need to be set up with different objectives than a normal drill day situation. Approximately two days per week should be set aside for match play. Team drill work is more helpful if matches are worked into the weekly schedule. If strength training facilities are available, they should be used two to three days per week, with one day between each training session for rest and on the alternating days sprint work or movement conditioning should be done.

DRILL WORK VERSUS MATCH PLAY

How much drill work should a team do? How much match play? What are the advantages of each? Individual team players would probably opt for a lot more drill work than match play. Drill work is fun and without pressure. The body can do its thing without interference from the mind and the emotions.

Drill work sessions are effective if players can work on grooving particular shots and learning new ones (shining existing tools and adding new ones). But, if only drill work is done, only the physical one-third of the player is used. With the many fine facilities, teaching devices, ball machines, and teaching pros in America today, many players have become great rallying machines. They are able to duplicate most of the shots that the pro players hit, but often with little or no understanding of how to use them. All the tools and materials to do any job are there, but there is often very little of the practical know-how, mental concentration, or perseverance to be successful. Because of this, the coach should do the best job possible to make his athletes work mentally and emotionally as well as physically.

In match play a player is forced to test and learn how to use the skills and tools that are already in his tool box. Moreover, he learns to win and to lose and, most importantly, to compete. The best shots in the world will not help a player if he has no knowledge of when and how to use them, and that comes only from match play. Ideally, the coach should schedule both drill work and match play in a timely way so that the player benefits from both and grows at a maximal rate.

ADMINISTER DISCIPLINE

Everyone wants discipline and love, and administering discipline is the most sincere way of showing concern and love. "Tough love," as counselors and psychologists refer to discipline, simply means taking the time to do what a person needs to provide necessary parameters and restraints. What a tragedy today that this very basic human need is often neglected.

Figure 18-3. Players can work on grooving shots and learning new ones in drill work sessions.

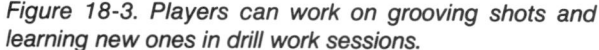

On one of my recruiting trips, I sat on the plane next to a counselor for youthful drug offenders. After we had talked for awhile, he asked me why I thought kids from wealthy or parentless homes become involved with drugs. I replied, "I guess because they have too much time on their hands, too much money." But he said, "No, the real reason is that the child is crying out for discipline." Discipline is a parent's way of showing love. In caring enough to punish a child, a parent cares enough to be involved in what is happening to the child, and he cares enough to make a decision that the child is not yet equipped mentally or emotionally to make. Basically, he takes the time and risks having the child dislike him. The child whose parents do not take these measures will look for ways to attract the discipline that he needs and wants. Sometimes the youngster will resort to drinking or drugs or breaking laws as ways of looking for the restraints that are supposed to come from somewhere. It is very sad that so many people feel that it is best to let youngsters make decisions for themselves without giving them specific guidelines during their formative years. These youngsters are neither equipped nor ready to deal with such responsibility. Like horses, children want to know their parameters. The first thing that horses do when they are put into a new pasture is to run to every corner of the field to find out the boundaries. Only after they have done this do they settle down and become content.

I saw the application of this truth from what took place at the home of a good friend of mine who has a 16-year-old daughter. In South Carolina it is quite the social thing for high schoolers to go to Myrtle Beach for spring break. I watched a very interesting scenario unfold as the mother denied her daughter's request to make this trip with her friends. It started with the girl's saying, "All my friends are going." The mother replied, "I don't care what your friends are doing." The daughter responded with, "How can you be so unfair? I hate you, I hate you," and the door slammed behind her as she rushed upstairs to cry. The mother looked at me and said, "It's so hard. I feel I'm doing right, but I hate to see her hurt so." Five minutes passed, and the young girl returned down the stairs and telephoned her friend, and said, "My mother won't let me go. I hate her. She's so mean, and I'm so mad." As she hung up the phone, I saw her look directly at the wall and breathe a large, peaceful sigh. She walked calmly upstairs to do a reading assignment. I thought, "Oh, my gosh, this girl is really happy that she's not going. She knew that it was an opportunity for trouble, and the bottom line is her mother took the responsibility of having to go against her friends off her shoulders."

Discipline Within a Team Structure

After my conversation on the plane, I came to realize the importance of good discipline within a team structure. No matter how players fight it and no matter how often they deny it, their greatest need in a competitive situation is discipline. It takes personal discipline to excel on the practice court and in match situations, and to do the routine details that no one likes to do. The coach provides the discipline of structure and administration of punishment, and this sometimes dictates that he set down unpopular requirements and restraints and punish or correct players when their actions are wrong.

In 1986 I learned a great lesson about the need to discipline players when a team rule has been broken. We had just lost a tough 5-4 match to Pepperdine, the number two ranked team in the United States. Two of the players, the number one and number five men on the team, had lost tough three-set matches to Pepperdine players, and both those matches were pivotal for the team. After a tough loss, like the one we experienced that day, we would usually go through a very intense drill session for about 15 minutes so that we not only took some of the sting off the loss, but also enabled us to go away from the courts with confidence. After this particular match, though, we had to leave immediately to catch our flight back to the East Coast for two more matches. I gave a talk to the guys about how proud I was of their effort and sorry that we had come up short. At the airport I checked the bags and rode the escalator up to where my team was waiting. As I got to the top of the escalator, I could not believe what I saw. Sitting at the bar directly ahead of me, for me and the whole world to see, were my number one and number five players, drinking a couple of beers. I am very strict on trips and never allow drinking, and this rule is well known by the team.

I stormed into the bar and screamed at the top of my lungs for the two players to get out into the hall. All the people in the bar immediately stopped drinking and talking. The players slid out into the hall, sheepishly acting as if they had not done anything wrong. I continued to yell. I was almost out of control as I screamed, "How could you do this to our program? How could you break a rule so flagrantly? Get out of my sight, just get out of my sight!"

It was still about an hour and a half before the flight took off, and I went to the farthest place in the terminal to brood. "How could my players be so stupid?" I thought. My mind was made up, though, and as soon as we got back to Atlanta to change planes, I sent those two players back to Clemson on a bus. The rest of the team and I went to Washington, D.C. area to play two conference matches. This was very tough because we now had a crippled lineup and had to use two freshmen in critical positions. Fortunately, though, we succeeded in barely winning the two matches. This situation had actually strengthened our team because we had developed great confidence after winning in spite of the absence of two starters.

The two players were very remorseful when we returned. They walked into my office and sat down for a meeting. My first question to them was, "Why were you guys so stupid to drink beer right out in the open knowing you were going to get caught? You could have gone to any other bar in the airport and gotten away with it. You could have put the beer in a plastic cup and sat in the back of the bar, and I wouldn't have known the difference. Why did you so blatantly break a team rule?" The older player looked at me and said, "Coach, I don't know why we did it. Right before you walked up the steps, John said, 'Hey, Coach will be here soon, and we're going to get caught.' It is as if we both knew we would get caught." As he said this, it dawned on me that these were the players who had lost two very tight three-set matches in our battle against Pepperdine. Could it be that they felt guilty and wanted to be punished? Could it be that they felt that they had let the team down but could not admit it? Had they sabotaged the situation so they would be caught? I asked them if they had ever heard of self-sabotage. I explained it to them, and they looked at each other and were quiet for a minute. I told them that as long as they gave 100 percent effort on the court, they would never let the team down. But their reaction to losing was wrong, and if they wanted to play on the Clemson team that year they would have to meet me at the track the next two days and run Dawn Patrol. They took their punishment and the incident was forgotten, but a great lesson was learned, not just by the players but by me as well.

When people fail, they feel guilty and feel the need to make things right and to clear the slate. It was not bad or wrong that the players lost, but they felt that they had let the team down. After they caused the situation to occur, they felt that it was critical that they be punished, because if they were not punished, they would have to carry their self-imposed guilt inside of them for a long time, and that would destroy their confidence. If I had said, "It's all right guys, I'll have a beer with you. It's not a big deal. We had a rough day today," it would surely have hurt the team, but most importantly it would have hurt these two players. They wanted to be punished even though there was no reason for them to be punished. Subconsciously they had planned a situation out of their guilt for what they had perceived as a failure.

After realizing this, I saw the importance of having a workout after a tough loss so that the players can get out some of their negative emotions. It is bad that 18 and 19-year-old young men and women carry around guilt because of their failure in performance, but it is hard for some of them not to, because so much emphasis is placed on success and failure. Only after a lot of maturing can a person walk away from a setback without carrying some of these feelings around.

METHODS OF DISCIPLINE

Team Discipline

Once the team policies are established, the rules and disciplinary actions for rule infractions should be handed out and explained in detail to the players at the first team meeting of the season. The rules should be specific and enforceable, and they should be enforced, or they cease to be effective. If there are too many rules, it can be impractical to enforce them. The well-respected coach Tom Parham once told me, "If you've got them, you better enforce them," and he continued, "I've got three rules for my team—no drugs, no drunks, no bums, and that covers it all. I enforce these and things work out pretty smoothly."

The coach does not have a lot of flexibility in enforcing the team policies—he must make sure that the rules are followed by every member of the team. It is a good rule for a coach to treat everyone the same and handle everyone differently. Problems can quickly arise when allowances are made for different team members, because team members will suspect preferential treatment because of a player's rank. In fact, the coach may want to make a special effort to be even a bit tougher on the top players on the team. Once the players know what is expected of them and that the rules will be enforced fairly, they will almost always respond favorably. Establishing these parameters takes considerable pressure off the players and gives them the chance to train wholeheartedly.

A coach should set team policies in the following areas, and he can add rules in other appropriate areas:

1. Academic standards
2. Team and individual image
3. Conduct on court and off
4. Competition standards at home and on the road (dress, routines)
5. Training (on court and off)
6. Lineups, practice schedules, use of equipment

Individual Discipline

The purpose of discipline is to help each player reach a point where he can achieve self-discipline. All team rules will be bent or broken at some time, thus forcing the coach into the position of having to discipline a player or players. There is always an initial testing period in which even the most cooperative of the players will sometimes break a rule.

This usually happens three or four weeks into practice when the newness of the training has worn off and the players have become familiar with the coach. The coach's role is a tough one, because he must be distanced enough from his players to administer discipline, but close enough to show a lot of concern for each player.

If a rule is broken by a team member, immediate disciplinary action must be taken. A good procedure is to have a progression of disciplinary actions for repeated infractions. For example:

Disciplinary Action—Slight Infraction

1. Talk to player, inform him of his infraction.
2. Have player do Yard Patrol (yard or maintenance work).
3. Have player do Court Patrol (have him pick up balls or do the manager's work instead of playing during practice hours).
4. Have player do Dawn Patrol (meet the player at 6:00 A.M. for a morning running workout).
5. Sit the player in the stands to watch practice.
6. Have the entire team run stadium workout or sprints for the infraction of the individual player while having the individual sit out of the running.

Disciplinary Action—Serious Infraction

Suspend the player indefinitely from the team, and as a last resort, dismiss him completely. A good coach will always feel bad about having to discipline a team member. But if players are treated in a consistent manner early in their careers, by the time they become juniors or seniors, they will usually help in training the young players on the team.

Athletes, especially very talented ones, are like thoroughbred racehorses. If left alone with no reins or restraints, they might run around the track on their own, but more likely, they will trot over to the pasture and graze in the sweetest grass they can find. The coach supplies the reins; at first it might be like guiding a bucking bronco stubbornly down the turns of the racetrack. As the athlete becomes better trained, the coach can gradually decrease the pressure on the reins until finally he throws them down and says, "Run, baby, run." As bad, though, as not guiding the thoroughbred that is untrained is to hold back and overly restrict the thoroughbred that is ready to run on its own. The best coaches know when and how to hold back and when and how to let the athlete go. The journey to this point begins with discipline.

Use On-Court Coaching Whenever Permitted

Although most team or individual matches prohibit on-court coaching of players, it is allowed in some situations, such as the Davis Cup play and college team matches. Although most of the coaching must be done before the match begins, a coach may use some of the following guidelines if he is allowed to coach during the match:

1. If it's not broken, don't fix it. Too often the temptation for the coach is to overly advise instead of letting the player win on his own merit. The coach needs to read the situation void of his own emotions.

2. Leave the player alone until the emotion from the start of the match has settled. Nothing will register with the player if the emotion of the match is controlling his thoughts.

3. Knowing when to coach:
   a. Watch for the first bad mistake when your player is behind. This is an indication that the player is starting to crack.
   b. Watch for the first (checkout) wasted shot when the player is ahead. This is an indication that the player does not want to take care of the dirty work ahead.
   c. Watch for initial changes in body language. This is the first indication that the match is in trouble.
   d. Watch for too many change of directions with shot selection. This is an indication that the player wants out of the pressure of staying in points.

4. How long to coach:
   a. Stay with your player during a loss. This is when your player needs help. Do not let him go down alone.
   b. Try not to be on the court when a player wins. The win should be to his credit and on his own doing. This will give confidence.

5. What to look for and correct:
   a. Is the player attacking the opponent's weakness?
   b. Is the court positioning good?
   c. Is the player running the right play and controlling momentum?
   d. Are the errors aggressive ones?
   e. How is the player reacting to his and his opponent's winners and errors?

6. Priority for player to execute:
   a. The first priority is for a player to have confidence in his own game.
   b. The second priority is to break down the opponent's game.

7. Coach's reaction to player and the coach's body language:
   a. Maintain confident body language on the side-

line and appear to be in control of the situation.
   b. Reinforce and confirm effort after loss of a point. Positive reaction to the player's hustle and effort when he loses a point keeps his confidence at a good level.
   c. No reaction after the player wins a point. This is often hard to do, but not reacting to good shots in the middle of a match keeps the player in balance to continue execution. Congratulations can be given after the match is over.
8. Other guidelines:
   a. Wait until after the first game of the next set to coach. There is usually too much emotion, high or low, for anything to make much sense immediately after a tough set.
   b. Do not upset MO or cause overreaction through untimely coaching. Ask yourself, "Is this exactly what I need, or is it a reaction to my emotions?" A few timely words are all that are usually needed.
   c. When in doubt, do something to change MO. When the player is definitely going to lose, if he continues in the same routine, try for a MO switch. Do not give up. The scoring system in tennis allows the chance of a MO switch at any point.

Figure 18-4. Use guidelines for on-court coaching.

On-Court Coaching—Sometimes You Have to Resort to Something Crazy

At the 1987 NCAA Tournament, I coached a doubles team of Craig Boynton and John Sullivan. They were playing a very tough first-round match against the number eight seed from Cal-Berkeley. Our team was explosive and capable of beating anyone on a given day.

Sullivan-Boynton jumped out to a quick lead and won the first set. The second set was a struggle, but they finally got a service break and went up on the team 5-3 in the second set, serving for the match. John Sullivan, a sophomore at the time, was very excited about being in his first NCAA event. He had played extremely well, but as it came time to serve the match out, I saw the signs of his pressing and the balance of pressure changing. I was certain that he was going to have a hard time with this service game. Sure enough, a double fault and an overhead into the net left the team down 0-30, and the match seemed to be changing. A missed volley and double fault later, and Boynton-Sullivan had just lost a love game. They crossed sides to receive serve, still leading 5-4, with a chance to win the match.

I recognized the shift in momentum and realized that the next three games would be lost very quickly unless something was done. I walked over and tried to talk to John and Craig, but they did not want to hear a thing I had to say. They brushed me off and said, "No problem, Coach. We have it under control." I said, "Guys, you really don't. You're pressing and you're really not doing the things you need to do." They replied, "No, coach, we're really fine, just leave us alone." As I got up to walk away, I realized my talk to them had been totally ineffective. I knew the next three games would be lost, and I knew the momentum switch would cause a quick third set to be lost also. I thought to myself, "There is no way I can walk away and let this happen."

At other times, I may have been more aggressive verbally and yelled at the players to shake them up. But this time I walked to Sullivan, picked up his water, and dumped half of it on his head. He turned around and gave me a long, silent stare and I said right then, "You guys played like crap that game, get yourselves in gear!" Sullivan kept looking at me in surprise and disbelief, and then he let out a laugh, and as he did it seemed that his whole body let go and relaxed. I walked off and stood about 50 yards away.

The California team had been ignited and played extremely well, but the most important thing that happened was that the Sullivan-Boynton team, so shocked at what I had done, maintained their level. Although they did not break serve, they arrived at 5-5 with their game and emotions intact and a good chance of winning the match in a tiebreaker or the third set. As it turned out, the match went to 6-6 and Boynton-Sullivan won a tough 7-5 tiebreaker.

Looking back, I am still surprised about the tactic I took, and I still do not know what motivated me to pour the water on John. I just knew I had to do something. In no way did I want to be degrading to a player or lessen his self-respect, but I figured there was no way in the world to get him out of his panic. The hope of any coach is to learn the best way to get a player's attention. When in doubt, it is better to do something than to do nothing at all and sit idly back and watch your players disintegrate because of their inability to keep the right balance of pressure on themselves throughout the match. I hope it can be a much more conventional and acceptable move than the one I used.

SUMMARY

There seems to be no harder job in coaching than getting individuals to function as a unit. In an individual sport such as tennis, the variables are many. A team of talented individuals cannot be successful, though, unless they bond together. The coach's job is to guide the individuals through many tough obstacles to accomplish goals and, little by little, bonding will take place.

Administering discipline, holding team practices, providing on-the-spot coaching, and working for the total development of each of the individuals are all details that are critically important. Although different methods and approaches may be used, the objective should be to allow each spoke of the team wheel to do his job to the best of his abilities.

CHAPTER 19

USE TIMELY POSITIVE AND NEGATIVE FEEDBACK

"Being behind someone means being there to kick him in the rear end as well as pat him on the back."
—Chuck Kriese

When to praise, when to criticize? We would all be great leaders, motivators, and coaches if we knew just when, where, and how to do each. For years the popular conception was that coaches gave only criticism and negative feedback to their athletes. Perhaps this is still true in the early part of a coach's career because it is usually easier to see what someone is doing wrong than knowing how to help him do it right. Since the 1960s, however, the use of positive feedback has increasingly become the rule rather than the exception for coaches, with the unfortunate result that, all too often, mediocrity has been rewarded and acceptable standards of performance have been lowered. This, in turn has brought about more mediocrity in our educational system, and, more dangerously, produced a nation of result-oriented rather than process-oriented people. Educators are now realizing that learning and growth do not occur from placing an emphasis on results, but rather from the process of working for a result.

So where is the balance between positive and negative feedback that a coach should use with his team? A coach should not beat down his players, nor should he reward mediocrity.

The following guidelines for the use of positive or negative feedback should prove effective. However, each situation is unique and may require special handling.

POSITIVE FEEDBACK

Positive Feedback Should be Used Before Competition

Before competition, positive feedback should be used exclusively. The day before or the day of competition is definitely the time to reinforce a player's strengths and emphasize the good points of his game. Overly analytical pre-match discussions of technique only serve to point out minor flaws that really cannot be corrected at such a late stage.

This realization should help the coach treat his player like the trainer treats the prize fighter. The coach should emphasize that the opponent will be tough but that his player is ready, sharp, and looking good. A player must respect his opponent, but at the same time he must have complete trust in his own strengths and skills. This is not a time for building the opponent's strengths in any way because discussion of the opponent's good points only makes him a tougher foe. Whatever the coach may be feeling, he should offer only positive reinforcement on game day and the day before.

Positive Feedback Should be Used Less at Practice Sessions than on Game Day

The practice session is the time to be a perfectionist with the athlete. At practice sessions, the coach should be picky when analyzing the athlete's game, and he should not accept anything but the top effort and performance from his athlete. The coach should be selective in the timing and amount of positive feedback he gives each athlete. Unlike pre-competition periods, practice sessions give the athlete time to regroup from this criticism and develop a tough exterior that will help him under match pressure. It is a good idea for the coach to let his players know that practice has to be the toughest time and that he will continually expect high intensity and an excellent performance. If the coach allows a weak performance in practice, he will get a weak performance in matches.

The ability to tell the athlete what he needs to hear and not what he wants to hear is an important one for the coach to acquire. This is tough to do because of the coach's very human need to be approved of and liked. From the outside it is easy to say, "Why isn't that coach tougher on his athletes, or why does he give in to all their whims?" The fact is, it is very hard to carry out the tough assignment that makes players unhappy, even though a coach's best coaching instincts tell him it's what they truly need. Players often look away, frown, grumble, or even walk away when the coach gives tough instructions. But the bottom line remains—the coach should have the athletes do what they need to do, not what they want to do. When these become the same, the coach is on the way to developing great players and a great team.

Figure 19-1. Use positive and negative feedback when appropriate.

Positive Feedback Should Not be Used for Mediocre Performances

What a coach praises in a player is usually the performance that the player will give the next time. It may be difficult for a coach not to get excited and praise any accomplishment of a team member, especially if that player is a low achiever. The coach must have a good perspective on what is truly a superior achievement for the individual as opposed to what is a mediocre achievement. This is hard to judge because what is mediocre for one athlete may be superior for another and vice versa.

The athlete himself is ready for any type of praise after a win, whether it is warranted or not. Again, what he needs and what he wants may be two completely different things. A coach's praise at the wrong time can make the athlete pleased and satisfied, whereas withholding a compliment at the wrong time may be discouraging for the athlete.

Neither the coach's need to give positive feedback nor the athlete's need to receive positive feedback should override what the athlete truly needs for his growth and development. Again, the coach's perception of what his player needs is the most important factor for productive use of positive reinforcement.

Positive Feedback Should be Used More with Less Experienced Players

Just as the newborn is sensitive to his new environment, so the rookie athlete is sensitive to his new situation. Veterans have tougher exteriors and are usually better able to handle the coach's criticism. Veterans also have a track record and the confidence to persevere through tough times. The young player will surely have obvious doubts from time to time. No matter how confident the rookie may appear, he will need positive feedback to make it through the initial tough times. The job of the coach is to help the young player get through this transition period without babying him along. The tough job is to be objective about successes, failures, and improvement areas, while giving as much sincere positive feedback as possible.

Positive Feedback Should be Used in the Presence of Others

To praise in public and criticize in private is one of the first rules of leadership. Sometimes a negative revealed to the athlete's peers can do a lot of harm. On the other hand, team meetings or other public occasions are excellent times to give sincere and truthful praise of a team member. People, especially young people, tend to express and develop the qualities that are affirmed in them. When affirmed in front of peers, positive affirmation has an even better effect.

Everyone works for and truly enjoys recognition. Positive recognition in the presence of others is an excellent coaching tool.

Positive Feedback Should be Used After a Loss

Positive reinforcement can be difficult to give when both the coach and the player are emotionally involved and if the match is an important one. Often the coach's disappointment is directed toward his player. This frustration surely needs to be vented, but the most available target is not always the best target. After a tough loss, the athlete and the coach need to have some time for their emotions to settle.

In almost all cases, the athlete who has diligently prepared for a competition will care enough to give 100 percent. He may have a tendency to withdraw energy when he is in a losing situation, but in more cases than not, if the athlete has trained hard, he will also play hard. It is a shame that so many people equate losing with a poor effort. The belief is that if someone tries hard enough, he will win. This is not always true, especially in a sport such as tennis in which creative skills, talent, and confidence are so important.

As difficult as it may be, the time after a loss is an excellent time for the coach to praise the positive aspects of the player and to help rebuild his confidence in his skills. No matter how self-assured the athlete may appear, inside he will be shaken up. To achieve his best performance, an athlete must find the balance between his confidence, trust, and belief in himself and his humility, respect for the opponent, and acceptance of his own shortcomings. When a tough loss or a great win upsets this balance, it is the coach's job to boost up the wounded ego or to bring down the high-flying ego.

Positive Feedback Should be Used Less Often After a Win

A player will not be short of pats on the back following a win. Parents, teammates, girlfriends, and friends will sing his praises. The compliment that comes from the coach always means the most, but it is not always essential for the coach to praise the athlete. A coach should point out the good things in the player's game, but the period after a win is an excellent time for him to be critical about things that need to be improved. The coach must be the judge of how much positive feedback to give. Sometimes a coach can slow the player's progress by over-rewarding what should be a routine success. Even an exciting and big win may be put in a different perspective by considering the player's total development. Early celebration and an abundance of praise may prevent the athlete from performing up to his capability his next time out. A football team has a week between games to go through the whole process of win—celebrate—come back down to earth—work hard—prepare for next ball game—take care of all pre-game details. The tennis player sometimes has only an hour or a day to go through this whole process. If he needs praise and celebration after a win, these must be short so that preparation for the next match can begin. In recognizing these facts, the coach should be very selective in his praise of a player immediately after a win. Credit should always be given, but the balance should be there as well.

Negative Feedback Should Not be Used Before Competition

If it has not been taken care of before you get to the battlefield, it probably is too late. There is no sense in pointing out the small wart on the pretty girl's face right before the beauty pageant. Pointing out flaws and weaknesses in a player's game before he takes the court does no good and can do a lot of harm. It would be like the manager of a boxer who says something like, "We should have worked more on your left jab before the fight. I hope it will hold up," or the coach at the Super Bowl who says "We've got to hope they don't throw the ball a lot, our secondary just isn't ready."

Pre-match tension is enough to cause the athlete to have some doubt. This is the time for the coach to say, "We're ready, the hay's in the barn, and the horses are at the gate. It's exciting to play today, and your game looks sharp," just like the boxing manager who says, "You're fit, you're fast, you're sharp, and there's none better."

Negative Feedback Should be Used After Competition

Nothing said in the way of criticism immediately after a match will work positively. After a loss the player is so scared and vulnerable that it will probably only do harm to point out his flaws. The best thing for the coach to do is to wait until the emotion of the situation has settled and then talk to the athlete. Specific points should be made in a constructive manner and in a way that does not attack the player's own self-concept. If there is enough time, the day following the match is the best time to point out flaws and weaknesses in the player's game. If there is not enough time, the coach should wait at least for an hour or so to let the emotions settle.

NEGATIVE FEEDBACK

A good example of negative feedback is the stereotype of a drill sergeant who never gives praise and continually berates his recruits' confidence and self-image. Although the drill sergeant's approach is appropriate for the needs of military recruits, badgering or belittling does little good for athletes, but timely use of negative reinforcement can greatly help them. How to use it, when to use it, and which players to use it on are keys to its effectiveness.

Negative Feedback Works Well in Practice

Practice is the time to expect and to get perfection. Since there is no opponent to supply pressure, the coach should provide it. In the pressure-free environment of practice, play can appear to be good without really being good. Great coaches nitpick in practice so that, in a match situation when real pressure exists, the player can execute.

USE TIMELY POSITIVE AND NEGATIVE FEEDBACK

It is easy for a coach to be lulled into a false sense of security because his team performs well in a practice situation when there is no pressure. A good rule of thumb for the coach is to be very fired up and emotional, always expecting perfection during practice sessions. On game day he should be more relaxed and accepting, and allow his players' creative juices to flow. Ideally, practice days should contain repetitive, obsessive work, and each athlete should be pushed hard by himself or his coach. Match days should be easier, and the coach should cultivate a creative and inspired atmosphere that allows the creative and inner talents of each athlete to surface.

Negative Feedback Should be Used More with the Older Team Members

The veterans of the team are more resilient and tough and can best handle negative reinforcement from the coach. Familiarity with the coach's methods prevents the older athlete's confidence from being damaged as easily as the younger athlete's. It is a tough job for the coach to always get maximum effort from an older member of the team. Motivation provided by the coach in the early part of a player's career must lead ultimately to an inner motivation on the part of the athlete. A good method of keeping motivation is to give responsibility to the junior or senior team member. With this added responsibility, the team member senses trust from the coach and will better understand the coach's negative feedback and tough criticism of the weak areas in his game.

Negative Feedback Should be Done in Private

"Don't hang out your dirty wash in public" as the saying goes. The rule to praise in public and criticize in private can once again be applied. People tend to become what we label them. Scolding or criticism of a player should be done in the office or in another private area. This allows the athlete to avoid being put in a defensive position in front of his peers, and it preserves his ego and self-esteem. In a disciplinary situation, the privacy of an office allows the athlete a chance to state his opinion and to get things off his chest. In front of a team this might not be appropriate and might make the coach defensive. Coach-player confrontations that occur in front of the team will (and must) be won by the coach because he has the designated power and authority. Often a situation that could have been taken care of in the privacy of an office is allowed to escalate when handled in front of others.

Negative Feedback Can be Used After a Win

The time immediately following a win is an excellent time to critique and be picky about your player and his tennis game. The player is probably flying high and, once again, one of the coach's jobs is to bring his player's emotions down to a workable level. The performance, and not necessarily the win or loss, is what should be analyzed.

After a win, a coach may have a tendency to praise the athlete and to feed that emotion that the athlete wants fed. But if winning is a chance for growth and confidence building, the coach must be objective enough to reward or punish the player's performance and not just the result.

Good Judgment Should be Used in Giving Negative Feedback After a Loss

This is a delicate situation, because the athlete is already vulnerable and sensitive. If his game is criticized, it must be done in an objective manner. Again, it is best to wait until the emotion of the situation has settled.

Once again, the older members of the team are better equipped than the younger members to handle criticism following a loss. The coach must use good judgment and timing in the use of negative reinforcement after a loss.

When Using Negative Feedback, Always Build the Player Back Up Before Dismissing Him

Just as a surgeon never performs an operation without closing the incision, so a coach should never punish, criticize, or overly critique an athlete without building him up again. A good method is to say something like, "Your actions stink, and I expect more out of you. This is not up to your standards and quality. You really messed this job up, but I believe in you and know that you will get the situation corrected." Or, "The team and I want you on this team because of your good qualities, and I know you will be able to handle this tough situation." Ideally, the action and the person can be separated, and the player can leave with his self-esteem intact, knowing what he has to correct.

LONG-RANGE MOTIVATION FOR PLAYER DEVELOPMENT

Affirmation is the key word in confidence development. Ultimately, a coach's trust and belief in his players as people and athletes will overcome any short-term ups and downs that occur. In the four years that a coach works with a player, immediate positive and negative reinforcement must take place and, in addition, the overriding tone and the underlying current provided by the coach must be filled with trust and confidence.

Just as the player must believe in the coach, so must the coach believe unconditionally in the player. The player usually accomplishes what the coach expects him to accomplish. He seldom accomplishes more, and he usually accomplished less. Positive affirmation of positive qualities and acceptance of those qualities that cannot be changed must be the long-term goal for the coach.

THE COACH'S CONFIDENCE IN HIS PLAYERS

There are some players a coach finds it easy to have confidence in and others with whom it's more difficult. But, sooner or later, there comes a critical point when a coach has to let go of the reins completely and say to the player, "You're on your own." As mentioned earlier, it is like training a thoroughbred racehorse. First, you pull the reins tight in order to get the stallion to move in the direction you want. Little by little, you let go of the reins until at some point you drop them completely and let him run. If you hadn't been strict and pulled the reins tight at first, the stallion would do whatever he wanted and react only on instinct.

Like thoroughbred racehorses, the best athletes need to have their energies directed positively. Emotion plays a big part in the development of a lot of top athletes. The coach must discern the direction the athlete needs to go in and give him guidance. Some athletes never seem mature enough to allow the coach to give up the reins completely. Usually these are the quiet or shy athletes who look as if their confidence is always close to breaking.

During the 1980 season, I had a player named Dick Milford who was our number six player and played number three doubles. At this point in my career, Clemson had never won the conference championship and we had just moved into a national ranking for the first time in the history of the school. My tendency then as a coach was to be tentative and calculate all moves so that we would not lose what we had gained. Dick's junior year had been difficult—he had had a lot of trouble with self-confidence, and some of the other players on the team had started to lose confidence in him as well. After a player's first year or so, when the initial enthusiasm of being a college athlete has worn off, he will often go through a slump.

Dick's slump started his junior year and went on for eight or nine months. Both he and I had worked very hard in overcoming the trouble he was having and in trying to pull him out of his slump. It was truly not a matter of hard work, though, because Dick was one of the hardest workers I have ever had on a team.

I learned a great lesson about having confidence in a player during an early February tournament in Arkansas, in a match against Brigham Young University. We were down in a team match 4-2 after singles, and when doubles play started it looked as if we had a good chance of making the match a close one. We then won number one and number two doubles. The entire team match came down to the number three doubles match, in which I really felt we were outmatched.

Dick's partner was a player named Mitch Mitchell, and they were totally dominated in the first set 6-2. As the second set started, I knew the only chance we had was to play much more aggressively. Dick usually chipped all of his returns, making it easy for the other team to gain control of the point. Early in the second set, I walked to the court and told Dick to hit out on the ball aggressively even if the balls went into the fence. If we were going to lose, I wanted us to lose with aggressive mistakes and not by trying to place every ball. Mitch Mitchell played the ad court and almost never missed a return of serve, thereby allowing us to take this gamble in the deuce court. Dick followed my instructions and hit the first two balls into the backstop, but I kept insisting that he hit out on the ball. Somehow, Dick finally connected with a few balls, and the change of play and his aggressiveness got us back into the match. At 5-5 of the second set we got a service break and held on to serve out the set.

In the third set our team made some early mistakes and got behind 4-2. The BYU team went ahead 5-3 and we held serve to make it 5-4. On the next return game, with no ad scoring, it came down to a single point, which we won to make it 5-5. I, of course, instructed Mitch to take the sudden death point, and he made a fine return. Then at 6-6, we went into a tiebreaker. At that time we played nine-point tiebreakers, which meant that at 4-4, one point decided the whole match. Dick's play had been sporadic. Sometimes he made contact with the ball, sometimes he didn't, so the safe play was to allow Mitch to take the 4-4 point if we got to it. The BYU team served to make the score 4-3 with two more serves coming up. Mitch made a fine return to make the score 4-4. Six hours of a very tough team match had come down to a single point. The suspense was both exciting and terrifying.

The obvious coaching decision at this point was to have Mitch take the return. I knew he would put the ball in the court, and I knew he would put tremendous pressure on the serving team by returning the serve. This was the calculated and best play. But there were other considerations in the decision that I had to make. One was our best opportunity to win the team match. But I also knew that Dick had been struggling with his confidence for some time. I knew that if Mitch made the return, winning or losing the point, Dick would be in the same dilemma in future matches. I knew what I had to do if I truly cared for Dick's development. Both players looked up at me and said, "Who should take it?" Without hesitation, I said, "Dick, you take the return." He looked at me in surprise and then turned around and looked to where the rest of the team was sitting. As he did so, the team stood up and cheered for him saying, "Go Dick! Do it, Dick!" Then I saw a big smile come across his face and saw any fear he might have had turn into courage. He spread his legs wide and got a good base as he readied to return serve. Although Dick had been hitting out on his return the entire match and had done fairly well, I felt that at this point he should go with his bread and butter and what he did best. I called from the stands, "Dick, chip and charge the way you like to do it." I had not let him chip a ball the other two sets and now I was asking him to do it at the biggest point of the match and probably the biggest point of his career. Dick had been chipping and charging for the ten years he had been playing tennis, and he seemed confident that he would make the return.

The BYU player missed the first serve, which made it easier for Dick to chip and charge on the second. The second serve bounced up high on Dick's backhand. Dick sliced from high to low to put the ball down at the server's feet and closed off the net. The server made a good first volley but Dick was already on top of the net, and he drilled a volley between the players for the match win.

I have never had a more exciting moment as a coach. The players cleared out of the stands and grabbed Dick into their arms. I was thrilled not only with Dick but also that I had elected to go with the boy's confidence and the thing that would be better for his growth. It is something I have always remembered, and any time I've been in a similar situation, I've always gone with the decision that was important for the growth of the player. The wins, I feel, will always take care of themselves. The players have few such growth opportunities.

Four more times in that season (the best season in the history of Clemson tennis), the team match came down to Dick's match. One was against Georgia in Athens, and Dick hit the shot that let us beat the Bulldogs for the first time in over 10 years. Another was our first NCAA Tournament victory over Princeton, in a dramatic come-from-behind match, that we won with another 7-6 in the third. In each of these, when the match got close, Dick played aggressively, assertively, and without fear. I know for a fact that if I had not given him the chance to return serve and win that team match, not only would his game not have come around that season, but our team may not have also. Perhaps even the Clemson tennis program would have been delayed in becoming a nationally recognized program for a year or two more.

Later, after Dick's graduation, I received a letter from him that meant more to me than just about any letter I have ever received from a player. It talked about my trust in the players, and how I set high expectations for them, and how even though we had not won the national championship his senior year, in the end, there was not one member of the team who truly did not believe that the team could accomplish such a goal. He stated that it was truly amazing that a group of guys who started out in last place in the conference as freshmen had accomplished so much. The team had experienced a great victory in the tremendous growth that the team members had made.

SUMMARY

The coach's use of positive and negative feedback in the proper manner and with the proper timing is critical to a player's growth. Immediate feedback is essential, and the coach should try to incorporate positive and negative feedback in his daily work with his players. When mistakes are made, they should be made with sincerity and with the right purpose in mind. These will be interpreted in the right way by the team members even if what the coach does is not exactly the right thing. In many ways the wrong action is better than no action.

A coach's belief in, and affirmation of, positive traits in the athlete is the only way for a player to develop long-term confidence. The coach's trust must exist through good times and bad.

CHAPTER 20

TRAIN YOUR TEAM'S DOUBLES SKILLS

"Be a go-giver as well as a go-getter."
—Anonymous

In team tennis, doubles becomes one of the focal points of concern in the training routine. Most of the pressure of a team match is in doubles because the climax of the match usually occurs there. The whole point is to arrive at the season finale with three well-tuned teams.

In college tennis, players keep the same partner for two to three years. In the junior ranks, and also in the pro ranks, players often switch partners and doubles routines because of the logistics of different schedules and because of the many different training sites. Regardless of whether your partner is a regular one or not, most of the same basic principles for good doubles play still apply.

With four people instead of two to cover just a bit more court than in a singles match, the doubles match relies more heavily on court positioning than on shot making. Shot making seems to be of greater importance in singles play because there a player can be forced off balance and out of position much more easily. In singles, the court position to shot making ratio could be rated at about 65 percent to 35 percent; in doubles it is probably just the opposite: 35 percent to 65 percent.

The doubles game is also more repetitive than singles, and the doubles player finds himself playing the same type of point again and again, whereas in

Figure 20-1. The doubles match relies more heavily on court positioning than on shot making.

singles it often seems that no two points are the same. Playing good doubles, then, is a matter of taking care of fundamentals over and over while being flexible enough to make a subtle change when needed.

The coach's first task is to teach his players their specific jobs and responsibilities at each position they play on the court. Each player will play about one fourth of his points as the server's partner, and one fourth of his points as the receiver's partner. If each player knows his responsibility at each position, the doubles match can be played with much more confidence.

The specific jobs of server, server's partner, receiver, and receiver's partner should be worked on at every doubles practice until players understand them and can effectively carry them out. They are the fundamentals for playing doubles effectively and if learned well, establish a firm foundation that can be built upon.

THE FUNDAMENTAL POSITIONS: THE SERVER, RECEIVER, SERVER'S PARTNER, AND RECEIVER'S PARTNER

Server and Receiver Fundamentals

The positions of server and receiver must be played well for a doubles team to be effective. It is critical that the server master the fundamentals of a good second serve and a solid first volley. Equally important is a solid crosscourt return for the receiver. These skills are so important and basic that I spend the first two months of the fall season playing one versus one (invisible partner doubles), or crosscourt serve and volley matches where records are kept and results used to rank the players for later doubles pairings. Also, the players are only allowed one serve, which helps them learn an effective second serve under pressure. The players get tired of playing the same crosscourt game over and over, but after the second month they are skilled at second serves, first volleys, crosscourt returns, and quick volleys. Figure 20-2 shows the boundaries for these games. (My thanks to James Wadley, tennis coach at Oklahoma State University, for helping me to establish this approach to teaching doubles.)

Figure 20-2. Boundaries for half-court serve and volley games.

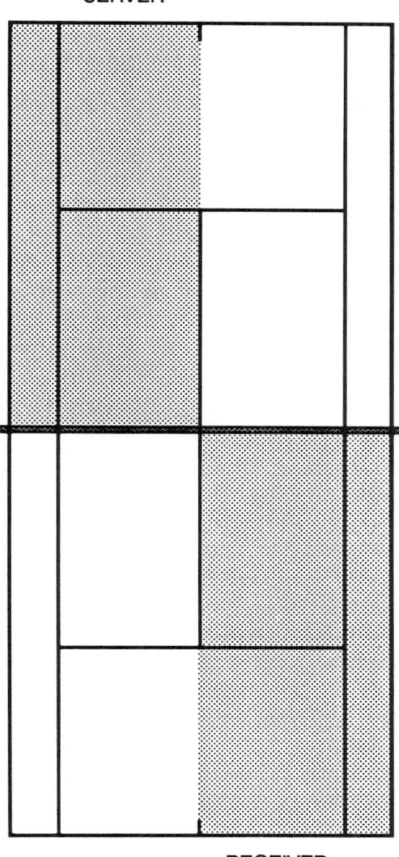

THE SERVER'S JOBS

Job One: Make the First Serve

This is the most basic job because the receiver naturally thinks defensively on the first serve, whereas on the second serve he thinks offensively. A big first serve about once a game works well to keep the receivers off balance and out of a groove, but a high percentage of first serves is critical to be successful.

Job Two: Serve to the Middle of the Deuce Court and to the Player's Body in the Ad Court

The angle of possible return that the receiver has is critical to holding serve effectively in doubles. A wide serve opens up the court for the receiver to hit a sharp angle back or to go down the alley past the net man. In the deuce court, a serve to the backhand or the middle of the court keeps the court closed and allows the net man to poach effectively to help the server hold serve. SD on Figure 20-3 shows the best place to serve in the deuce court. In the ad court, the server may be concerned with a serve to the middle because the receiver gets to hit a forehand. A serve wide to the backhand still makes the alley vulnerable, and it allows a sharp angle crosscourt return. For the best serve into the ad court, the server should aim at the receiver's left leg to deliver a ball into his body. The angles are kept close, and the receiver's stroke is jammed. A wide serve can be used effectively, but it must be used with the right timing. Even though some aces will be hit, in doubles even more than in singles, the purpose of the serve is to set up the second shot. Smart placement of the serve makes holding serve much easier (SA on Figure 20-3).

Figure 20-3

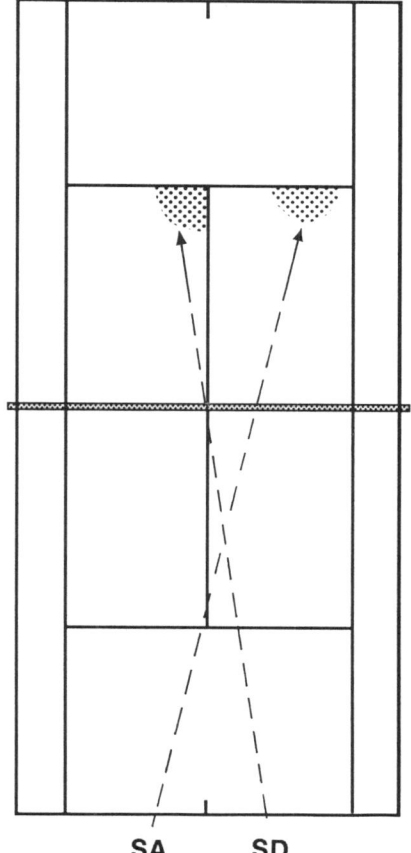

Job Three: The First Volley Should go Down the Middle

For the same reasons that a wide serve should not be used very often, so the first volley should not be angled unless it can be hit for a winner.

A first volley to the middle again keeps the angles closed and prevents the receiving team from making an offensive shot. If the first volley is close enough to the middle of the court, the receiver will probably lob, which is what two players who are on the net would favor (see Figure 20-4).

Figure 20-4

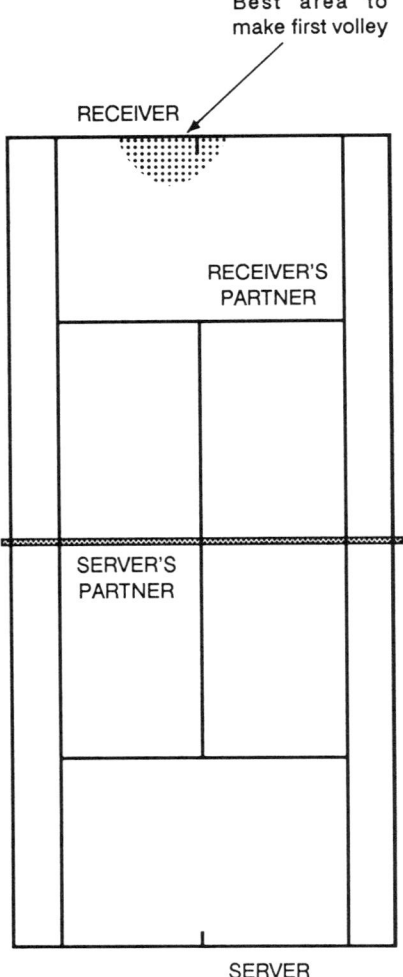

Job Four: Move in as Close to the Net as Possible to Make the First Volley

The difference between hitting an offensive or a defensive first volley is the server's positioning close to the net. An offensive or put-away volley is possible on high returns if the server can move in quickly. A low ball will have to be dealt with more conservatively.

Job Five: The Server Should Assume Responsibility for all First Volleys

Miscommunication between the server and partner is often what causes a break of serve. The most common scenario is when the server's partner starts to poach on a floating ball at the net and then changes his mind, leaving the server unready to make the volley and upset at his partner for not taking the ball. This only has to happen once for the server's partner to become either tentative or overly aggressive the next time in trying to make things happen. Miscommunication can be prevented with the rule that unless a planned poach is called, the server is responsible for all first volleys. If the server's partner rushes across with a swing and a miss, the server still backs him up. This allows the poacher at the net total freedom to move on any ball that floats, making him a significant threat. The server is the backup man, and his partner is the cutoff man. The partner should cut off any ball that he can reach, but if he cannot hit a solid volley, he should allow the server to play the first volley. When the server knows that he is responsible for all first volleys, he is able to put the right amount of pressure on himself to allow him to hold serve a bit easier.

Job Six: Use the I Formation for Change-up

The I Formation (sometimes called the Australian Formation) can be used as an excellent tactic when a receiver is in a groove and not missing any returns. Even if this formation does not make him miss returns, it will at least change his groove and perhaps change the flow of the returning team's confidence. The I Formation forces the receiving team to change the direction of the ball on the return in order to go down the line instead of crosscourt. This changing of direction usually causes errors on the service return.

Figure 20-5. The I Formation

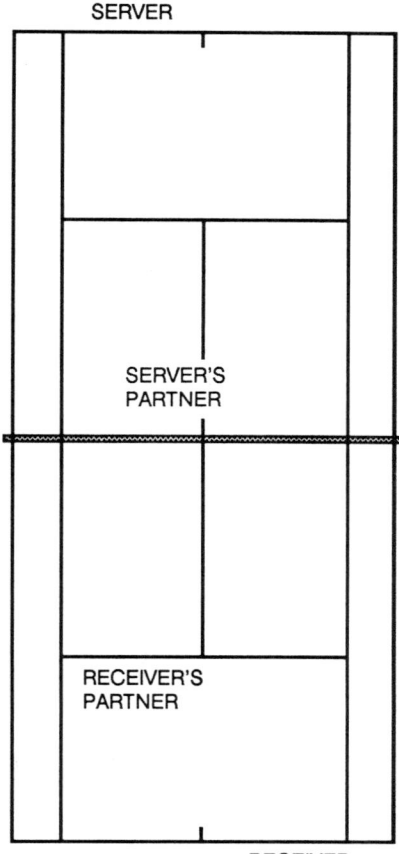

One seldom-noticed advantage of the I Formation is its ability to handcuff the receiver's partner and prevent him from making any poaches. It works very well to take away this element of a receiving team.

A good idea on service placement is to realize that a wide serve allows the receiver angles to hook the ball down the line, pinning the net man down. The serve to the opponent's body is best, but the serve to the middle of the court can work well also. The I Formation should be practiced often so that the doubles team is comfortable with it in pressure situations.

THE RECEIVER'S JOBS

Job One: No Returns Wide or in the Net

This is the only what-not-to-do in this section, and it acts as a reminder that the return should be hit over the net and through the opponents. It is a good idea for the receiver to completely block the poacher out of his mind as if he were invisible or nonexistent. It is best not to change directions on the return, as this reduces the percentages for an error (see the section on transition shots in Chapter 6). The rule is basic, but it should be ingrained in the player's subconscious. A ball hit wide or in the net is an immediate loss of the point and the mortal sin of a returner. Most returning errors in doubles are a result of pressing or trying to make the shot be too good. The player's "regular stuff" is good enough, as long as the rule "No balls wide, no balls in the net" is followed.

Job Two: Determine which Formation to Use and which Play to Run

Option One: Move into the net behind a weak serve. Controlling the net is a big advantage in doubles, and when a receiver can take the net away from the serving team, it becomes easier to break serve. The return does not have to be hit hard, only deep into the court so the point can be won on the next volley. If the serve is weak, the receiver's partner must be sure to move in also.

Option Two: Return low at the server's feet, allowing the returner's partner to cross for a winning poach. This is an advanced play that can be used effectively with the combination of a good returner and a good volleyer as the receiver's partner. The idea is to hit low and aggressive returns that will force the server to pop the first volley up. The receiver's partner can be intimidating to the server by leading him to press and make errors at critical times in the match.

Option Three: Play both players on the receiving team back and try to take the net off the first weak ball. Dan Magill, tennis coach at the University of Georgia, uses this formation exclusively, and until my team was defeated by his team's use of this style at the 1986 NCAA Championships, I would seldom use it. The objective is to take a bit of pressure off the receiver in having him make a great crosscourt return every time. With two players back, the serving team has a tough job to put away the first volley. As soon as the first volley is made, the receiving team hits through the serving team until the serving team pop up an easy ball that makes for an easy winner for the receiving team. The offensive top spin lob is also thrown in to keep the serving team from closing the net too tight. Of course, the serving team gets its share of winners, but also make many errors from being forced to handle so many volleys. This formation does take practice, but if mastered it can beat any opponents who are not good volleyers. The best doubles teams, though, will usually beat a defensive doubles team which uses this both-players-back formation. Top-flight doubles is won at the net and players should definitely learn offensive tactics as well. The optimum would be to use the both-players-back receiving formation at strategic times. The coach's job is to judge the ability levels of his players and to decide which formations to use.

THE SERVER'S PARTNER'S JOBS

Job One: Direct the Server's Placement of his Serve

Much as a catcher does in baseball, the net man can give a signal that dictates the type or the placement of the serve. This is a very simple combination that works well in holding serve. If the server is directed to serve to the middle, then his partner knows to move a step toward the middle with or without the fake of a poach. There are other combinations that can also be used.

Directing the serve with signals works better than calling poaches with signals because once the poach is called, the net man is forced to cross even if the server has hit a poor serve. When the server's placement is planned, the server's partner can watch for that specific serve and react accordingly. Poaches can still be planned, but it is recommended that they be called verbally so as not to have any mistake in communication. To be effective, signals must be kept simple and specific.

Job Two: The Starting Position Should be a Step Farther Back with Weight on the Inside Foot

The starting position should be a position that allows the net man to be able to move quickly on any floating ball. The weight should be on the inside foot, and the net man should position himself a step or two farther back to be able to lean in as the receiver makes contact with the ball.

Job Three: Move for a Poach on all Floating Balls

An important key to holding serve more easily is for the net man to move on any ball that floats. This aggressive play will often take the receiver's concentration off making a solid return and help score many points for the serving team. If the server's partner is tentative and does not move, the receiver has a great opportunity to get into an excellent groove on his return. The already stated rule for the server's assuming responsibility for every first volley allows the net man great freedom to be aggressive in the hunt of floating balls.

Job Four: Poach with Lateral Movement

Poaching with sideways or lateral movement gives the net man good balance for reaction to a ball that may be hit behind him or in an awkward position. The poacher often makes the mistake of running through a poach out of balance instead of moving laterally for the poach.

Job Five: Stay Aggressive at the Net

The server's partner should not stand still, but should either fake or cross. His job at the net is to distract the concentration of the receiver through his aggressive play. This helps his partner tremendously in holding serve. Even making eye contact with the receiver can sometimes help tremendously. He should look for, and poach on, any floaters. If nothing else, he should draw fire from the receiver. Holding service is always done with the help of a good partner at the net. He should stay active and make things happen.

THE RECEIVER'S PARTNER'S JOBS

Many players do not recognize the importance of the receiver's partner. But, if this position is played well, it can be the game breaker and the difference between a good or a great doubles team. The receiver's partner has specific jobs in helping to break service.

Job One: Start at the Service Line and Square Off Facing the Server's Partner

If the receiver's partner is at the service line, it will:

1. Allow him to help make the service line call.
2. Put him in a position out of the way of the return of serve.
3. Most importantly, give him an opportunity to react to a poach that the net man may make.

The primary reason for squaring off toward the net man is that the net man has the first play on the ball after the return. Therefore, the receiver's partner's attention should be focused on this position, allowing the best opportunity to negate a poach through the middle. Once the ball has been returned past the net man, the receiver's partner should then take care of his next job.

Job Two: Take Three Steps to Close Off the Net

Immediately after the ball is returned past the net man, the receiver's partner should take three steps straight in to close off the net. This puts pressure on the server's first volley and allows the receiving team to take advantage of a good return of service. Staying at the service line and not moving in does nothing except to put the receiving team in a crippled situation.

Job Three: Inside-Inside or Outside-Outside Coverage

Once the receiver's partner has closed off the position on the net, his other attentions should be directed to the server's first volley. If the ball is returned low and to the inside of the court, the receiver's partner should move to the inside lane to cut off the first volley. This puts tremendous pressure on the server's first volley. The server can try to hook a backhand volley from the inside to the outside behind the poaching receiver's partner. This will force the server to change the direction of his first volley that will very often lead to the serving team's errors at critical times in the match. If the receiver's return goes to the outside or the server's forehand, the outside or line must always be covered.

Job Four: Play Both Back for a Change-up or a Different Look

As explained earlier, it is often a good tactic to play both back for a different look to the servers. This should be done at strategic times according to the type of pressure the serving team needs to have put on them.

WORKING AS A TEAM IN DOUBLES

How to Pick a Partner

Before choosing a partner, it is important to understand what makes a good doubles team. There are countless examples in the professional ranks of two fairly good players who, when combined, make a great team. A good doubles team should be put together with a player who can attack and put balls away (the hitter) and a partner who makes few or no errors (the setter). The setter allows the hitter to do his work, and the hitter provides the element of recklessness and aggression that the setter cannot. Two setters together would fall prey to a more aggressive or a more consistent team, whereas two hitters on the same team would be hot or cold, either scoring great wins or very bad losses. The combination of a good hitter and a good setter works well if the two players get along with each other.

The temperaments and personalities of the doubles partners should complement each other in the same way that the game styles do. Two aggressive personalities do not work well together because they may end up fighting. Two passive personalities usually cannot make up their minds. Although neither personality must be overbearing, a comfortable mesh between them works well.

Figure 20-6. The personalities of doubles partners should complement each other.

WHO PLAYS WHICH COURT?

The decision of who should play the ad court and who should play the deuce court is based on who returns best in each court. Another important factor to consider is that the best returner should play the ad court, since that is where most of the big points are played. With the exception of the 40-15 and the 15-40, games are always won or lost in the ad court. Positioning the better returner in the ad court helps very much in keeping the pressure on a serving team that leads to a service break.

WHAT ABOUT A LEFT-HANDER?

A left-hander on a team usually adds a good dimension to the team's effectiveness. The left-hander's shots provide different spins and variety for the opponents.

Although some teams prefer to have a lefty play the ad court for crosscourt returns, my preference is that the lefty play the deuce court, allowing both player's forehands to be in the middle for ground strokes and for poaching. Of course, both players must be able to handle the wide serve to the backhand well.

MOVEMENT AND TRACKING FOR THE DOUBLES TEAM

It is often said that two players moving well as a doubles team appear as if they are connected invisibly as they flow in unison from side to side and up and back.

The Inside-Inside/Outside-Outside Rule for Tracking

Tracking, or the ability to cover the opponent's possible shots at the net, can be done effectively by following the rules of inside-inside/outside-outside for your doubles team. The rules are that if your shot goes to the outside (your opponent's forehand in the deuce court or your opponent's backhand in the ad court), you or your partner must cover the outside shot possibility with the other player moving to cover the middle lane. The sharp crosscourt angle is not the priority because it is such a difficult shot to make. This outside-outside rule should force the opponents into trying this type of low percentage shot.

The rule for shots to the inside, or the middle of the court, is that both you and your partner lean to the middle for the main coverage with less attention given to the shot from the middle of the court to the outside. Figures 20-7 and 20-8 show inside-inside/outside-outside coverage at the net:

Figure 20-7. Inside-inside coverage on a ball to the middle.

Figure 20-8. Outside-outside coverage on a ball hit wide.

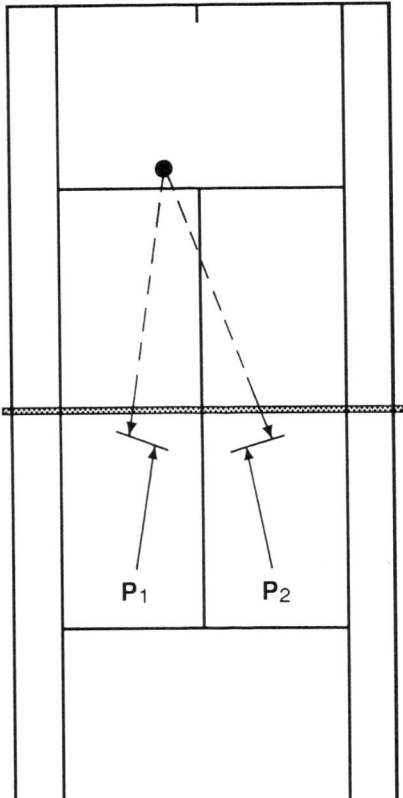

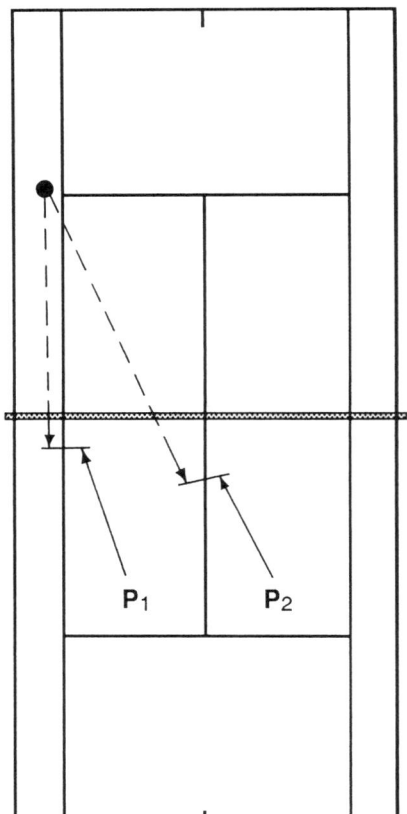

These same rules apply to any situation when a player and his partner are at the net. Drills should be done with two up and two back, or all four players up, to practice good teamwork in tracking and coverage.

OTHER QUICK REMINDERS ABOUT EFFECTIVE DOUBLES PLAY

1. Control the net and you will control the match. This is almost always true. With two players covering shots, it is hard to put balls away or to be effective without taking the net. Work as a team on closing off the net.

2. Go down the line or down the middle to set up your partner. A crosscourt shot from the baseline against two net men is like a shooting gallery for the team on the net. A down-the-line or down-the-middle shot, if kept low, will usually set up a player's partner.

3. Good positioning, not great shots, wins most often in doubles.

4. Hit to the middle of the court on any ball that cannot be angled off for a winner. Remember that an angled shot opens the court up for your opponent's offensive shot.

5. Hit through your opponents, not around them. This simply means that good doubles teams do not go for great shots but keep angles closed while working to gain better positioning on the net.

6. MOVE, MOVE, MOVE, AND CLOSE, CLOSE, CLOSE for better court positioning.

SUMMARY

Figure 20-9. Doubles play—your role at each position.

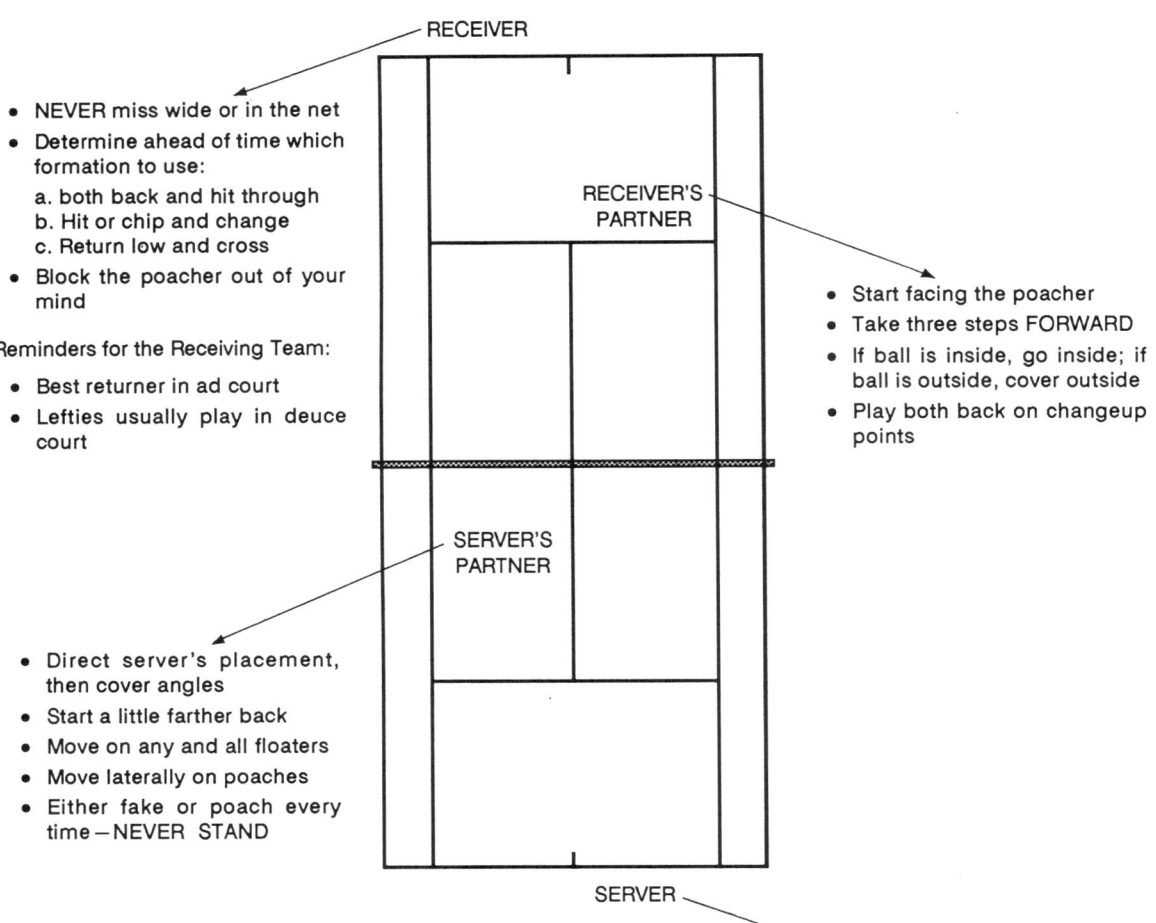

- NEVER miss wide or in the net
- Determine ahead of time which formation to use:
  a. both back and hit through
  b. Hit or chip and change
  c. Return low and cross
- Block the poacher out of your mind

Reminders for the Receiving Team:
- Best returner in ad court
- Lefties usually play in deuce court

- Start facing the poacher
- Take three steps FORWARD
- If ball is inside, go inside; if ball is outside, cover outside
- Play both back on changeup points

- Direct server's placement, then cover angles
- Start a little farther back
- Move on any and all floaters
- Move laterally on poaches
- Either fake or poach every time—NEVER STAND

- Make high percentage of first serves; hit an agressive serve two times per game
- Serve down the middle, and ad court into body
- First volley deep to middle
- Get one step farther in to volley
- It's the server's responsibility to make all first volleys
- Use the I formation of changeup

Reminders:
- Control the net and control the match—be one step closer
- Do not go crosscourt from backcourt. Use the middle of the court to set up the point
- Setter in ad court; hitter in deuce court
- Good positioning, not great shots, wins in doubles play
- MOVE, MOVE, MOVE—CLOSE, CLOSE, CLOSE
- Use the middle on any ball that you cannot end the point on
- Hit through your opponents, not around them

CHAPTER 21

USE EFFECTIVE DRILLS TO SHARPEN YOUR TEAM'S SKILLS

"Either you're green and growing, or you're ripe and rotting."

—Don Keller, guidance counselor, Clemson University

THE CONCEPT OF DRILL WORK

Drills help a player learn new skills and shots that would be difficult to learn by just playing sets. These shots can be developed and grooved until the player is ready to incorporate them into his game and tool box of skills.

In order for a drill to be effective, it must simulate as closely as possible the shots or situations that occur in a match. The most sophisticated drills do not have merit unless they prepare the individual for the situation he will be in under the pressure of competition. Drills should be simple and specific, and each player should know what he is trying to accomplish.

There are six groups of drills in this section:

1. Feeding drills—important for basic stroke development
2. Breakdown or one-on-one rallying drills—for practicing not changing the direction of the ball
3. Two-on-one drills—for practicing changing the direction of the ball
4. Match simulation drills
5. Serving drills
6. Simulated set play

1. FEEDING DRILLS

Feeding drills have the most benefit when a skill is first being learned. The primary purpose of feeding drills is to allow the player to groove a particular stroke or shot, and this is done by having the coach feed balls to a particular area of the court for the player to make return shots. The coach should try to feed balls with a variety of spins and placement so that the player learns to handle balls of various degrees of difficulty. Although feeding drills do instill confidence, it is quite difficult to simulate the same spins, power, and rhythm that occur in a game rally. Each feeding drill should be repeated anywhere from eight to 12 times, depending on the player's fitness and ability.

A feeding drill.

1. Wide-Middle Forehand Drill

Objective: To work on wide forehands and forehands from the middle position. The major emphasis is on improving movement and setting up for the forehand from any position on the court.

Description: Standing just behind the service line, the coach (C) feeds a balls deep and wide to the forehand side (1), making the player (P) stretch to return it. The coach then feeds a ball to the middle (2) so the player has to move very quickly in recovering to the middle to hit a forehand. The coach continues hitting balls wide (3) and to the middle (4), mixing up the feeds. He should also feed balls to the backhand corner so that the player can hit inside-out forehands.

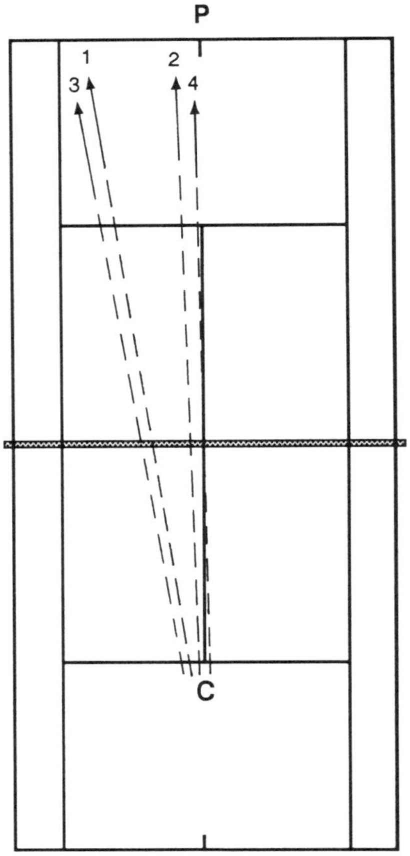

2. Wide-Middle Backhand Drill

Objective: To work on wide backhands and backhands from the middle of the court, with the major emphasis on the player's movement and balance in setting up for the shot.

Description: The coach (C) stands behind the service line and feeds a ball wide to the backhand side (1) so the player (P) has to stretch to return it. The coach then feeds a ball to the middle of the court (2), forcing the player to back up into a position to make this backhand shot. The coach continues to hit balls wide (4) and to the middle (3) of the backhand side. As the player becomes more proficient in setting up for each shot, the coach should also feed balls to the forehand side of the court to force the player to develop even better court movement in setting up for balance.

Figure 21-1

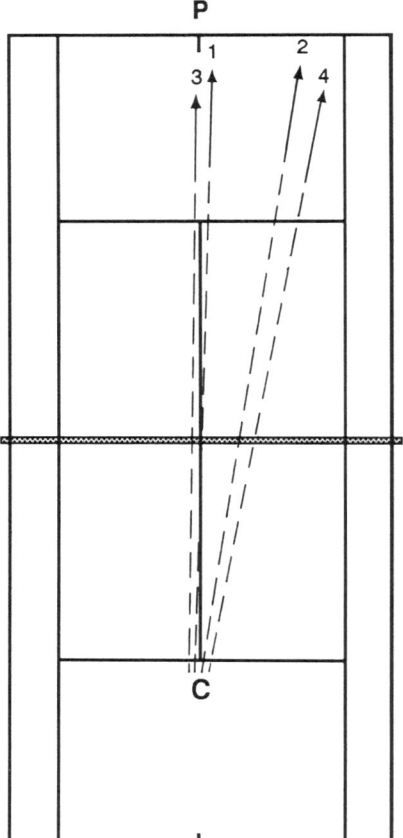

Figure 21-2

3. Wide-Middle Volley Drill (Forehand and Backhand)

Objective: To work on stretch volleys and volleys from the middle position. The improvement of movement and balance is emphasized.

Description: The coach (C) feeds balls alternately wide and to the middle of the deuce court, forcing the player (P) to stretch for a wide ball (1 and 3) and then recover to the middle for a cramped volley (2 and 4). The drill should also be performed with the player in the ad court so he can work on his backhand volley.

4. Stretch Ground Stroke Drill

Objective: To groove the forehand and backhand while working on footwork and lateral movement.

Description: The coach (C) stands behind the service line and feeds a wide ball to the forehand side of the backcourt (1). The player (P) moves from the center of the backcourt to return the ball, and then recovers to the middle by using good lateral footwork. The coach then feeds the player another wide ball to the forehand side (2) and continues the drill with two consecutive feeds to the backhand side (3 and 4). The player should aim his returns either crosscourt or down the line.

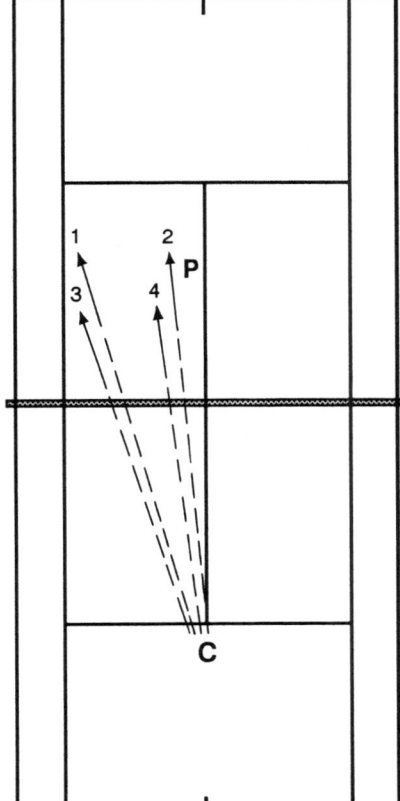

Figure 21-3

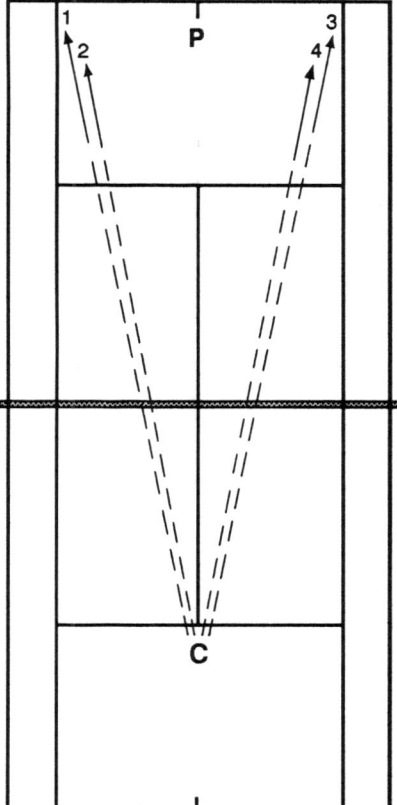

Figure 21-4

5. Stretch Volley Drill

Objective: To improve movement at the net and to learn how to make the volley when he is fully stretched out.

Description: The coach (C) stands four to five feet behind the service line and feeds balls to the outstretched reach of the player's (P) forehand and backhand volleys. Special emphasis should be placed on the player's recovering back to the middle after each shot before stretching for the next ball. The player should hit the ball deep to the baseline or make a drop volley.

6. Six Ball Drill: All Court Coverage

Objective: To combine the stretch forehand and backhand ground strokes with the stretch forehand and backhand volleys.

Description: The coach (C) stands four to five feet behind the service line. He feeds balls to the player (P) so that the player has to move from one corner to the other and stretch to return the balls (1 and 2). He then brings the player into the net by feeding him a short ball (3). The player hits the approach shot, and then the coach feeds balls to the player's forehand and backhand sides so he has to stretch to volley back (4 and 5). The coach can add an overhead as the last shot.

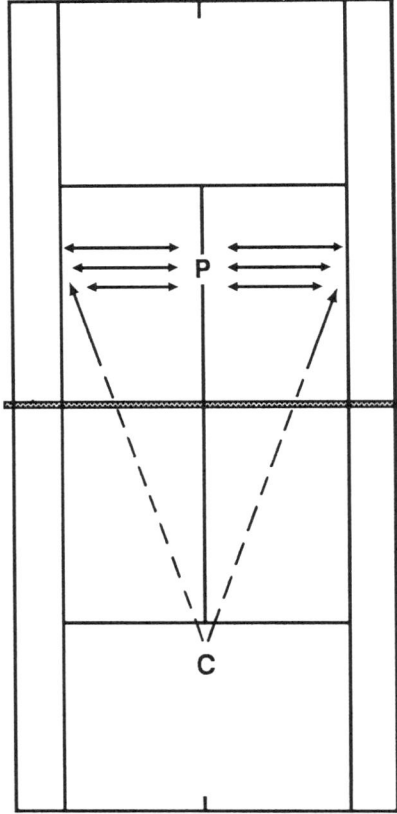

Figure 21-5

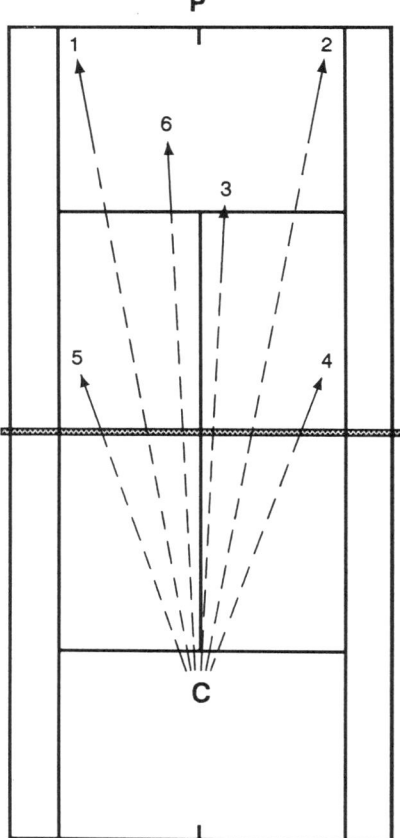

Figure 21-6

7. Kill Shot Drill

Objective: To develop the player's kill shot, or a shot that is virtually impossible to return.

Description: The coach (C) feeds weak balls to different positions on the court (1, 2, 3, and 4), and the player (P) moves to every ball and hits only a forehand or a backhand. This forces the player to develop his footwork and court movement and to learn to hit an aggressive shot off a weak ball. The player should try to hit each shot as aggressively as possible, and shot placement can be made to either corner.

8. Volley-Close-Smash Drill

Objective: To develop forward and backward movement.

Description: The coach (C) feeds a low volley to the feet of the player (P), who starts behind the service line (1). The second volley should be a floater that the player closes on to angle away, and the third shot should be an overhead that the player moves back for and puts away (2 and 3).

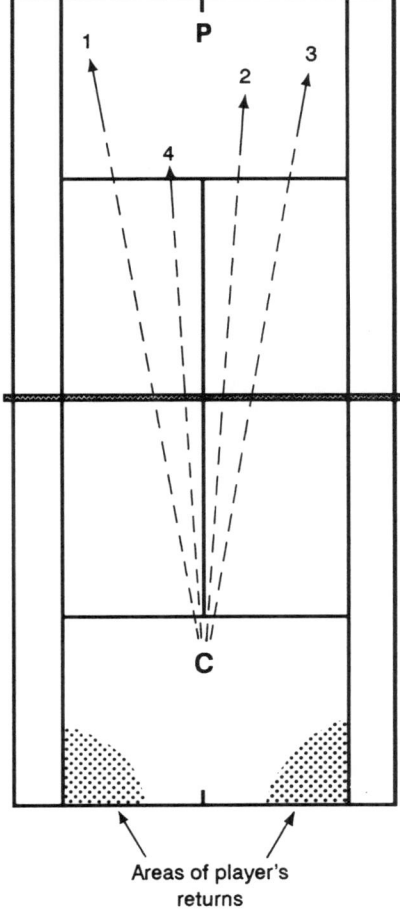

Figure 21-7

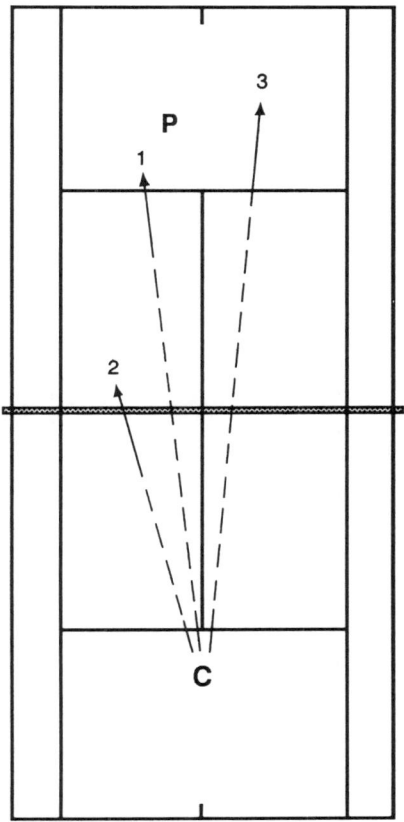

Figure 21-8

9. Low Ball-High Ball Drill

Objective: To work on forward and backward movement and to improve low volleys and overheads.

Description: The player (P) starts behind the service line and moves up quickly to take a short volley out of the air (1), and then the coach feeds an immediate overhead beyond him (2). The player has to move back quickly for a smash (3) and then close again for a short volley (4).

10. Drop Shot Drill

Objective: To improve forward movement for running down drop shots.

Description: The player (P) starts on the baseline. The coach (C) is at the net and drops a very short ball over the net to the right or the left (1 and 2). The player races from the baseline to make the shot, and back pedals to the start again.

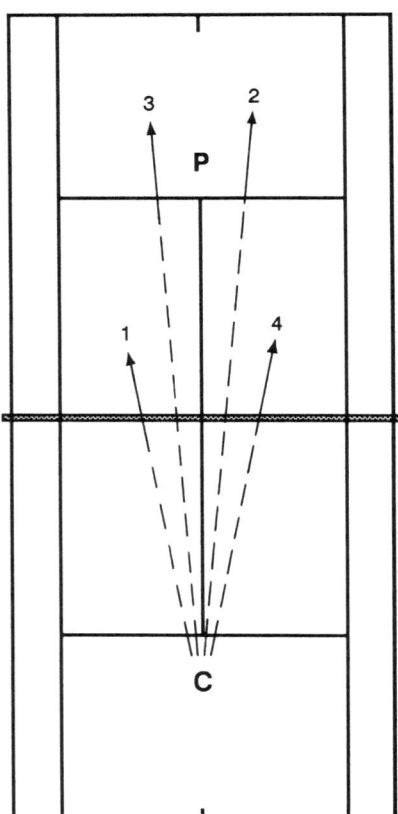

Figure 21-9

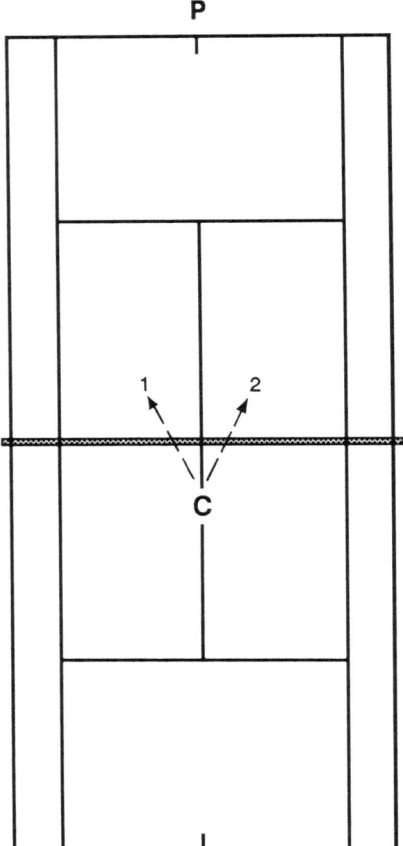

Figure 21-10

11. Change of Direction Drill (Ground Strokes or Volleys)

Objective: To learn how to change the direction of the ball on ground strokes, and how to improve court movement. The player will also learn his limitations with each shot.

Description: The coach (C) feeds balls from the deep corner of the court to different places all over the court (1-5). The player gets to every ball and hits shots of different speeds and spins to the opposite corner. This can be done with the player at the net, or with the coach up and the player back, or with both the player and the coach at the net.

12. No Change of Direction Drill (Ground Strokes and Volleys)

Objective: To learn how consistency can be developed when the ball is hit right back to where it came from (at a right angle). There is a difference when the player tries to change the direction of the ball. The player will also learn his limitations on each ball.

Description: The coach (C) feeds balls from the deep corner or the side net position. The player (P) has to get to every ball (1-5) and hit it right back to where it came from. This drill can also be done with both the coach and the player up, or with one up and the other back.

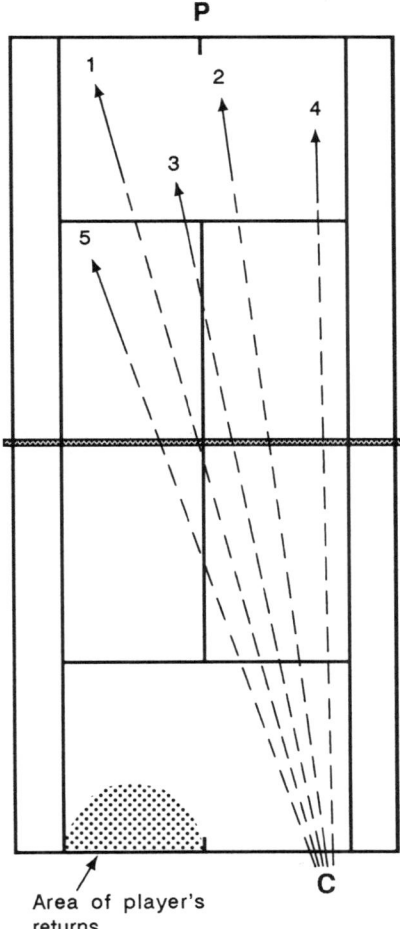

Figure 21-11

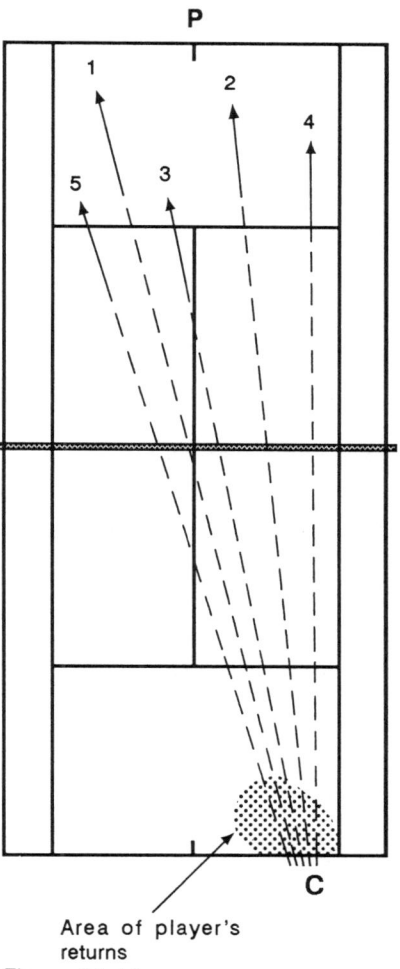

Figure 21-12

13. The Boykin Bring in Drill

Objective: To learn to use the short angles that are necessary to stretch, and to work on coming to the net and playing from an uncomfortable position.

Description: The coach (C) stands behind the baseline and feeds balls to different areas of the player's court. The player (P1) drives two or three balls deep and then hits a very short angle to the wide part of the service box. If a second player (P2) is used in the drill, he is forced to the net, so the first player hits a passing shot. The drill should be used in preparation for competition against a player who dislikes net play.

14. Approach-Volley-Smash Drill

Objective: To improve upward and backward movement, and to improve the approach shot, volley, and overhead smash.

Description: The coach (C) feeds balls from three to five feet behind the service line. The player (P) starts in the middle of the backcourt area. The coach feeds the player an approach shot (1) that he slices, and then he comes into the net. The coach then feeds the player a volley (2) followed by an overhead (3) that makes the player move all the way back to the three-quarter court area again.

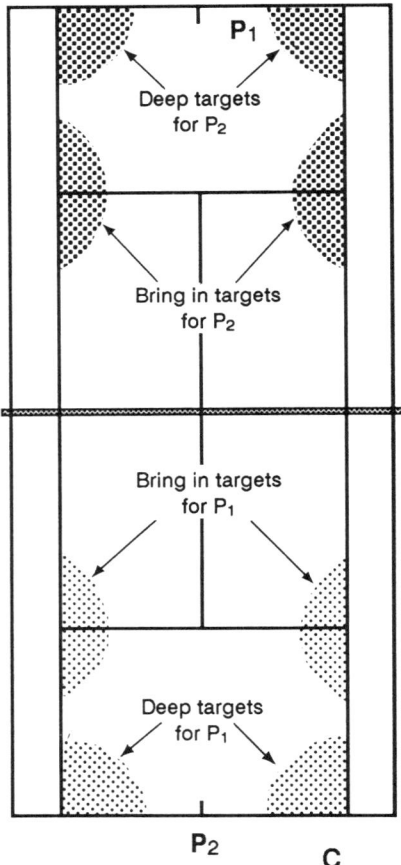

Figure 21-13

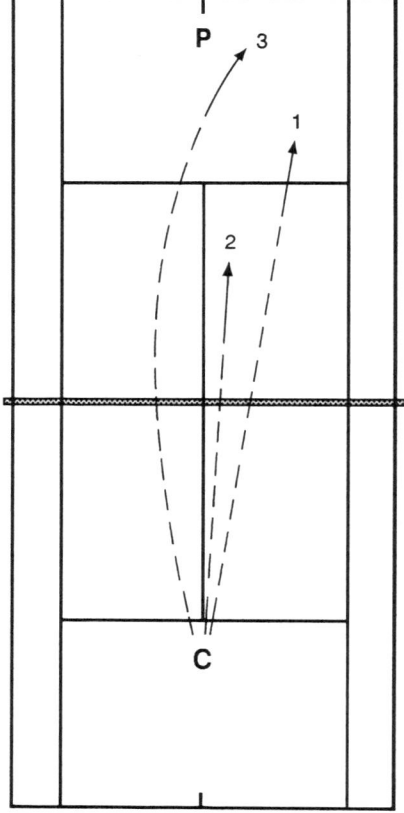

Figure 21-14

CHANGING THE DIRECTION OF THE BALL VERSUS NOT CHANGING THE DIRECTION OF THE BALL

During a point of tennis, a player may choose to change or not change the direction of the flight of the ball. Not changing the direction of the ball (hitting the ball back to where it came from) allows the player to hit the ball at a right angle. This is very forgiving to slightly mishit shots and also for more difficult shots such as the return of serve, first volleys, passing shots, approach shots, and balls placed so that a player is stretched and becomes off-balance or out of position to return them. It is a good rule to not change the direction of the ball on any shot that cannot be controlled.

Changing the direction of the ball (hitting the ball to the open court), on the other hand, is a much riskier proposition. Only a slight change in the angle of the racquet face can misdirect a ball out of bounds or into the net. The temptation is to hit the ball to the open court, away from the opponent. However, this is not always a good idea because of the greater chance for error and because a poorly hit ball will sit up, thereby giving the opponent an opportunity for a put-away on his shot.

Of course, put-aways usually have to be hit to the open court, or with a change of direction. The key is for a player to recognize his limitations with each ball hit in a rally, whether he is in the backcourt or at the net. If the shot cannot be adequately controlled or be put away for a winner, the direction of the ball should not be changed. Returning the ball back to where it came from keeps the player in position and sets him up for the next ball, thereby making it difficult for the opponent to make a winner. If the ball can be controlled or put away, though, the player should hit it to the open court.

Players who compete on extremely fast courts quickly learn that few or no changes of direction can be made. Also, against extremely hard hitters, it is an excellent tactic not to change the direction of the ball, because this will reduce errors and allow the player to use his opponent's pace more effectively for his own shots. It may also tempt the hard hitter to go for the open court too often.

The following rallying drills teach players how and when to use either a change of direction or no change of direction.

2. BREAKDOWN (ONE-ON-ONE) RALLYING DRILLS

In these drills the player returns the ball to where it came from and tries not to break down in his execution or his concentration. The drills show the use of a coach and one player, but they can be done with two players, or with two players and a coach with the coach acting as a feeder.

A breakdown drill.

15. Ground Stroke Breakdown Drill

Objective: To learn how to cover the court and make deep shots with no change of direction.

Description: The coach (C) feeds the ball from the corner of the court (1). The player (P) rallies the ball back to the coach, and the coach hits each successive shot to a different area of the court (2, 3, and 4). The coach stays in the corner, and the player moves for every ball to any place on the court. The rally continues until either the player or the coach misses. Score should be kept. After the game, the coach should go to the opposite corner and repeat the drill. *Note:* If a ball sets up, the player can finish off the shot by returning it to the open court.

16. Volley Breakdown Drill

Objective: To learn to cover the net well and to return all balls without a change of direction to set up the next ball.

Description: The coach (C) feeds a ball (1) from the corner to the player (P), who stands at the net. The player volleys the ball back to the coach, allowing the coach to hit another shot to make the player stretch in another position (2). The coach should mix in hard and soft balls as well as wide balls and balls to the middle. Score should be kept, and the drill should be done to the opposite corner as well. *Note:* If a ball sets up, the player can finish off the shot by returning it to the open court.

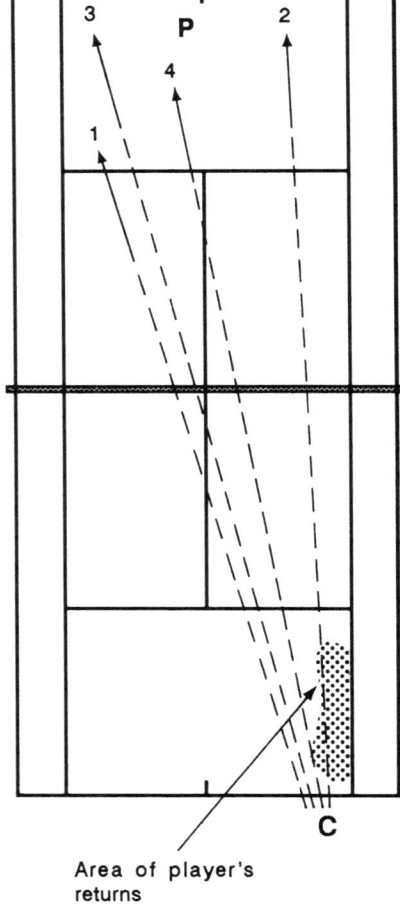

Figure 21-15

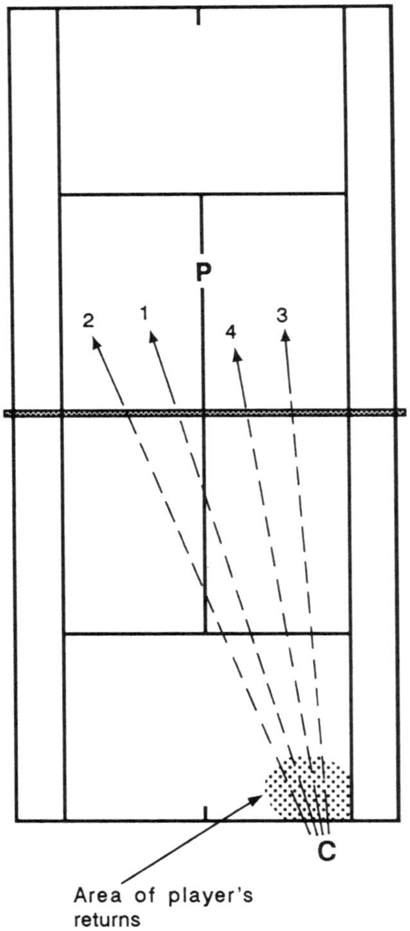

Figure 21-16

17. Passing Shot Breakdown Drill

Objective: To learn how to hit first passing shots back to where they came from, and to learn which balls to change the direction of and hit to the open court.

Description: The coach (C) stands in the rear corner position of the service box. He feeds a ball to the player (P), and he and the player rally. The player must hit every shot of the rally back to the coach. The coach runs the player to different areas of the court. Score should be kept, and the drill should be done from the opposite short corner. *Note:* If an easy ball sets up, the player can finish off the shot by returning it to the open court.

18. Quick Volley Breakdown Drill

Objective: To learn not to change the direction of the ball on a stretch out volley, and to train the hands to be quicker.

Description: The coach (C) stands at the rear corner of the service box, and the player (P) is at the service line. The coach makes shots on both sides low to the player's feet (1-4) to make him stretch and bend to direct them back to the coach. Score should be kept, and the drill should be done from the other side of the court.

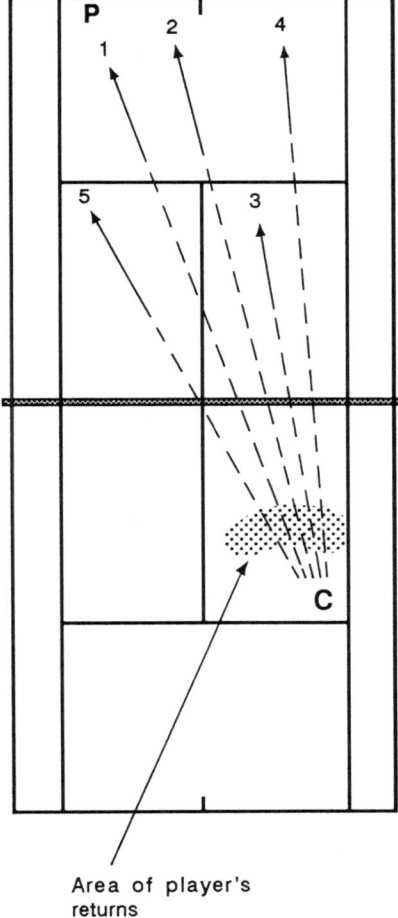

Figure 21-17

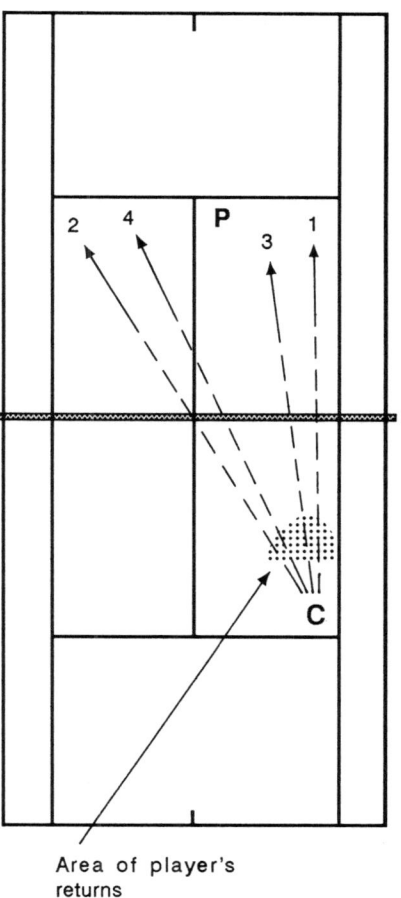

Figure 21-18

19. Overhead Breakdown Drill

Objective: To learn a consistent and reliable overhead smash.

Description: The coach (C) stands to one side behind the baseline and as close to the fence as possible. The player (P) stands close to the net. The player is forced back with a high defensive lob (1). He makes an overhead smash and then tries to close back on the net. The coach then hits another lob up (2) and continues (3 and 4) until the player is fatigued. The drill should be repeated with the coach feeding balls to the other side of the court.

20. Offense-Defense (Weapon) Drill

Objective: To turn the player's favorite stroke into a good weapon.

Description: Standing to one side and as far back from the baseline as possible, the coach (C) delivers very easy balls and lofty balls to the player's midcourt area (1, 2, and 3). The player (P) moves around the ball to use his favorite stroke and hits the hardest shot possible that he can still control back to the coach. The coach continues to float balls to the player until the player is fatigued. The drill should also be done with the coach feeding balls to the other side of the midcourt.

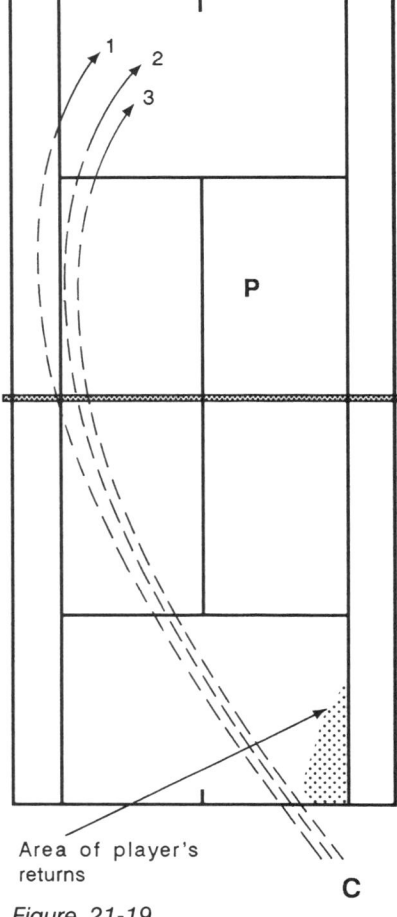

Figure 21-19

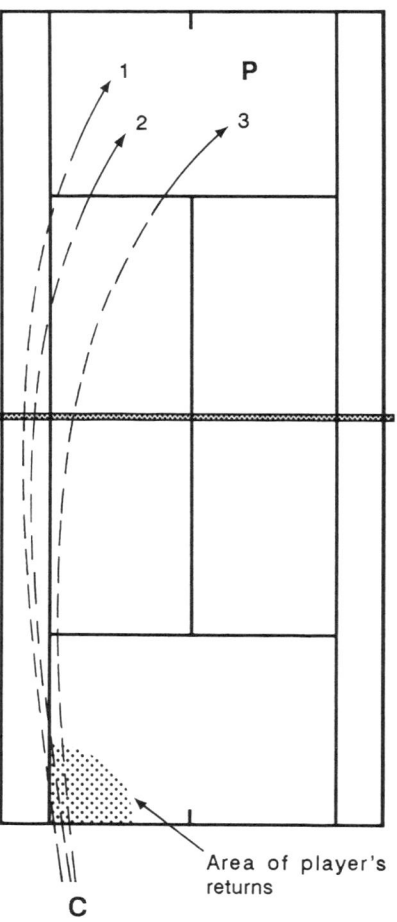

Figure 21-20

21. Three-Quarters Court Closing Drill

Objective: To learn half-volleys and work on transition with midcourt balls on the way to the net.

Description: The coach (C) stands in the right or left service box to feed the ball. The player (P) starts inside his baseline in the backcourt area. The coach hits the ball to the player's feet (1), and the player makes a pickup and proceeds into the net. The coach, having the better court position, keeps hitting to the player's feet (2-5). As soon as the player misses, he backs up to the baseline and starts again. A drill is successful when the player makes it all the way into the net to put a volley away.

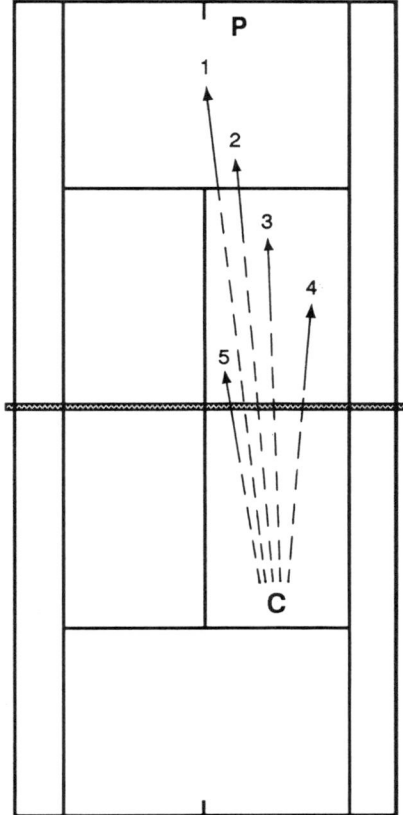

Figure 21-21

3. TWO-ON-ONE DRILLS

Two-on-one drills are used routinely to teach players their limitations on every shot, and they are a great way to learn racquet control and good court movement. Players must also learn to hit balls on the run, and in very different positions. Harry Hopman, the famous Australian Davis Cup Coach, made two-on-one training popular worldwide. He trained his Davis Cup teams and many other international champions in this way.

The player who is being drilled should concentrate on hitting through the two players on the other side of the court, never missing wide, and never missing in the net. The player should concentrate on hitting the ball back to where it came from on shots that he cannot control or is off balance on. He can try to change the direction of any ball that pops up to make a penetrating shot. Training in this manner takes on many of the proportions of match play.

As illustrated in the following drills, two-on-one training can be performed in four different formations:

1. Two players on the baseline versus one on baseline—for ground stroke work.
2. Two players at the net versus one on baseline—for passing shots and reflex ground strokes.
3. Two players on the baseline versus one at the net—for deep volleys and consistency on volleys.
4. Two players at the net versus one at net—for quick volleys and reflexes.

These drills can be executed with three players; with three players and a coach, who acts as the feeder; or with two players and a coach.

Two-on-one workout.

22. Two-on-One Baseline Rally Drill

Objective: To learn good movement consistency and depth while learning the limitations of each shot and whether or not to change the direction of the ball.

Description: Two players stand at the baseline (P1 and P2), while the third (P3) positions himself at the opposite baseline. P1 and P2 work rallies to P3 as he covers the entire court.

23. Two-on-One Passing Shot Drill

Objective: To work on movement, quick reflexes, the ability to hit on the run, and deciding whether or not to change the direction of the ball.

Description: Two players (P1 and P2) are at the net, while the third player (P3) stands at the baseline. P1 and P2 hit balls to any spot on P3's side of the court. P3 has to move to each shot and hit back through P1 and P2. P3 will quickly learn which balls to change direction and which not to change direction. He should try never to hit shots wide or into the net.

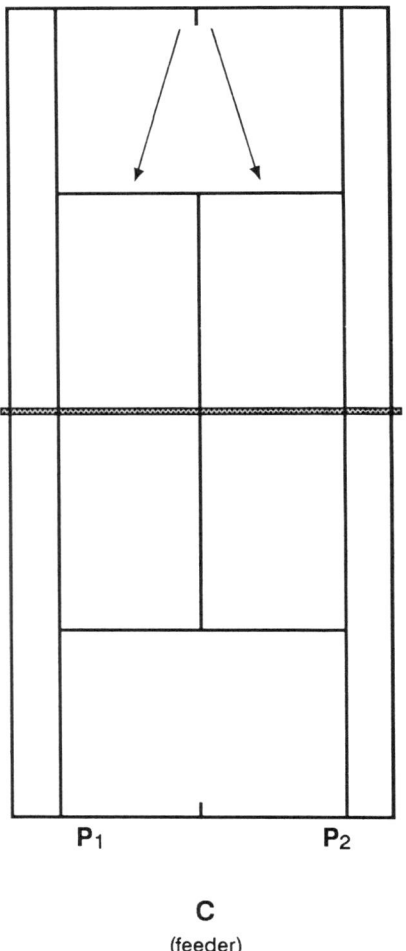

Figure 21-22

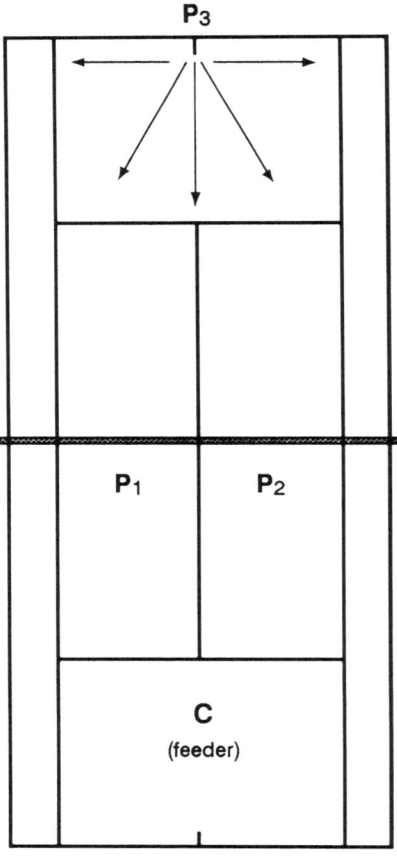

Figure 21-23

24. Two-on-One Deep Volley Drill

Objective: To develop good movement and consistency of volleys.

Description: Two players (P1 and P2) are on the baseline, and the third player (P3) is at the net. P3 plays each ball hit to him, returning it with a deep volley to either side of the opposite court.

25. Two-on-One Quick Volley Drill

Objective: To improve reflexes and learn limitations in a quick volley situation.

Description: Two players (P1 and P2) are at the service line and face the third player (P3), who stands at the opposite service line. P1 and P2 hit balls at P3 and P3, in turn, reflexes quick, crisp volleys back through his two drill partners.

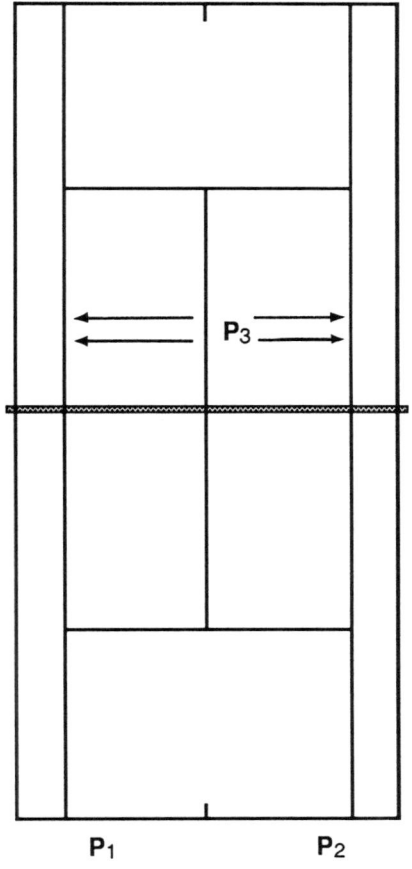

Figure 21-24

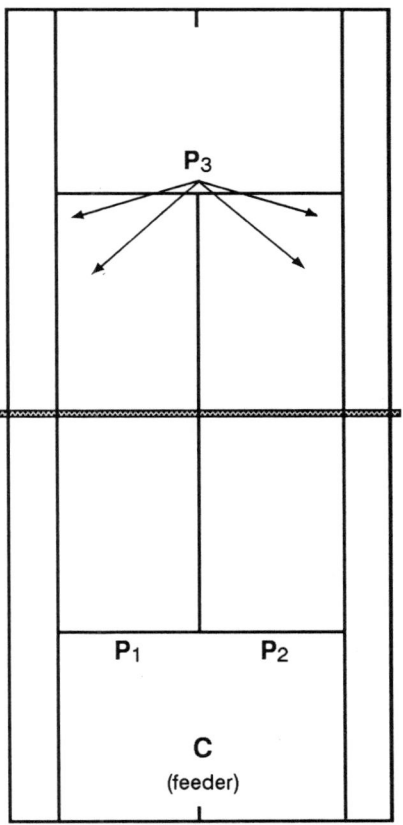

Figure 21-25

26. Two-on-One Offense/Defense (Weapon) Drill

Objective: To create a good weapon from a player's favorite stroke. This drill is also excellent for learning correct footwork when setting up for floating balls.

Description: Two players (P1 and P2) are far behind the baseline, and the third player (P3) is at midcourt on the opposite side. P1 and P2 alternately deliver very soft floating balls to P3 (1-4). P3 moves around each ball and uses his favorite stroke to hit it, regardless of where it lands. Unlike the one-on-one drill, the player has his choice of hitting to either corner of the opposite side of the court.

27. Two-on-One Three-Quarters Court Closing Drill

Objective: To learn to hit half-volleys and to make reflex shots on the way to the net.

Description: Two players (P1 and P2) stand at the net. The third player (P3) starts at three-quarters court or toward the rear of the backcourt. P1 and P2 take turns hitting balls down and toward P3's feet as he tries to work himself to the net (1-6). If P3 misses a shot, he backs up and begins again. A successful drill finds P3 all the way in the net for a finishing volley.

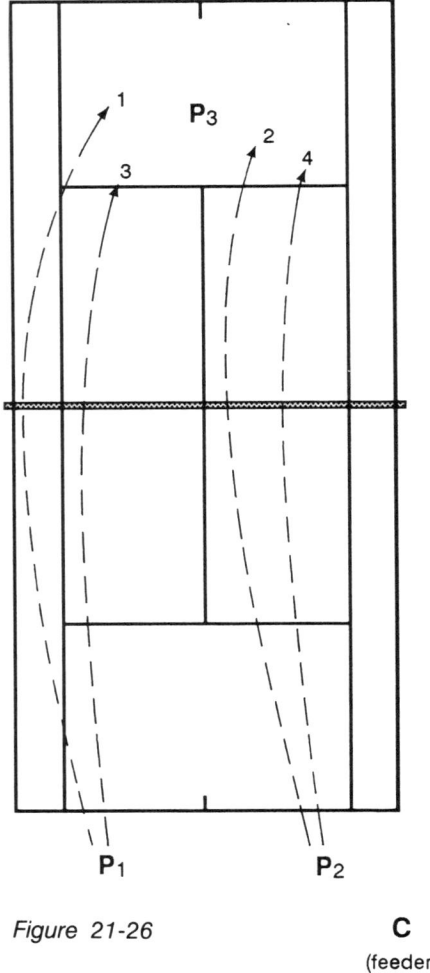

Figure 21-26

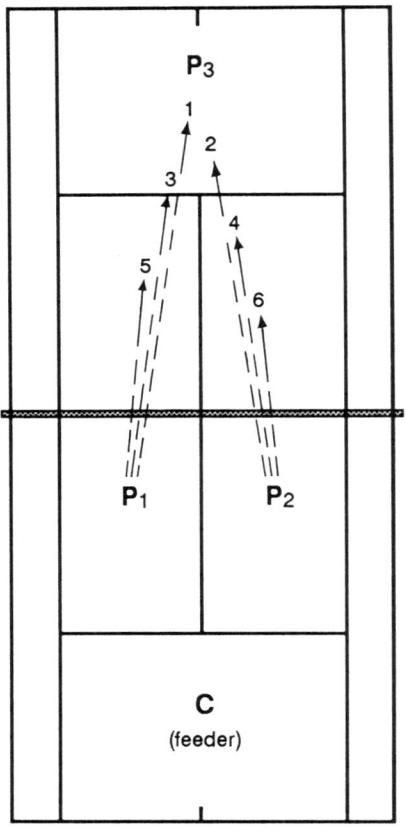

Figure 21-27

THE KRASS QUICK VOLLEY DRILLS

"Quick hands and quick feet make for volleys that are hard to beat." These three quick volley drills pay big dividends to a player who wants to develop quick reflexes and control of the racquet head. Players should be encouraged to be very aggressive and intense during these high-paced drills.

A Krass quick volley drill.

28. Shoe Shine Volley Drill

Objective: To develop skills in handling the low volley and half-volley and to develop the skill of placing volleys at the other player's feet.

Description: Both players (P1 and P2) stand behind the service line for the entire drill. Using one-half of the singles court as the boundary, each player tries to hit his volleys to the other player's shoes. Good footwork and use of legs is important. *Note:* The coach can also feed balls from a side position.

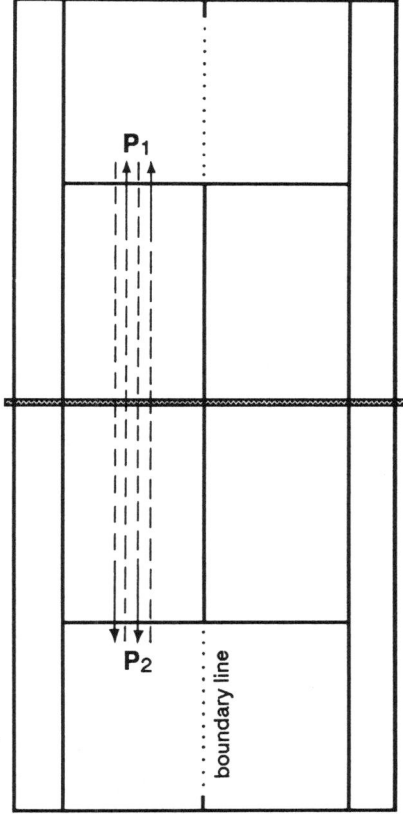

Figure 21-28

29. One-on-One Closing Volley Drill

Objective: To learn how to close on the net and to develop quick hands, feet, and reflexes.

Description: Both players (P1 and P2) stand in the backcourt. Using one-half of the singles court for the boundary, each player tries to close to the net and win a quick volley point. Score should be kept. *Note:* The coach may also start the ball out from a side position.

30. Two-on-Two Doubles Tracking Drill (Inside-Inside/Outside-Outside)

Objective: To work on quick volleys and to learn how to track as a doubles team. This drill is excellent practice for doubles movement.

Description: Four players (P1 and P2, P3 and P4) start at their respective service lines. The coach feeds balls to different positions, forcing both pairs to shift or slide together in order to cover the returned shots. Players should also attempt to close together on the net as the drill progresses. This drill can also be done with two players on the net and two on the baseline.

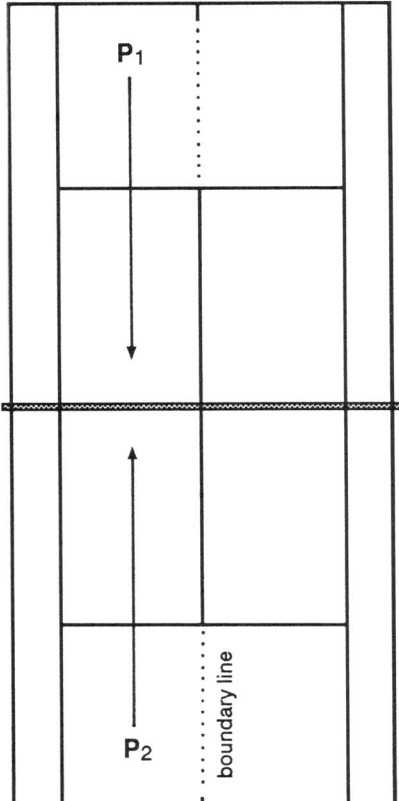

Figure 21-29

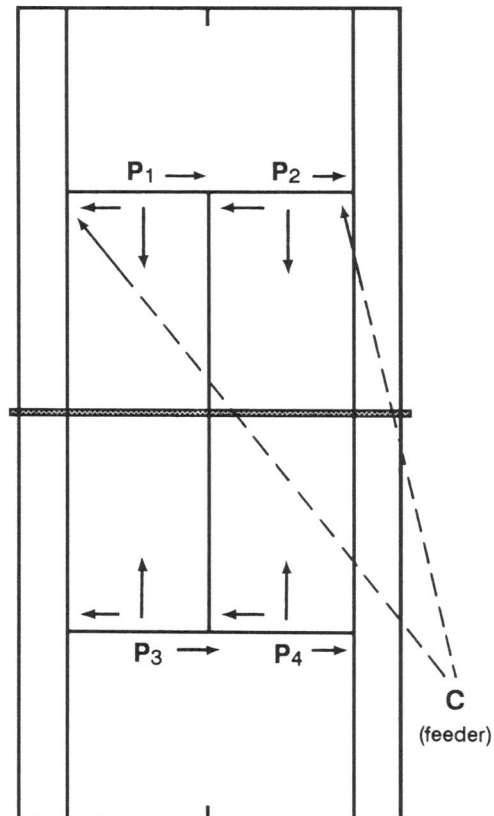

Figure 21-30

4. MATCH SIMULATION DRILLS

There are certain patterns that closely simulate situations that occur again and again during match play. The following drills contain some of these patterns that the player can use to develop his skills in playing points in various shot sequences. Although most points cannot be planned from start to finish, the first two or three exchanges usually work well to set up some sequences, and these drills will help the player obtain a good understanding of this concept.

31. The Serve and Volley-Volley Drill

Objective: To work on service placement to the middle of the court, and to work on the first and finishing volleys.

Description: Only one serve is allowed in this drill. The receiver (P2) must return the serve (1) through the middle of the court (2), thereby allowing the server (P1) to make the first volley (3). This first volley should be hit back to where it came from (4), or to the middle of the court. The server then closes off the net and tries to put his second volley away (5). The receiver is allowed to pass on the second ball as well.

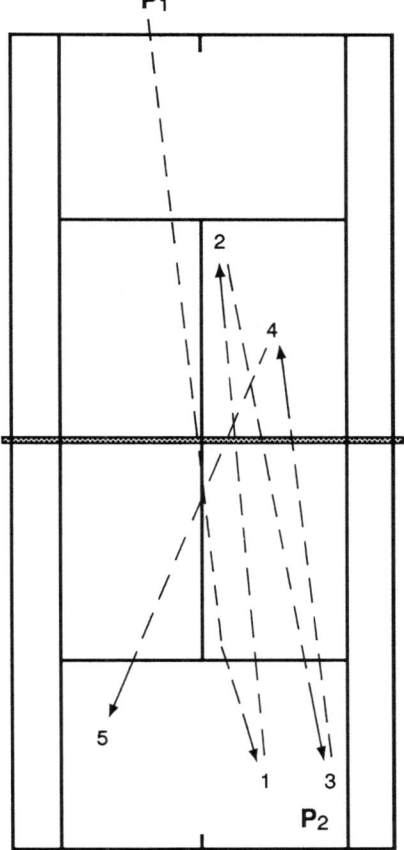

Figure 21-31

32. The Wide and Glide Drill (Serve Wide and Approach)

Objective: To learn how to pull the receiver out of court and then approach the net.

Description: The server (P1) slices the serve wide into the deuce court or kicks the serve wide into the ad court (1). The receiver (P2) makes his return cross-court (2). The server makes an approach shot off the first return (3) and comes to the net for the finishing volley (4 and 5). The server makes an approach shot off the first return and comes to the net for the finishing volley.

33. One Serve Receiver Attacks Drill

Objective: To put pressure on the server's second serve, to teach the receiver to come to the net on a return of serve, and to work on the server's passing shot when he is pressed.

Description: The server (P1) is allowed one serve (1). The receiver (P2) must return the serve (2) and come to the net. The server tries to hit a passing shot (3). The receiver now tries to win the point (4) at the net position. Score is kept as in a regular set.

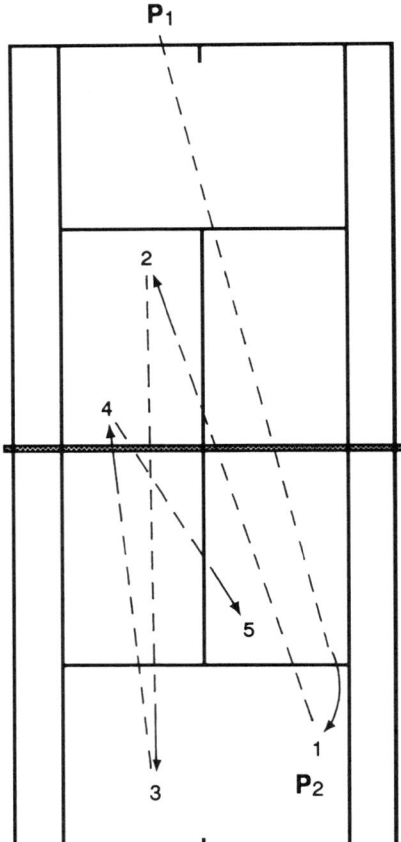

Figure 21-32

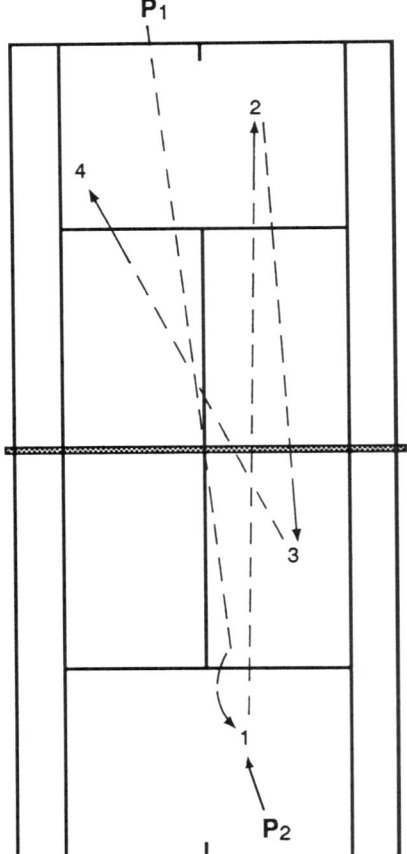

Figure 21-33

34. Crosscourt Volley with Approach Shot on Short Ball Drill

Objective: To learn the importance of crosscourt rallies, to learn to keep the court closed, and to learn the skills of making consistent crosscourt rallies and down-the-line approach shots. Description: The two players exchange deep crosscourt forehand or backhand shots (1-3) until a short ball is hit (4). This short ball is the cue for the player to make a down-the-line approach shot (5) and to play the point out. Score should be kept.

35. Crosscourt and Down-the-Line Rallies Drill (Control Drill)

Objective: To become proficient at changing the direction of the ball during the rally.

Description: One player (P2) rallies from the baseline, directing his balls crosscourt, and his partner (P1) returns the balls down the line. This forces the players to run from side to side and change the direction of the ball. Score should be kept, and then the drill should be reversed. Players performing this drill should be concerned with consistency.

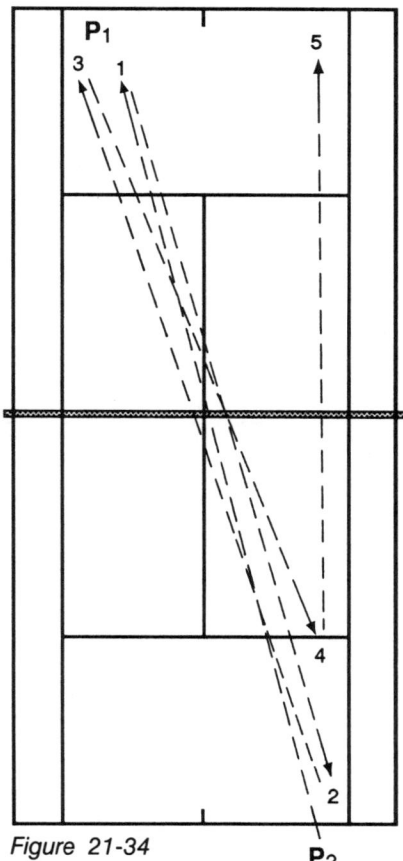

Figure 21-34

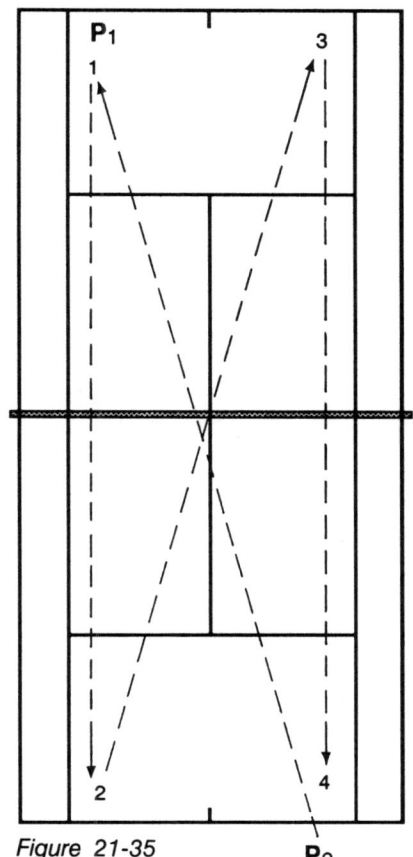

Figure 21-35

36. Two Volley Passing Shot Drill

Objective: To allow one player to work on the approach volley, and to allow another player to work on the first pass and the second passing shot.

Description: One player (P1) starts behind the service line and feeds a ball as an approach shot (1) to the other player (P2), who is on the baseline. P2 must hit his first pass back to P1 (2). Both P1 and P2 then try to win the point (3 and 4). Score should be kept.

37. Approach-Passing Shot Drill

Objective: To work on approach shots and passing shots.

Description: The coach (C) feeds balls from a position to the side and off the court. Two or more players (P1, P2, and P3) line up at the center of the baseline. One player (P4) is on the coach's side of the court at the baseline. The coach feeds a ball into the midcourt (1); each player takes a turn approaching the net with good under spin approach shots (2), while the player at the baseline tries to make his passing shot (3). Score should be kept.

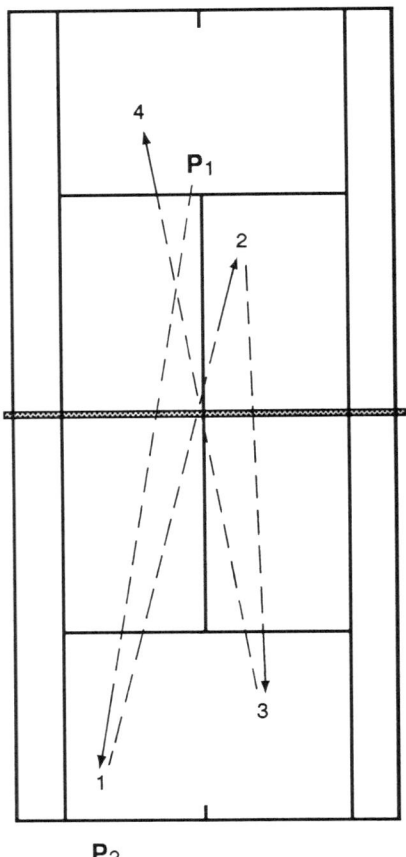

Figure 21-36

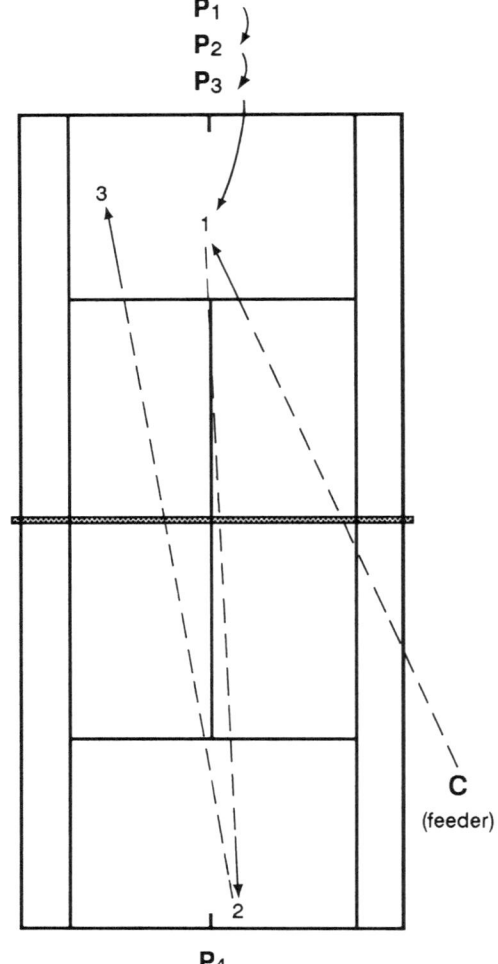

Figure 21-37

USE EFFECTIVE DRILLS TO SHARPEN YOUR TEAM'S SKILLS

38. One-on-One Stretch Pass and Volley Drill

Objective: To work on stretching to make down-the-line passing shots and stretch crosscourt volleys.

Description: The coach (C) feeds the ball from a position either behind or to the side of the court. He hits a ball to the corner of the passing player's (P1) backcourt, forcing him to stretch for the ball. P1 must make a down-the-line passing shot (2) that the net player (P2) tries to cut off and angle crosscourt (3). The coach then hits a wide ball to the passing player's backhand side (4), and the drill is repeated (5 and 6). The passer may also hit his first shot crosscourt and then move in to finish the point with his second shot.

5. SERVING DRILLS

The following two drills may be used to help players improve their serves.

39. Wrist Serving Drill

Objective: To develop a quicker wrist snap for better racquet head speed on the serve.

Description: The server stands with the side of his body facing the net and both his feet placed firmly on the ground. As the toss is delivered, his whole body is frozen in this sideways position, and the only power used for the stroke comes from the snap of his wrist. It is very important that the feet, legs, hips, upper body, and head all stay sideways so that the wrist action is the predominant power source. The arm, wrist, and racquet head should become one and move like a whip with the racquet head cracking through the ball. The server should serve 50 to 75 balls before regular practice of the serve.

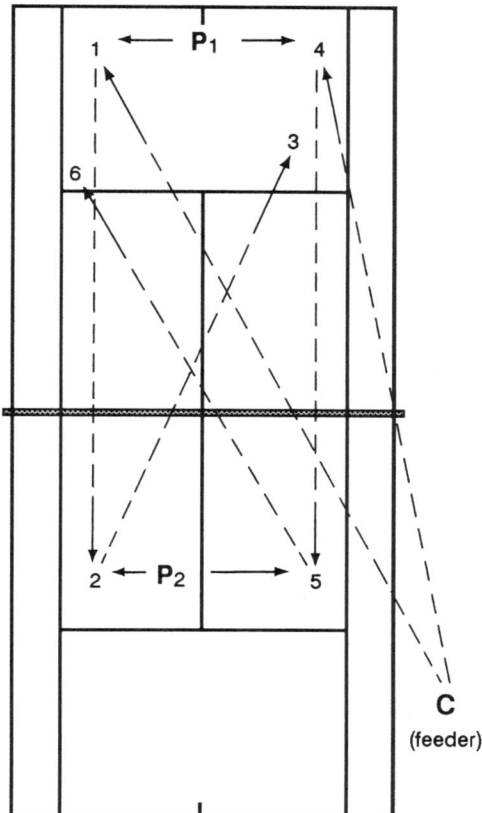

Figure 21-38

40. The Boykin Placement Cues Drill

Objective: To give the player a very basic concept of placement and accuracy.

Description: Just as a bowler looks at the arrows on the lane, and just as a hunter looks through the sight on his gun, so a server can look at an area of the net as a directional target for better service accuracy. A player can improve the placement of middle line serves by standing in the ready position and using the V-shaped area formed by the center strap and the opponent's center service line to direct a serve to Target 1. He can direct a body serve to Target 2 by aligning his opponent's feet with a corresponding spot at the top of the net. A wide corner serve to Target 3 can be directed by lining up part of the net with the target. The diagram illustrates serves to the deuce court, but these targets can also be used when serving to the ad court.

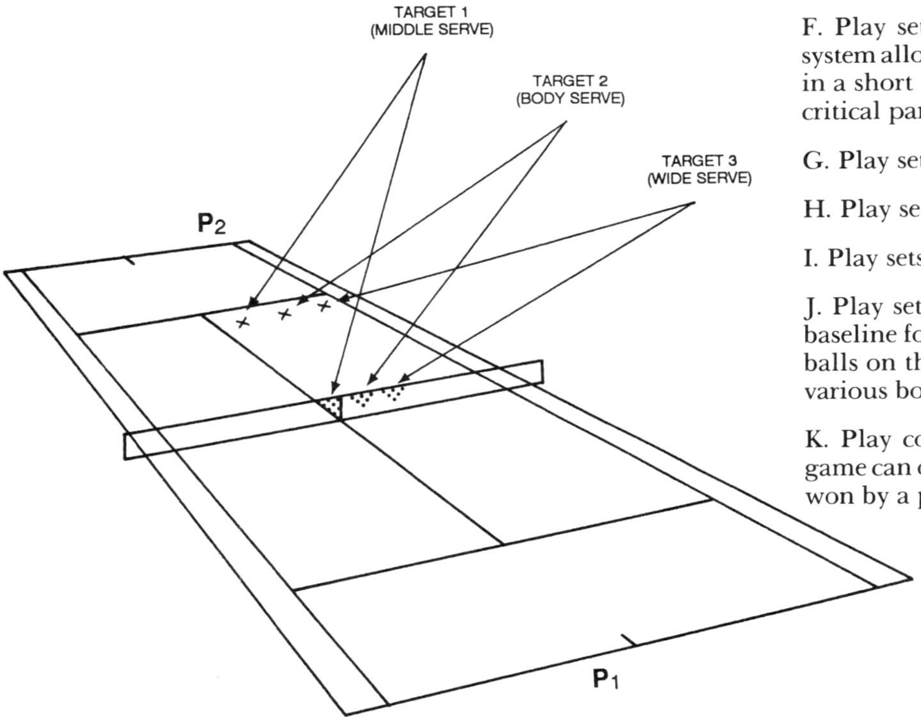

Figure 21-39

6. SIMULATED SET PLAY FOR PRACTICE SITUATIONS

A. Play a set, scoring on the service game only, as in volleyball and racquetball. This emphasizes learning how to hold serve.

B. Play a set, scoring on the return game only. This emphasizes learning how to break serve.

C. Play sets in which the server is allowed only one serve, and the receiver must come into the net. This teaches a good second serve as well as coming to the net on a return, and it helps the player develop passing shots.

D. Play a set, in which you must hold serve before you can turn serve over to the opponent. In the first service game, score starts at 0-40; the second service game starts at 0-30, the third game at 0-15, then 0-0, 0-0, as long as it takes to hold serve. This game teaches the server how to come from behind on his service game, and it teaches the receiver to take advantage of early opportunities. This concept works very well in doubles practice sets as well.

E. Play a set serving only to the deuce court, or serving only to the ad court, for the entire set. This allows the server a chance to groove his serve and to learn what his options and plays are to run in each court.

F. Play sets starting at deuce in every game. This system allows multi-sets or competitions to be played in a short time while placing emphasis on the very critical part of each game.

G. Play sets allowing only one serve.

H. Play sets allowing only serve and volley.

I. Play sets allowing no net play.

J. Play sets in which players must stand inside the baseline for all shots. This teaches the player to take balls on the rise and to deal with strange shots and various bounces.

K. Play conversion sets (three points in a row). A game can only be won if three consecutive points are won by a player.

SUMMARY

Nothing can be a substitute for the pressure of actual match play, but drills do work as excellent physical and mental grooving devices. The important emotional training that allows the mental and physical to run can only be trained through the pressure of competition.

NOTES

Chapter 2

[1] Edward L. Fox and Donald K. Matthews, *Interval Training*, Philadelphia, W. B. Saunders Co., 1974, p. 184.

[2] Fox and Matthews, p. 184.

[3] Fox and Matthews, pp. 24-25.

Chapter 4

[1] Barry I. Johnson and Jack K. Nelson, *Practical Measurements for Evaluation in Physical Education*, Minneapolis, Burgess Publishing, 1969, p. 100. All further definitions in this chapter are from this source.

[2] Bass, Ruth U. "An Analysis of the Components of Tests of Semi-circular Canal Function and of Static Dynamic Balance," *Research Quarterly* May 1939, p. 33.

[3] William S. Zorbas and Peter Karpovich, "The Effect of Weight Lifting Upon the Speed of Muscular Contraction," *Research Quarterly* May 1951, pp. 145-148; Bruce M. Wilkin, "The Effect of Weight Training on Speed of Movement," *Research Quarterly* October 1952, pp. 361-369; John W. Masley et. al., "Weight Training in Relation to Strength, Speed, and Coordination," *Research Quarterly* October 1953, pp. 308-315; John P. Endres, "The Effect of Weight Training Exercise Upon Speed of Muscular Movements," Masters Thesis, University of Wisconsin, 1953. Edward Chui, "Effect of Systematic Weight Training on Athletic Power," *Research Quarterly* October 1950, pp. 188-194.

Chapter 5

[1] Frank Lisciandro, *The Sugar Film,* Santa Barbara, CA, Image Associates, 1980.

Chapter 16

[1] Joseph B. O'Xendine, "Emotional Arousal and Motor Performance," *Quest* 13 (1970), p. 29.

Chapter 17

[1] Grawunder, Ralph and Marion Steinmann, *Life and Health*, 3rd edition, New York, Random House, 1980, pp. 28-29.

Chapter 18

[1] Taibi Kohler, *Personality Types*, Kohler and Associates Processed Communication Managers.

BIBLIOGRAPHY

Bass, Ruth U. "An Analysis of the Components of Tests of Semi-circular Canal Function and of Static Dynamic Balance." *Research Quarterly* May 1939:33.

Benjamin, David. *The ITCA Guide to Coaching Winning Tennis.* New York: Prentice-Hall, 1988.

Chui, Edward. "Effect of Systematic Weight Training on Athletic Power." *Research Quarterly* October 1950:188-194.

Endres, John P. "The Effect of Weight Training Exercise Upon Speed of Muscular Movements." Masters Thesis University of Wisconsin, 1953.

Fox, Edward L. and Donald K. Matthews. *Interval Training.* Philadelphia: W. B. Saunders Co., 1974.

Grawunder, Ralph and Marion Steinmann. *Life and Health.* 3rd. ed. New York: Random House Inc., 1980.

Hoffman, Marshal and Gabe Mirkin, M.D. *The Sports Medicine Book.* Boston: Little, Brown and Co., 1978.

Hoyt, Creig, et. al. *Food for Fitness.* 6th ed. Mountain View, CA: World Publications and Bike World Magazine, 1978.

Johnson, Barry I. and Jack K. Nelson. *Practical Measurements for Evaluation in Physical Education.* Minneapolis: Burgess Publishing Co., 1969.

Kohler, Taibi. *Personality Types.* Kohler and Associates Processed Communication Managers.

Kraft, Steve and Connie Haynes. *The Tennis Player's Diet.* New York: Doubleday and Co., Inc., 1975.

Lisciandro, Frank. *The Sugar Film.* Santa Barbara, CA: Image Associates, 1980.

Masley, John W., Ara Hairabedian, and Donald N. Donaldson. "Weight Training in Relation to Strength, Speed, and Coordination." *Research Quarterly* October 1953:308-315.

O'Xendine, Joseph B. "Emotional Arousal and Motor Performance," *Quest* 13:23-31, 1970.

Sprague, Ken. *The Athlete's Body.* Los Angeles: Jeremy P. Tarcher, Inc., 1981.

Wilkin, Bruce M. "The Effect of Weight Training on Speed of Movement." *Research Quarterly* October 1952:361-369.

Zorbas, William S. and Peter Karpovich. "The Effect of Weight Lifting Upon the Speed of Muscular Contraction." *Research Quarterly* May 1951:145-148.